Transnational Corporations and China's Open Door Policy

Transnational Corporations and China's Open Door Policy

Edited by
Teng Weizao and N.T. Wang

Lexington Books
D.C. Heath and Company/Lexington, Massachusetts/Toronto

Library of Congress Cataloging-in-Publication Data
Transnational corporations and China's open door policy.

 Includes index.
 1. International business enterprises—China—Congresses. 2. China—Foreign economic
relations—Congresses. I. Teng, Weizao. II. Wang, N. T. (Nian-Tzu), 1917–
HD2910.T73 1988 338.8′8851 87-45763
ISBN 0-669-16967-6 (alk. paper)

Published simultaneously in Canada
Printed in the United States of America
International Standard Book Number: 0-669-16967-6
Library of Congress Catalog Card Number 87-45763

The paper used in this publication meets the minimum requirements of American National
Standard for Information Sciences—Permanence of Paper for Printed Library Materials, ANSI
Z39.48-1984.∞

88 89 90 91 92 8 7 6 5 4 3 2 1

Contents

Part III Chinese Policies and Experiences 181

Preface and Acknowledgments

One of the innovations of the international community in recent years is the establishment of a machinery by which issues concerning transnational corporations can be aired and practical measures in dealing with them can be discussed and negotiated. Within the framework of the United Nations, this machinery is path-breaking in at least two respects. One is the subject matter itself since until the creation of the United Nations Commission on Transnational Corporations, these activities were not recognized as appropriate topics for intergovernment deliberations. The second is participation by experts in their individual capacity from various backgrounds in business, labor, or academia. Formerly, they were at most involved in the background in intergovernment bodies.

The editors of this book have participated in the work of the United Nations machinery at various stages. We have been impressed by the importance of transnationals to world development and are convinced of the usefulness of parallel work outside the United Nations so that the issues under consideration can be more specific and the environment can be less subject to concerns regarding national positions and diplomatic rules.

When China decided to pursue an open door policy, the implications were far-reaching. Suddenly, there was a real need for the Chinese to understand transnational corporations and vice versa. The idea of an international conference on transnational corporations and China's open door policy that would promote such an understanding was born. However, the logistics of organizing a conference of over one hundred participants was overwhelming. It was not until winter 1985 that concrete plans were formulated and the cooperation of all those involved secured.

We are grateful to all the participants for their contributions to the conference, which took place in Tianjin, China, October 27–30, 1986. Although considerations of space and balance have prevented the inclusion in this book of a number of the papers presented, many of them will be published elsewhere, including the companion volume in Chinese. Our thanks go especially to <u>Li</u> Lanqing, at that time vice mayor of Tianjin, who set the tone of the conference in his opening statement: to the members of the presidium and chairmen of sessions, who managed the proceedings efficiently, but whose papers are not reproduced here—notably Clement G. Kahama, (ambassador of the Republic of Tanzania), S. Balde of UNESCO, <u>Liang</u> Xian of China Merchants, Wilfried R. Vanhonacker of Columbia University, K.C. Mun of Chinese University of Hong Kong, Walter A. Buhler of Arthur Andersen, Vichai Trangkasombat of Coca-Cola, and David Sycip of Asean Finance Corporation. Almost one hundred people were involved, day and night, in the conference preparations. Unfortunately, they are too numerous to mention.

The conference benefited from direct financial contributions from UNESCO and indirectly from major donors to the China-International Business Project of Columbia University—notably, Maria Lee, the Bei Shan Tang Foundation, the General Electric Foundation, Merrill Lynch, Hong Kong Shanghai Banking Corporation, and AMAX Foundation.

This book would not have been possible without the generous help of Marianna E. Oliver, who worked closely with the editors on the text.

Introduction

In recent years, the Chinese attitude toward transnational corporations has changed dramatically. This change is reflected in official pronouncements of the open door policy. Transnationals are no longer viewed as tools of capitalist exploitation but as agents and resources that can serve the purposes of Chinese development.

Nevertheless, the precise role of transnational corporations and the rationale of the Chinese open door policy have rarely been brought together and articulated in China. In academic as well as policy discussions, transnational corporations remain mystified. They continue to be monopolist by definition. There has been little empirical study of their activities and operations, if only because of lack of information. Even for those whose operations take place in China, such as joint ventures and cooperative arrangements, detailed reporting, not to say analysis, is scanty, apparently influenced by considerations of confidentiality. Those whose task it is to deal directly with transnational corporations are faced with a dilemma. On the one hand, they are anxious to conclude arrangements speedily so as not to be accused of obstructing China's open door policy. On the other hand, they are reluctant to make any decisions that might in retrospect be regarded as not protecting the national interest.

This dilemma is rooted in the intellectual basis of China's open door policy as well as in the bureaucratic rules of the game. One school of thought is wary about the link between the policy and bourgeois liberalization. It frowns upon all the "polluting" influences, ranging from pornography to rock music, from humanism to Western-style democracy. Although this school is countered by assurances that the open door policy and the campaign against bourgeois liberalization are complementary rather than conflicting, and that the open door policy is a long-term decision that will not be altered when political leaders change, the cautious see advantage in hedging. Moreover, the rationale of the open door policy permits both broad and narrow interpretations. In a broad sense, an open door policy recognizes the common heritage of human ingenuity and wisdom, which cannot and should not be confined within national boundaries. In economic terms alone, a nation's long-term survival in a competitive world depends on the ability to engage in activities that can stand comparatively with the rest of the world. In a narrow sense, an open door policy is identified with a development strategy that is export-oriented or that welcomes the inflow of foreign investment and technology.

In such circumstances, transnational corporations' perceptions of Chinese policy is also somewhat uncertain. Many of them are influenced by their personal inclinations and experiences. Those who have been impressed by the genius of Chinese innovations throughout history are convinced that the folly of self-imposed isolation and ossification will not be repeated, while those who fear the continuity of Oriental despotism are less sure. Similarly, actual experience in dealing with the Chinese has also varied considerably. Some look forward to continuing and expanding relations that fit into their global strategy, while others have been thoroughly frustrated and vow never again to be involved with China.

The Nankai Conference was organized to promote an understanding of transnational corporations as well as of China's open door policy. It also sought to provide a guide to policies by sharpening new tools of analysis and evaluating experiences in other countries. The participants included academicians in various disciplines, government officials, and transnational executives. Over sixty papers were presented. Most authors departed from their written texts and expanded their arguments significantly in introducing their papers. A major part of the conference was devoted to informal as well as formal exchanges of views.

For convenience, the chapters based on the conference are organized in three parts.

Part I gives a theoretical and empirical overview of transnational corporations (or multinational enterprises—the terms may be used interchangeably). It summarizes the salient developments to date as well as the arguments of major schools of thought. The lead chapter by John Dunning poses the fundamental question of whether a new theory of transnational corporations is required given the significant changes in the world environment. These changes include the continued trend toward globalization of the world's major enterprises, increased two-way flows of investment, shifts in the geographic pattern of transnational corporation activities, and an increasingly conciliatory attitude toward them. The result is an eloquent defense of his eclectic theory, which can serve as a framework for explaining a variety of phenomena. This is not surprising since the eclectic theory is already a synthesis of numerous less comprehensive theories. As in the case of the paradigms of general theory, such as supply and demand, almost any particular explanation can be fitted in. At the same time, in view of the fact that the numerous changes in the environment are expressly considered for the first time in this framework, the chapter represents an important extension of Dunning's theory as expounded earlier.

Chen Yin-fang observing the same set of changes in the environment, attempts to answer the important question of whether transnationals have a positive or negative impact on development—of the Third World in particular. His recognition of the basic positive ingredients of the transnationals' contribution to productive forces is in striking contrast to most of the writings of his compatriots since the 1950s. The main point, however, is that while one should not deny possible conflicts between the transnationals and the host developing countries arising from differences in their objectives, from certain activities such as transfer pricing and restrictive business practices, or from lack of concern on the part of the transnationals for less developed areas), emphasis should be placed on the policies and measures that developing countries themselves can adopt in order to utilize the capabilities of the transnationals.

A further exposition of the theoretical basis for an open door policy in a developing country is provided by Xian Guoming. This basis is not derived from the pronouncements of Lenin or Mao, but from Western thought—notably, the theory of internalization. In spite of certain limitations of the theory, the key role of transnationals in the contemporary international division of labor is affirmed. Such division of labor in accordance with the law of comparative advantage is seen to have accelerated the development of all countries, and developing socialist countries should participate in it through the pursuit of a long-term open door policy.

Jack Behrman, more specifically, suggests that appropriate government policies toward transnationals need to be designed according to the different orientations and strategies of different types of transnationals. Since resource seekers, market seekers, and efficiency seekers have different strategies, different government policies should be designed in order to obtain the most effective contribution from each. One of the conclusions reached is that transnational corporation codes of conduct are often ineffective or even counterproductive because they are either too vague or too specific. This argument, however, is countered by Jun Nishikawa, in chapter 6 as well as by Carsten Ebenroth and Joachim Karl in chapter 11.

Policy dilemmas for developing countries in respect to transnationals in knowledge-processing industries, notably computers and telecommunications, are emphasized by Edward Roche. This sector lags in most developing countries as compared with the rapid pace of innovation in developed economies. If a developing country adopts a relatively open policy in order to allow technological diffusion from transnationals, the domestic industry may be unable to withstand superior competition. On the other hand, if barriers are erected against such diffusion, the domestic technology may soon become out of date. Indeed, there are already vast amounts of wasted investment, both in human resources and in hardware, rapidly becoming obsolete in developing countries. Correspondingly, international arrangements also lag behind the problems and opportunities brought about by the microelectronic revolution.

A more forceful reminder of possible negative aspects of transnationals is offered by Jun Nishikawa. Not only does he see inherent conflicts between transnationals and host and home countries, but also a linkage between transnationals and the current world crisis. The conflicts are regarded as inevitable given the pattern of international division of labor, transfer pricing, restrictive business practices, and the control over subsidiaries desired or brought about by transnationals. The world crisis, in his eyes, ranges from unemployment and stagflation in developed countries to crushing external debt and abject poverty in developing economies. His recipe for action is adequate control of transnationals at the international, national, and local levels. In particular, he envisions a new society in which human beings, with the aid of solidarity of labor, will control transnationals and not vice versa.

Part II provides an international perspective. The experience of other countries in their relations with, and policies toward, transnationals are just as valuable to China as the lessons from China are to the rest of the world. Stefan Robock characterizes the posture of the United States government toward inward and outward international direct investment as essentially "no door" rather than an open door policy. With very few exceptions, there are no special institutions or procedures to screen the inflow or outflow of foreign investment. After a review of the trend and pattern of investment behavior of U.S. private enterprises with different strategies, he concludes that attracting U.S. investment to China depends mainly on the economic, political, policy, and administrative situations in the host country. The main determinant of U.S. investment decisions is profitability. Resource seekers will weigh the attractiveness of various host countries. Market seekers must have the ability to repatriate some of their profits though they may be required to earn some foreign exchange. Import-substituting industries can eventually be converted to export industries.

The new open door policy of India in the 1980s is the theme of Anant Negandhi's chapter. The important point is that China is not the only developing giant to pursue such a line. The policy is examined in the context of the historic evolution of Indian industrial policy. Although as of the 1986 conference, it is too early to tell how the policy will be received in India, an analysis of the impact of earlier policies of restricting inward investment and payments for technology transfers indicates the contending forces. These are implicit in the positive effects of earlier policies—namely, the development of indigenous entrepreneurs and technological capabilities, and in their negative aspects, notably the monopolist domestic market and the stagnation of industrial and technological programs.

In contrast to the praise heaped by many observers upon the Thai model of development, Suthy Prasartset laments the utter dependence of Thai society on transnationals. Trade dependence, financial and debt dependence, technological dependence, and cultural dependence are all the results of transnational corporate control of local productive processes and the weakening of the indigenous bourgeoisie. Technological domination by transnationals, in particular, reveals itself in restrictive contractual arrangements, high fees, and pervasive transnational influence. Transnational control over important branches of industry is exercised through technology, market channels, imports, finance, and management as well as through equity investment. The message for Chinese policy is that if China's present selective relinking of its economy with the transnationals goes beyond a certain point, there is a danger that it will result in financial and technological dependence as well as in cultural disruption through the emulation of transnationalized life-styles and tastes.

The case of Hungary is of special interest because its experiments in new relations with transnationals as well as experiments in overall reform of the socialist economy started much earlier than in most other socialist countries. Mihály Simai identifies the evolutionary process of this new relationship. Before the second World War, the view of transnationals was dominated by ideological and political preoccupations. Transnationals were characterized as monopoly capitalist and not seriously studied as potential partners or possible organizational models. The increasing role of transnationals and the expansion of Hungary's trade with the West demanded a new approach. As the experience of this trade proved largely satisfactory, and the political environment became more favorable, many forms of cooperation with transnationals were established. Since 1986, there have been qualitative changes in this cooperation as a result of the ongoing economic reforms and the establishment of a new legal framework that facilitates transnational capital inflow and free trade zones. However, the extent of transnational corporation involvement to date remains limited.

Common to both developing and developed countries is the international environment. Carsten Thomas Ebenroth and Joachim Karl note in chapter 11 the renewed importance in recent years of foreign direct investment. There has been a change in attitude on the part of most developing countries about the impact of such investment, and their debt crises have enhanced the attractiveness of alternative sources of finance. Contrary to the view expressed by Behrman earlier, Ebenroth and Karl underline the usefulness of an international code of conduct. Such a code could serve as a GATT for international investment. The draft United Nations code can already provide a guide to negotiating and interpreting bilateral investment contracts. It can also improve the investment climate of developing countries and ease the current debt crisis.

Part III deals directly with China's open door policy. The relevant papers presented at the conference were very many and voluminous, covering a wide range of topics, from strategic considerations to specific policy, sectoral, and geographic issues, from macro development to experience at the enterprise level. Only a few of these papers can be included in this book.

The chapter by Zhang Yangui provides a forceful reminder that the decision to adopt an open door policy raises the follow-up question of the choice of competing strategies. After an assessment of the external and internal environments, a strong argument is presented for a mixed approach embodying import substitution, export promotion, and export substitution as well as resource exploitation, thus rejecting simpler or mutually exclusive solutions. Import substitution becomes the dominant area for attracting foreign capital, mainly because it is appropriate for the basic industries. These may be sunset industries in developed economies, but they are sunrise industries in China. This strategy fits with the redeployment of industries in the global strategy of transnationals as well as with China's development plans. However, export promotion is suitable for light industries, notably textiles, which are labor intensive and which must earn foreign exchange in order to support import-substituting industries. Export substitution, defined as a transition from labor-intensive exports to technology and capital-intensive exports, is also feasible because China, like India, has some fairly advanced basic industries. Some of China's natural resources, such as agricultural and mineral products, have export surpluses and will continue to provide a substantial portion of export earnings. This mixed approach is to be accompanied by the use of various forms of cooperation in different industrial sectors and geographic regions. It also requires close coordination of the various components of the strategy.

Some of the strategic considerations are echoed in chapter 13 by Wang Zheng Xian. In particular, import substitution is affirmed as part of a general policy of welcoming foreign direct investment. Skepticism is expressed about the usefulness of existing cost-benefit analysis techniques in selecting projects, in view of the lack of efficient markets and the tenuous estimates of shadow prices and indirect effects. Despite the general conclusion that the positive effects of foreign direct investment are likely to outweigh the negative ones, the chapter is in agreement with many foreign observers that China's investment climate remains a problem.

An external view of China's policies and relations with transnationals is offered by S. J. Noumoff. The problems confronting China since the historic decision of the Third Plenary of the Eleventh Central Committee are found to be enormous despite the correctness of the general policy line. The uneven development of regions is both deliberate and unavoidable since it is beyond

China's means to develop all areas simultaneously. Yet, the internal transfer of skill and technology from the more prosperous to the less prosperous areas may not be sufficient in spread and scale to avoid inequities. While many positive experiences with transnationals are reported, the negative experiences should not be lost sight of. The negative features include the receipt of outdated technology, overvaluation of foreign technology, undervaluation of Chinese contributions in joint ventures, vague contractual arrangements, and lack of Chinese participation in foreign marketing. All these are illustrated by cases such as the Remy-Martin of Tianjin wine joint venture, the Wuhan iron and steel works equipment acquisition from Japan, the Baoshan steel complex, a Chengzhou watch factory, and a shirt project. The inescapable conclusion is that it was nonsensical in the past to adopt a contemptuous attitude toward all things foreign. It would be equally nonsensical now to worship them.

Some of the problems in China's relations with transnationals arise from a lack of mutual understanding of each other's laws and regulations. Preston Torbert's chapter documents problems in technology transfer between Chinese and U.S. parties. A mutual understanding will allow each side to realize that certain demands that may appear unwarranted can result from legitimate considerations. This is illustrated by U.S. parties' refusal to give bank guarantees, insistence on a breakdown of technology payments and a prohibiting of sales to other countries of products made with imported technology, and uncertain interpretation of the effect of takeovers or contracts. It is therefore suggested that each party should listen carefully to the other's demands and find out the reasons underlying them.

The problems of transnational management of human resources in China are examined in a field study reported by Murray Bovarnick. Those concerning transnational expatriates in China may come as a surprise both to the casual observer and to the Chinese themselves. For example, the total cost of maintaining a U.S. manager in China runs as high as $250–300,000 per year, reflecting the demanding nature of the work and the unfamiliar and even harsh environment. Among transnational corporations, there are, however, few China-specific policies and practices concerning the selection, orientation, career development, compensation, leave, and education of expatriates. Recognizing that China is not just another developing country, suggestions are made for specific policies for expatriates there, such as measures to provide a supportive environment, special qualifications, more intensive orientation, and longer assignments.

The last chapter, prepared by N. T. Wang, sums up the simple truth that both transnationals and China have been travelling along an untrodden path in their new relations. The errors made in the beginning stages may in retrospect appear totally avoidable or even laughable. Yet, opinions are often formed on the basis either of preconceptions or of outdated empirical evidence. In interpreting the findings presented in this book, it is necessary to remember that China is undergoing important changes and that so are the transnationals. Both may slide down the learning curve. The chapter identifies progress in many respects. At the same time, it should not be assumed that the learning process is automatic; much conscious effort is needed.

A careful study of past experience in relations with transnational corporations, in China and in other countries, together with a forum for exchange of views, should help all parties to profit from a steeper incline of the learning curve. It is hoped that the conference and this book will make a small contribution to this end and will stimulate further efforts elsewhere.

Part I
Transnational Corporations: Theory and Practice

1
Transnational Corporations in a Changing World Environment: Are New Theoretical Explanations Required?

John H. Dunning

T he activities of multinational enterprises (MNEs) continue to grow apace. Throughout the world recession of the late 1970s and early 1980s and, more recently, the renewed prosperity of at least some leading industrialized countries, the total sales—and the foreign component of these sales—by MNEs, has outstripped both world output and world trade. This chapter will concentrate on the changing pattern of MNE involvement in the 1970s and early 1980s and the implications these changes have had on our theorizing about such involvement.*

A Statistical Overview

Through the early 1980s (as the tables in appendixes 1A and 1B reveal), the United States and the United Kingdom remained the world's largest foreign direct investors. Of a total international direct capital stake of around $600 million in 1983, U.S. MNEs accounted for two-fifths and U.K. MNEs for 12 percent. But, the share of new investment accounted for by these countries is declining. In 1960, for example, Germany and Japan accounted for only 2 percent of the world stock of foreign direct investment; by 1983, their share had increased to one-fifth. By contrast, the combined share of the traditional investors—the United States, the United Kingdom and the Netherlands—had fallen from over three-quarters to under two-thirds.

One of the most intriguing phenomena of the late 1970s and early 1980s has been the emergence of some industrializing less developed countries as outward direct investors. By 1980, MNEs from India, South Korea, Hong Kong, Singapore, and Brazil—to name the leading capital exporters from the

---

* For the purposes of this book, the terms *transnational corporation* and *multinational enterprise* are synonymous. This chapter draws substantially on writings published elsewhere by the author.

Third World—had invested more than $18 billion mainly in other developing countries, but also (particularly in the technology-intensive and service sectors) in Europe and the United States. Although their share of the world foreign capital stake is still small, it is likely to increase substantially in the late 1980s as these countries develop their own particular competitive advantages.

In the early 1980s, as table 1–1 and figure 1–1 show, the outflow of new foreign investment—particularly from the United States—has been cut back sharply, mainly due to the appreciation of the U.S. dollar, the recovery of the U.S. economy and the debt crisis faced by several developing countries. At the same time, the growth of intraindustry activities by MNEs in developed countries (e.g., the cross-hauling of international production in motor cars, color television sets, tires, and pharmaceuticals has continued, as has the trend toward symmetry of inward and outward investment flows by the leading capital exporters. In the mid-1960s, when the United States's technological and economic hegemony was at its peak, the ratio of its outward to inward direct capital stake was 5.0; but then, as first Germany (F.R.) and then Japan grew in stature, the ratio declined. By 1985, the U.S. outward/inward capital stake ratio had fallen 1.3, while between 1975 and 1985, the rate of increase in the latter was four times that of the former. By contrast, the German outward/inward capital stake ratio trebled from 0.40 in 1960 to 1.20 in 1980. In Japan, inward direct investment flows in the first half of the 1960s were in the region of one-half of outward flows, but by the last three years of the 1970s, they had fallen to just over 4 percent.

The geographic composition of the activities of MNEs also changed in the 1970s and early 1980s. The United States, Western Europe, and industrializing Asia (except India) all attracted an increasing share of new investment, while that going to the more traditional recipients (e.g., Canada, Latin America, India, and Australia) fell. In the United States, most MNE activity in the late 1970s took the form of acquisitions or part acquisitions of companies by European investors. There were several reasons for this. Relative to the major European currencies and the yen, the dollar was undervalued. The stock market was depressed, and U.S. internal energy prices were below international levels. By mid-1982, both the dollar and U.S. share prices had recovered, and the rate of foreign acquisitions was drastically cut back. At the same time, the earlier retrenchment by some MNEs of their foreign investment (to prop up ailing industries at home) was stemmed.

MNEs have a wide industrial spread in their foreign activities, but in the past decade, the most rapid growth has occurred in high technology manufacturing sectors, in information-intensive service sectors (especially in finance, insurance, and business services), in trade and distribution, and in tourist-related activities. Due inter alia to the expropriation of the assets of mineral-based MNEs in several developing countries, the share of the foreign

Table 1–1
Outward Direct Investment Flows by Region and Selected Countries, 1968–83

	Average Annual Value of Flows (SDR millions)				Share of Total World Flows (Percent)			
	1968–73	1974–80	1981–83	1983 Only	1968–73	1974–80	1981–83	1983 Only
All Countries	12,653	27,100	29,071	28,421	100.0	100.0	100.0	100.0
Developed countries	12,576	26,746	27,529	27,520	99.6	98.7	92.7	96.8
United States	7,112	12,319	2,760	4,607	56.2	45.5	9.5	16.2
Europe	4,422	10,674	16,749	14,488	35.0	39.4	57.6	51.0
EC[a]	2,352	6,054	9,246	8,302	18.6	22.3	31.8	29.2
United Kingdom	1,710	3,771	5,499	3,692	13.5	13.9	18.9	13.0
Other Europe	361	849	2,005	2,494[e]	2.9	3.1	6.9	8.8
Canada	348	1,493	3,233	4,253	2.8	5.5	11.1	15.0
Japan	567	1,729	3,882	3,374	4.5	6.4	13.4	11.9
Other developed countries[b]	147	531	905	798	1.2	2.0	3.1	2.8
Developing countries	57	354	1,601	900	0.5	1.3	5.5	3.2
OPEC countries[c]	25	112	1,072[c]	387	0.2	0.4	3.7	1.4
Western Hemisphere[d]	17	153	262	267	0.1	0.6	0.9	0.9
Africa[d]	5	7	17	7	*	0.1	0.1	*
Asia	10	72	250	239	0.1	0.3	0.9	0.8
Middle East[d]	1	8	40	–10	*	*	0.1	*
Other Asia and Pacific[d]	10	65	211	249	0.1	0.2	0.7	0.8
Estimate for unreported flows	0	0	59	1	0	*	–0.2	*

Source: International Monetary Fund. *Balance of Payments Statistics, 1984 Yearbook,* part 2, vol. 35; *1983 Yearbook,* part 2, vol. 34; *1982 Yearbook,* part 2, vol. 33; *1981 Yearbook,* part 2, vol. 32; *1980 Yearbook,* part 2, vol. 31; *Supplement to 1979 Yearbook,* vo..30; and *Supplement to 1977 Yearbook,* vol. 27.

Notes: All countries total includes IMF estimates for unreported flows, identified in this table as "Estimate for unreported flows." Since these estimates are not allocated by country, developed and developing countries' totals do not add to all countries' total. Otherwise, columns may not add to totals because of rounding.

* Less than one-tenth of one percent.

a. Belgium, France, Germany F.R., Italy, Luxembourg, and the Netherlands.

b. Australia, New Zealand, and South Africa.

c. Outward direct investment flows from Kuwait for 1981 and 1982 have been adjusted by 2,253 millions SDRs and 505 mill:on SDRs, respectively. The data for Kuwait were adjusted based on U.S. data showing direct investment capital inflows to the United States from K.iwait, which represent outward direct investment flows related to acquisitions of U.S. companies, transactions identified in public sources.

d. Excludes flows from OPEC countries, which are shown separately.

e. Switzerland reported outward direct investment flows to the IMF for the first time in 1983, valued at 459 million SDRs.

Figure 1–1. Outflow of Foreign Direct Investments of Developed-Market-Economy Countries by Region of Origin, 1950–83 (billions of U.S. $ at 1975 prices and U.S. $ exchange rates)

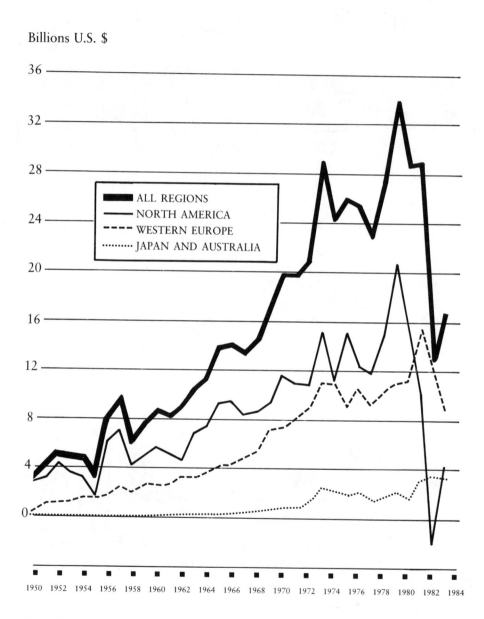

Source: United Nations Centre on Transnational Corporations.

capital stake directed to the primary sector of these economies fell from 23 percent in 1971–72 to 12 percent by the end of the decade, while that going to the manufacturing and services sectors rose from 59 to 65 percent and 18 to 24 percent, respectively.

Another important structural development of the period has been the growth of integrated production by MNEs in Western Europe and Latin America—particularly in cars, computers, agricultural machinery, and domestic electrical appliances—coupled with the emergence of Japan as an important foreign investor. In the early 1960s, Japanese MNEs had largely concentrated their foreign activities in South Asian developing countries and in industrial sectors in which Japan was least competitive or was about to become uncompetitive (e.g., textiles, iron and steel, and various primary goods sectors). More lately, as it has upgraded its domestic technological capabilities and has sought to penetrate the markets of foreign competitors (e.g., with motor vehicles and consumer electronics), Japan has begun to invest more in these sectors in Europe and the United States. In the United Kingdom, for example, there were in 1986 six Japanese affiliates that produced nearly one-half the color TV sets bought by British consumers. As Japanese exports become less competitive (due to higher real wage costs or import protection), import-substituting Japanese investment is likely to increase sharply.

In recent years, MNEs from almost every country have increased the component of their worldwide sales produced abroad. For all leading MNEs, this was 31 percent in 1977 and 34 percent in 1982.[1] For U.K. MNEs, it rose from 35 to 40 percent; for Swedish MNEs, from 40 to 50 percent; for Japanese MNEs from 4.1 to 7.1 percent.

Some industrial sectors are more internationally oriented than others and a few are completely dominated by MNEs. In 1982, 38 percent of the global sales of petroleum companies were derived from their foreign affiliates; higher than average ratios were also recorded by tobacco MNEs (44 percent) and consumer chemicals (including pharmaceuticals) MNEs (40 percent). By contrast, the sectors least involved in foreign production included aerospace (8 percent), textiles and clothing (18 percent), and paper and wood products (18 percent). Chemical, automobile, and food-processing MNEs are among those increasing the foreign component of their output between 1977 and 1982, while the share of this component fell in the case of office equipment and petroleum MNEs.

New Thinking on the Theory of MNE Activity

To what extent do the developments just described necessitate a reappraisal of the economic and behavioral theories of foreign direct investment and

MNE activity put forward in the 1950s and 1960s to explain what was largely a U.S. phenomenon and one generally confined to large MNEs competing in oligopolist markets? It is my belief that, while some of the partial theories of the 1960s are inappropriate to explain the events of the 1980s, the more general paradigms of international production developed by economists at the University of Reading since the mid-1970s—particularly when combined with recent advances in our understanding of the business strategy of MNEs—do fare well and offer a useful and operational explanation of the burgeoning foreign involvement in the Chinese economy.

Let us now trace some of the main theoretical insights of the 1970s and 1980s. Early attempts to explain the multinationalization of firms by drawing on traditional international capital theory were soon abandoned for two main reasons. First, foreign direct investment involves the transfer of resources other than finance capital and it is the expected return on these, rather than on the capital per se, that prompts enterprises to produce outside their national boundaries. Second, in the case of direct investment, resources are transferred within the same firm, rather than externally between two independent parties; in consequence, *de jure* control is still retained over their usage. Furthermore, in some cases, without this control (which is often necessary to capture the economies of common governance), the transfer of resources to a recipient firm changes its production capabilities. This is the essential difference between portfolio and direct investment.

Industrial Organization Theory versus Location Theory

If international capital theory could not explain the growth of MNE activity, what could? By the mid-1960s, two main approaches led the stage—namely, the "why" or "how it is possible" approach based on industrial organization theory and the "where" approach based upon location theory.

The Industrial Organization Theory Approach. This theory concentrated on identifying the characteristics of MNEs that gave them a net competitive advantage over other firms that might supply the same foreign markets. Though the gist of this idea was contained in the studies of Southard (1931) and Dunning (1958), it was left to Hymer's seminal doctoral thesis (1960) to refine and formalize it into a separate theory of foreign direct investment.[2] Based on an internationalization of Joe Bain's notion of barriers to entry, Hymer asserted that foreign direct investment presupposed that investing firms possessed assets (e.g., technology, access to markets, managerial capacity) that other firms did not have, and that these advantages could be sustained over time because of entry barriers. The identification and evaluation of these advantages commanded much of the attention of economists in the 1960s and early 1970s.

The Location Theory Approach. This second approach tried to answer the question "Why do firms produce in one country rather than in another?" Frank Southard followed this approach in his pioneering work on American Industry in Europe (1931), as did the authors of most of the early country case studies published between 1953 and 1970. In most cases, the influences of location were extracted from field study data and, occasionally, ranked in importance. Later, as more complete statistics became available, statistical analysis was used to identify the main factors leading to U.S. direct investment in Europe and Canada.

For the most part, these two approaches evolved independently of each other and, for this reason, if for no other, neither was wholly satisfactory. The industrial organization approach did not explain where competitive advantages were exploited; location theory could not explain how it was possible for foreign-owned firms to outcompete domestic firms producing in the later's territory. Neither approach grappled with the dynamics of foreign direct investment. In this respect, the work of Raymond Vernon and his colleagues on the product cycle theory (Vernon, 1966; Wells, 1970) was of pioneering significance, partly because it treated trade and investment as part of the same process of exploiting foreign markets, and partly because it explained how the process varied over time. To the questions "why" and "where," Vernon added the "when" to the theory of foreign direct investment. But even the Vernon theory was initially put forward to explain the growth of U.S. manufacturing investment abroad and, in the 1960s at least, relied exclusively on data about U.S. corporate activity.

Theoretical Advances in the 1970s and 1980s

Advances in the theories of international production in the 1970s have taken five main directions.

Extensions of the Industrial Organization Approach. There have been numerous variations of this approach; however, each has focused on identifying and evaluating the competitive advantages most likely to explain patterns of the foreign manufacturing activities of U.S.-based MNEs. The conclusions of many studies suggest that the firm- or ownership-specific advantages most likely to explain foreign direct investment fall into three groups: (1) superior management, technology, and innovatory capacity, (2) the ability to produce a differentiated or branded product, and (3) the advantages associated with geographic and product diversification. Limited testing has also been done on the industrial structure of foreign direct investment by other countries.

Extensions of Financial Theories. There has been a resurgence of interest in some of the financial aspects of the foreign activities of firms. There have been a series of strands, but most fall into one of two groups: first, those emphasizing the imperfections of capital markets and foreign exchange, e.g., Aliber (1970), (which, inter alia, explain why enterprises of one nationality may value assets denominated in a foreign currency differently from firms of another nationality), and, second, those extending portfolio theory to explain the industrial and geographic distribution of foreign activities and take account of risk diversification and the stability of earnings. Here the work of Lessard (1979) and Rugman (1979) is especially illuminating.

Extension of the Theory of the Firm. There have been several new theoretical advances in seeking an explanation for international production as an extension to the theory of the firm. This reflects a switch in attention from the act of foreign direct investment per se—which is now recognized as a particular form of involvement by firms outside their national boundaries—to the institution making the investment. Here, the MNE is essentially treated as a special case of a large diversified firm. Using the principles first expounded by Coase (1937) and Penrose (1958)—but more recently developed and extended by Arrow (1971), Alchian and Demsetz (1972), and Williamson (1975)—in their analysis of information markets and economics of vertical integration, economists such as McManus (1972), Buckley and Casson (1975), Magee (1977), Rugman (1981, 1982), and Teece (1981) have sought to explain the propensity of firms to engage in foreign direct investment in terms of the failure of the market (as an economic institution) to efficiently transact the exchange of intermediate products between independent sellers and buyers. Such failure may show itself, inter alia in high negotiation and transaction costs, particularly in markets in which knowledge of product availability and performance is asymmetric; in supply instabilities; in the protection of proprietary rights; in the absence of future markets; and the inability of the selling firm to extract the maximum price of the product or asset being sold, either because of buyer ignorance or uncertainty (e.g., in the case of a patent) or because the full benefit of a particular asset depends on its being used jointly with other assets that only the selling firm possesses. The higher these costs, relative to those of internalized decisiontaking, the more an enterprise is likely to wish to supervise its foreign investments.

This approach helps to explain by which route a firm chooses to exploit any advantages it possesses over its foreign competitors (although the route itself may sometimes affect these advantages), a question largely ignored in the early literature on international direct investment. The problem of choosing between the alternative ways of servicing a foreign market was first taken up systematically by Hirsch (1976), who identified the conditions under which a firm might exploit its ownership-specific advantages through exports or foreign direct investment. Later, this theme was extended by Lall (1980), Buckley and Davies (1979), and Giddy and Rugman (1979), who have also addressed the principles of choice between foreign direct investment and licencing as well as between exports and licencing.

Development of an Eclectic Approach. It was, however, the dissatisfaction with these partial explanations of international direct investment and their failure to integrate investment with trade or portfolio resource transfer theory that led economists to favor a more eclectic approach to the subject. This fourth line of development draws upon and integrates the three strands of economic theory just described. Its principal paradigm, described in Dunning (1981), is that a firm will engage in foreign direct investment if each of three conditions is satisfied:

1. It possesses net ownership advantages vis-à-vis those of firms of other nationalities in serving particular markets. These ownership-specific advantages largely take the form of the possession of intangible assets that, at least for a period of time, are the exclusive right of the firm possessing them.

2. Assuming condition (1) is satisfied, it must be more beneficial to the enterprise possessing these advantages to use them itself rather than to lease them to foreign firms to use—i.e., for it to internalize that use through an extension of its own activities rather than externalize it through market transactions with independent firms.

3. Assuming conditions (1) and (2) are satisfied, it must be beneficial for the enterprise to utilize these advantages in conjunction with at least some factor inputs (including natural resources) outside its home country; otherwise, foreign markets would be served entirely by exports and domestic markets by domestic production.

Table 1–2 illustrates the options of servicing a market, which are related to the presence or absence of these three conditions. The eclectic paradigm suggests that a country's propensity to engage in foreign direct investment, or to be invested in by foreign companies, depends entirely on the extent and form of the ownership advantages of its enterprises (whether or not these are internalized within these enterprises) and on how much the enterprises find it

Table 1–2
Market Servicing—The Options

Route of Serving Market	Advantages		
	Ownership	Internalization	(Foreign) Location
Foreign direct investment	Yes	Yes	Yes
Exports	Yes	Yes	No
Nonequity resource transfers	Yes	No	No

Table 1–3
Types of International Production: Some Determining Factors

Types of International Production	Ownership Advantages (the "why" of MNE activity)	Location Advantages (the "where" of production)	Internalization Advantages (the "how" of involvement)	Illustration of types of activity that favor MNEs
Resource-based	Capital, technology, access to markets	Possession of resources	To ensure stability of oil supply at a good price; control of markets	Oil, copper, tin, zinc, bauxite, bananas, pineapples, cocoa, tea
Import-substituting manufacturing	Capital, technology, management and organizational skills, surplus research and development and other capacity, economies of scale, trademarks	Material and labor costs, markets, government policy (e.g., with respect to barries to imports, investment incentives)	Wish to exploit technology advantages, high transactions or information costs, buyer uncertainty	Computers, pharmaceuticals, motor vehicles, cigarettes
Rationalized specialization (1) of products (2) of processes	The same as for import-substituting manufacturing, but also access to markets	(1) Economies of product specialization and concentration (2) Low labor costs, incentives to local production by host governments	(1) The same as for import-substituting manufacturing plus gains from interdependent activities (2) Economies of vertical integration	(1) Motor vehicles, electrical appliances, agricultural machinery (2) Consumer electronics, textiles, clothing, cameras
Trade and distribution	Products to distribute	Local markets; need to be near customers; after-sales servicing	Need to ensure sales outlets and to protect company's name	A variety of goods—particularly those requiring close consumer contact
Ancillary services	Access to markets (in the case of other foreign investors)	Markets	Broadly as for import-substituting manufacturing, rationalized specialization, trade and distribution	Insurance, banking and consultancy services
Miscellaneous	A variety, including geographical diversification (e.g., airlines, hotels)	Markets	A variety (see above)	A variety, including portfolio investment properties plus where spatial linkages are essential (e.g., airlines, hotels)

beneficial to exploit them in a foreign rather than a domestic location. It asserts that most kinds of activities by MNEs, irrespective of their country of origin or involvement, can be explained in this way, although the nature and significance of these advantages will differ according to country, industry, or firm-specific characteristcs. Table1–3 encapsulates the main features of this approach and illustrates the kinds of activities in which MNEs tend to play a dominant role.

Current Thinking on the Eclectic Paradigm. It is now generally accepted that the eclectic paradigm essentially draws its analysis and predictions from two strands of economic theory—the theory of international resource allocation and the theory of market failure.[3] Together, these theories help to explain both the origin of the ownership, location, and internalization (OLI) advantages created or acquired by firms and their strategic management of them.[4] It is, for example, widely accepted that a MNE's choice of location for exploiting its competitive advantages will be influenced by the distribution of immobile resources and by nonmarket forces that are country-specific; but, in explaining the *origin* of some kinds of competitive advantages, these considerations may be no less relevant. Why do some countries innovate more than others? Why do they generate different production technologies, management capabilities, marketing strengths, and entrepreneurial initiatives? Why does the nature of product differentiation vary across national boundaries? Why do some countries excel at some kinds of research development and design relative to others? For the kind of intangible assets that become the proprietary right of firms, but that, to be produced in the first case, need a certain production and marketing environment that is country-specific, this model holds well. Within both the developed and developing world, the patterns of both inward and outward direct investment—like those of trade—do differ between countries. So does the product composition of the world's largest companies (Dunning and Pearce, 1985). So also does the pattern of international patenting, licencing, and technology transfer (Pavitt, 1984; Cantwell, 1985).

To this extent, then, international production combines the export of intermediate products, requiring inputs in which the home country is relatively well endowed, with the use of resources in which the host is relatively well endowed. But if this were all there was to it, we would not need a separate theory of international production; an extension of international trade theory to incorporate trade in intermediate products and allow for the mobility of at least some factor endowments would be sufficient. On the other hand, attempts to explain patterns and levels of international production without taking the distribution of factor endowments into consideration is like throwing the baby out with the bath water![5] Clearly, their location is relevant to explain most resource-based investment and also (if one allows for nonmarket forces such as import controls, taxes, subsidies, and commercial policy) some import-substituting investment as well. It is likely to be most relevant in explaining North/South, and South/North, and South/South, and West/East international trade and production. We would also argue, that, as with trade, firms will normally first engage in international production to take advantage of the differences in the international disposition of resource endowments; hence, one would expect the early overseas ventures of developing countries to be at least partly explainable by a factor-endowment type of model.

The failure of the factor-endowment approach to fully, or, in some cases, even partially explain international production arises simply because it predicates the existence of perfect markets for both final and intermediate goods. In neoclassical trade theory, this leads to all sorts of unrealistic assumptions (e.g., atomistic competition, identity of production functions, the absence of risk and uncertainty, and, implicitly at least, that technology is a free and instantaneously transferable good between firms and countries). Economists have been grappling to incorporate market imperfections into trade theory since around 1950, but, in the main, their attention has been directed to final rather than intermediate goods markets. Because of this, they had paid little attention to the ownership and organization of production across, or indeed within, national boundaries, the implicit assumption being that this question is irrelevant to an understanding of the "where" of economic activity. In situations involving some locational choice between producing intermediate products at home or overseas, attention is directed to the influence on the export versus licencing decision of a foreign firm, rather than the export versus foreign production decision.

This peculiar lack of concern with ownership or governance questions in trade theory—which has spread to some writers, notably Kojima (1978, 1982), who derive their models of direct foreign investment from neoclassical trade theory—arises because such theory (again, implicitly rather than explicitly) assumes that all firms are single-activity or single-product firms. The effect on trade patterns of vertical integration or horizontal diversification of firms is not discussed in the literature. Since the options of (1) internalizing domestic production at different stages along the value-added chain and (2) buying inputs and selling outputs in the open market *within* a country have not interested trade economists, it is hardly surprising that they have been little concerned with issues of international production. Yet, as Casson (1986) has shown, the unique characteristic of the MNE is that it both is multiactivity and engages in the internal transfer of intermediate products across national boundaries. In other words, it produces at different points of the value-added chains and in different countries. Since firms producing at more than one point on the chain necessarily engage in intrafirm rather than, or in addition to, interfirm transactions, and are multiactivity, this implies the existence of some kind of market failure in the sense that, whether within or between countries, firms are motivated to replace the market as a transaction agent. When these activities are undertaken across national boundaries, there is international market failure. It is the difference between domestic and international market or market failure that distinguishes the multinational from the uninational multiactivity firm. It is the inability of the market to organize a satisfactory deal between potential contractors and contractees of intermediate products that explains why one or the other should choose the hierarchical route rather than the market route for exploiting different factor-endowment situations.

Several types of market failure are identified in the literature (Casson 1979, 1986). In a recent assessment of Stephen Hymer's contribution to the theory of the MNE, Dunning and Rugman (1985) distinguished between structural and transactional market failure. The former, which Hymer tended to emphasize, gives rise to monopoly rent arising from an imperfect market structure among competing firms that, through the internalization of related activities, can be increased and captured by the internalizing firm.

The second type of market failure arises from the inability of arms-length transactions to perform efficiently. This might come about for three reasons. The first, and perhaps the most important when considering the differences between international and domestic market failure, is the additional risk and uncertainty associated with cross-border transactions. The MNE, if nothing else, engages in foreign production to counteract environmental volatility (Kogut, 1985). Such risks are particularly noteworthy in raw materials and high technology industries that typically incur high development costs; where there is a danger of a disruption of supplies; where there is a likelihood of property rights being dissipated or abused by foreign licences; or where the threat of the preemption of markets or sources of supplies, or of an improvement in the competitive position by rival oligopolists, will encourage a follow-my-leader strategy by firms (Vernon, 1983).

The second reason for transactional market failure is that the market cannot take account of the benefits and costs associated with a particular transaction between buyers and sellers accruing to one or another of the parties, but that are external to that transaction. Where products are normally supplied jointly with others or are derived from a common imput or set of inputs, there may be good reason why the different stages of the value-added chain should be coordinated within the same firms. Cross-border transactions may give rise to additional advantages of common governance such as those that exploit the imperfections of international capital and exchange markets and of different national fiscal policies.

The third cause of transactional market failure arises wherever the market is insufficiently large to enable firms to capture economies of size and scope while facing an infinitely elastic demand curve. Such economies may be in production or in purchasing, marketing, research and development, finance, organization, and so on; they are essentially those that are external to a particular activity but internal to the totality of activities of a firm.

These and other market failures cause enterprises, be they uninational or multinational, to internalize individual productive activities—vertically, horizontally, or laterally. They do it partly to reduce the transaction costs of using markets and to exploit the transactional benefits of hierarchies—and partly to ensure that they gain the maximum economic rent (discounted for risk) from the asset advantages they possess. I repeat: the only difference between the actions of multinational and uninational firms in this respect is the added dimension of market failure when a particular transaction is concluded across the exchanges. Moreover, market failure may vary according to parties engaging in the exchange.[6] Here too, country-specific factors may enter the equation. Returning again to our parallel between a firm engaged in international trade and one in international production, it is quite possible that while the two may engage in exactly the same value-added activities, the former does so within a single country and exports its final product, whereas the latter undertakes at least part of its value-adding activities outside its national boundaries. This it will do because of the advantages offered by a foreign vis-à-vis domestic location.

Earlier, we suggested that at least some of the endogenous advantages offered by different locations are likely to be based upon the distribution of factor endowments; others, however, will have to do with market failure, which may itself be country-specific. Let us offer two examples. The first is transfer pricing; the second is the diversification of the investment portfolio to reduce risk.

If it is in the best interest of MNEs to allocate revenues or costs arising from the activities in one country to another in order to minimize its global tax burden as well as its exchange and other risks, then differences in corporation taxes between countries and the risk attached to holding assets in different currencies may prompt firms to try and counteract such market failure[7] by appropriate invoicing on intrafirm transactions, the use of leads and lags of payments, and so on. Clearly, the more countries in which MNEs operate, the more these country-specific market failures are likely to affect transborder resource allocation. Second, due to country-specific risks, a firm's decision of where to engage in value-added activities may well be related to the structure of its *existing* investment portfolio (Rugman, 1971). Given the same opportunity to make gross profits, one MNE or group of MNEs might view the advantages of a particular location differently from another MNE or group or, for that matter, a uninational firm. Other examples of firms being influenced in their choice of location by country-specific market failure are set out by Kogut (1985).

There are other ways in which market failure may affect the activities of

MNEs. So far, we have asserted that firms internalize markets to reduce transaction costs, including risks. We have suggested that this has a locational dimension. At the same time, the replacement of market transactions by hierarchical fiat may be undertaken to steal a march on competitors or to protect an existing market stance. The intention to capitalize on the internalization of external economies by coordinating complementary value-added activities is one example. As a firm widens its territorial horizons, it may well be able to exploit advances in information and communication technology better than its uninational competitors. At the same time, transactional competitive advantages may be difficult, if not impossible, to buy or sell on the open market, simply because their economic rent is related to the way in which resources are allocated rather than to the possession of resources per se.[8]

I have suggested that the ownership advantages of the transaction-cost–minimizing kind are likely to assume greater importance as a firm's foreign commitments increase. They are also related to the technical characteristics of the products produced and, particularly, the extent to which it is profitable to engage in the specialization of economic activities along the value-added chain or between different value-added chains. The literature suggests that there are certain types of production that lend themselves to an international division of labor and others that do not (Casson et al., 1985). Similarly, there are some activities that require closer locational linkages than others. Obviously, the greater the economies of scale or scope, and the less the need for activities to be spatially linked, the less concentrated, yet the more specialized, production in a particular location is likely to be. This is the case, for example, in much of North/South vertical production and some North/North horizontal production in specialized products. Usually, apart from resource-based investment and that involving high transfer (e.g., transport) costs, investment based upon this kind of ownership advantage is geared to supplying products with a high income elasticity of demand.

So far, I have not mentioned the economic environment in which international production takes place. The literature is full of illustrations of the way in which country-specific factors influence the generation of ownership advantages of firms, the location in which production takes place using these advantages as inputs, and the extent to which value-added activities are internalized in the same firm (Dunning, 1981). I have already identified the role of resource endowments in the creation and use of the ownership and locational advantages. As regards the internalization advantage, three factors are of crucial importance. The first is the level of economic development, as typified, for example, by the educational, legal, technological, and commercial infrastructure within which both foreign and domestic firms have to operate. The second is the structure of the economy (i.e., what types of economic activity are best suited to its resource patterns and size). The third is the role of national governments in fashioning both political strategy and economic policy and hence, influencing the amount and form of inward and outward direct investment.[9]

We shall confine ourselves to two illustrations. The first is the attitude of governments to being involved in the international economy. The fewer restrictions are placed on trade and commerce then, ceteris paribus, the more firms will locate their production units according to the dictates of production and transaction costs. But it is also the case that the fewer the restrictions on the movements of goods and services, the more MNEs can take advantage of other forms of international market failure (e.g., those arising from economies of scale, externalities, and risk). For example, without regional economic integration in Europe, the easing of trade restrictions within Latin America, and the establishment of export-processing zones in several Asian countries, much of rationalized and export-led manufacturing investment would not have taken place. Neither, indeed, would a good deal of international contracting of materials and parts by MNEs have been feasible.

The second illustration concerns the effect that government policy may have on the establishment of domestic linkages by foreign affiliates, and the form of such linkages. This might be partly affected by inducements to source locally, but no less so by the ability and willingness of governments to influence the supply capabilities of their own firms (e.g., by the improvement of training, technological, and industrial programs, by fiscal incentives, and by encouraging the appropriate kind of market structure).

Let us now conclude this general review of the determinants of international production. The unique characteristic of such production is that it marries the transborder dimensions of the value-added activities of firms with the common governance of those activities. While the former draws upon the economies of both the distribution of the factor endowment and the market as a transactional agent to explain the *location* of production independently of its ownership, the market-failure theory explains the ownership of activity independent of its location. The blending of the two suggests that market imperfections, specific to the transaction of intermediate or final goods across national boundaries, together with the desire of firms to locate the production of different stages of the value-added chain in different countries, should be the core ingredients of any eclectic paradigm of international production. The precise character and pattern of that production will depend on the configuration of ownership, internalization advantages of firms, and the locational advantages of countries. These, in turn, reflect not only the nature of the activities undertaken and the countries in which they are undertaken, but also the characteristics of firms themselves vis-à-vis their competitors, which will determine their strategy in international markets.

One aspect of the eclectic paradigm that interests me especially is how far these determinants and the balance between the factor endowments and market failure explanations are related to the stage of development of a country and its strategy for development and how these in turn influence the country's degree and form of international economic involvement. I have suggested that there are parallels between the internationalizations of production and trade. To start with, trade tends to occur between nations with markedly different patterns of resource endowments.[10] Later, depending on the way in which and the speed at which a country develops relative to others, trade is likely to be increasingly between countries with similar or converging patterns of resource endowments. In such cases, while part of trade may continue to be based on factor endowment differences or differentiated tastes, part will require a "market-failure" type of explanation."[11]

On the other hand, while trade (in its entirety) is always balanced (or nearly balanced), international production need not be. If such production is based on the transfer of intermediate products (such as technology) that require resources with which developed countries are comparatively well endowed or that are best exploited by large and diversified MNEs, one would expect there to be more concentration among the suppliers than the recipients of foreign direct investment and for MNEs to originate mainly in industrialized countries.[12] The factors uphold both these propositions.

A Macroeconomic Approach. The fifth theoretical development of the 1970s and early 1980s is that typified by the work of Kojima (1978, 1982), who prefers a macroeconomic approach to the explanation of international direct investment. Making use of the received theory of international trade, Kojima explains the propensity of countries to engage in international investment in terms of (1) their comparative advantage of particular resource endowments and (2) the market structure in which their enterprises operate. He argues, for example, that while postwar Japanese foreign direct investment has been primarily aimed at exploiting resources in which Japan has a comparative disadvantage, thus releasing capacity in the home country to produce goods that require resources in which it has a comparative advantage, U.S. foreign direct investment has been aimed at those sectors in which the home country has a comparative advantage and the host countries a comparative disadvantage. Kojima puts this "antitrade" type of investment down to the defensive competitive strategy of large U.S. MNEs operating within an oligopolistic market environment.

Although this argument is somewhat simplistic and not entirely borne out by the facts, Kojima has directed the attention of economists to some important resource allocation problems associated with foreign direct investment. His approach can be reinterpreted in terms of the eclectic theory in as much as he is arguing that for countries to make the best use of their human and physical resources, they should seek to encourage inward direct investment in those sectors that use location-specific (i.e., immobile) endowments in which they have a comparative advantage, and that use ownership-specific (and largely mobile) endowments in which their own enterprises have a comparative disadvantage; and to encourage outward direct investment in those sectors in which they require resources in which their enterprises have a comparative ownership advantage but which need to be combined with other (immobile) resources in which they are comparatively disadvantaged.[13] One suspects that in the 1980s, more attention is being given to the structural implications of both inward and outward investment than in the past.[14]

A Strategic Approach. The main criticism of all economic theories of the MNE is that they assume that firms will react to the same information confronting them (e.g., about cost, revenue, and markets) in a way that is consistent with similar, identifiable, and usually single objectives. It is argued that once a firm is faced with either structural or transactional market failure, it has behavioral options, the response to which will depend positively on managerial goals and perceptions of risk situations, an evaluation of the way in which related firms (e.g., competitors and suppliers) react to such situations, and the risk averseness of decisiontakers. Nowhere is this more clearly seen than where diversified MNEs compete as international oligopolists in uncertain markets. In such situations, the identification and evaluation of the variables that influence the strategy of firms may well be as important as identifying and evaluating the variables (e.g., of the OLI kind) that cause firms to consider their strategies in the first place.

The Response of MNEs to a Changing World Environment

Due especially to efforts of host governments to encourage more indigenous ownership in the affiliates of foreign firms, but also to the belief of some MNEs that they no longer need to exercise detailed control over their subsidiaries, an increasing proportion of foreign direct investment is now taking the form of joint ventures rather than wholly owned subsidiaries. In the early 1960s, about two-thirds of all foreign affiliates of MNEs were fully owned by them. By 1980, this proportion had fallen to around 55 percent; that it had not fallen further is partly explained by a parallel desire of larger MNEs—mostly from high technology sectors investing in several countries—to lessen the risks of their international operations by centralizing product and sourcing strategies and financial management. IBM is a classic case in point, but there are many others, particularly those finding it profitable to engage in international product or plant specialization and intrafirm trade.

Since the middle and late 1970s, there has also been a marked change in the way in which MNEs penetrate new markets. In 1960, about three-fifths of new entrants took the form of greenfield investment, and the balance the form of acquisitions, mergers, or reorganizations. By the early 1970s, the former proportion had fallen to around 50 percent and, by the end of the decade, to nearer 45 percent. The fall would have been even more pronounced but for the emergence of new MNEs from Japan and the less developed countries. It would appear that the larger and more diversified a MNE becomes and the later it enters into a market vis-à-vis its competitors, the more it favors acquisition rather than greenfield investment as an entry mode.

A further recent development has been the opening up of Eastern Europe and mainland China to the activities of foreign-based MNEs and an extension of Eastern European firms outside their national boundaries. According to one estimate, there were 544 foreign direct investments (mostly involving minority shareholdings) by the Soviet Union and Eastern European firms in 1978, with a total value of around $1 billion; while, in the reverse direction, the number of joint ventures involving Western firms in Yugoslavia, Rumania, Hungary, and Czechoslovakia was rapidly increasing. Again, it seems that a new era of East–West internationalization of production has begun.

Finally, I would emphasize the blossoming of various forms of nonequity foreign involvement by MNEs and other companies.[15] Contractual and co-operative ventures including technical assistance and licencing agreements, management contracts, franchising arrangements, turn-key operations, and subcontracting have mushroomed in the late 1970s and 1980s. They flourish particularly in sectors in which the technology, management techniques, or information about markets imported from abroad is fairly easily codifiable and where contractors believe their property rights are adequately protected by the terms of the agreement. Such is the case, for example, in the international hotel industry, where there is comparatively little equity investment by MNEs, but a great deal of contractual involvement by the big hotel chains such as Hilton International (U.S.), Grand Metropolitan (U.K.), and Meridien (France). This trend toward the unbundling of the package of resources provided by traditional foreign direct investment has also led to the growth of MNE consultants in the construction engineering and business service sectors.

The Future Scenario

To what extent are the trends just outlined likely to continue in the 1980s? What has been the influence of governments on the events of the 1970s and what is likely to be their role in the future?

First, the early 1970s were a time of rising confrontation between MNEs and many nation states, which seemed to reach its peak between 1973 and

1975, when oil prices quadrupled and the United Nations set up the Commission on Transnational Corporations to monitor the activities of transnationals and to assist developing countries' dealings with them. Coupled with the depreciation of the U.S. dollar in 1971 and a concerted movement by many developing countries toward economic self-reliance, the growth of international business seemed threatened. As fast as these conditions came about, however, others were set in motion that dramatically realigned the balance of power between MNEs and host governments and affected perceptions of what each could offer the other. The world economic recession of the late 1970s increased, rather than reduced, the need of all countries—particularly developing countries—for the investment, technology, and markets unique to MNEs; this, together with a move to the right by many governments, led to a more conciliatory and constructive attitude toward international hierarchies.

Second, the 1970s saw an intensification of competition between the world's leading MNEs as well as the emergence of new sources of finance capital, technology, and management.

Third, the countries or regions growing fastest in the world economy (e.g., Japan and some parts of Western Europe and East Asia) generally pursued welcoming policies toward inward direct investment; in addition, they had a well-trained and motivated labor force, adequate organizational and technological infrastructures, and an economic system conducive to private enterprise.

Fourth, within Europe and to a certain extent in Latin America, regional economic integration, by reducing trade barriers, has encouraged MNEs to engage in product rationalization and intraindustry trade and investment. In the 1980s, there have been further improvements in international communications.

Within this kind of scenario, we would expect that international business will flourish, but that its character will change and its structure will become a lot more diversified. The integrated MNE should remain a dominant force in technology- and information-intensive industries, particularly where production decisions and transactions are coordinated by international computing networks. With the advent of telematics, the opportunities for small firms to internationalize their operations will increase. At the same time, increasing risks of large capital commitments at a time of rapid technological change and the propensity for many diverse technologies to be involved in the production of a single product suggest that firms may wish to establish more cooperative links. There might be, too, a growth of time-limited equity arrangements, particularly in the less technology-intensive import-substituting sectors, with MNEs from Japan and the more advanced developing countries playing an active tutorial role.

At the same time, as mergers and rationalizations are part of domestic economic life—particularly in times of structural change—and as long as imperfections remain in international capital and foreign exchange markets, I foresee increases in both the exit and entry of MNEs and transborder acquisitions, and in cooperative agreements—particularly among MNEs in developed countries with one type of MNE (the multinational conglomerate) behaving more like an institutional than a direct investor. Finally, I envisage greater roles of governments as initiators and the international capital market as financiers of projects in which foreign firms will act more as contractors or subcontractors than as entrepreneurs. This is already happening in the Middle East, where huge new construction projects are being financed from oil money, under Korean management and with Sri Lankan or Philippino labor. Gone are the days when foreign companies *own* country-specific natural resources that are the basis of that country's comparative trading advantage with the rest of the world. This indigenization of assets will become more widespread in some manufacturing and service sectors—with the role of the foreign direct investor being increasingly that of a catalyst for self-development rather than that of an economic imperialist.

More generally, in many other ways the international economic climate of the last two decades of the twentieth century will be very different from that of the third quarter. Since the 1950s, the emphasis has been on technological innovations and productivity improvements—spurred on by the need to cope with rising living standards and labor shortages. This has generated competitive advantages of a capital- or technology-intensive kind. In the foreseeable future, in an industrialized world of limited growth and substantial unemployment, environmental concern, and the depletion of nonrenewable resources—and in a developing world increasingly conscious of its need to satisfy basic needs—the innovational emphasis may well be on materials and energy saving and on increasing agricultural output.

If this diagnosis is correct, it may be that the technological advances of the 1980s and 1990s will require a different kind of organizational form to exploit them. As some countires move toward a postindustrial stage of development, more innovations will occur in the service sector. (Already this has happened in the sphere of project management, consultancy, and data provision and interpretation.) It is by no means certain that the resource endowments needed for these innovations and their development will be those that generated their predecessors. Nor is it certain that the hierarchical structure of firms evolved during the 1960s and 1970s will be suitable for the remaining years of the twentieth century.

All this suggests constant shifts in the role of MNEs in the world economy and in their form of involvement. But this is no less true of the domestic business sector in many countries; very few firms supply the same product or markets as they did 50 years ago. Yet, whatever the problems of size and diversification, for every firm that cannot manage to cope efficiently, there is another that can—spurred on by some new technology or organizational advance that it can accommodate in its hierarchy. That, to my mind, is the test: the rate of growth of new innovations, institutions, and ideas on the one hand, and the willingness of countries to be economically interdependent on the other.

By the end of the decade, we would foresee a dual structure of MNE activity. The first group of firms, mainly made up of very large international hierarchies and in the vanguard of technological progress, will act as the pivotal firms with a galaxy of satellites—bonded to each other by equity ownership or a variety of collaborative arrangements. They are likely to be U.S., Japanese, or European in origin; their satellites will operate in different locations and be linked to the mother firms by a common technological base and production strategy. The major constellation of such MNEs is likely to be concentrated on a North/North axis, with some North/South involvement.

The second, and much larger, group of MNEs will consist of smaller-sized firms engaging in the more traditional import-substitution or resource-based investment. These will tend to be concentrated in more mature industrial sectors, producing goods and services, that do not depend on the kind of linkages of the first group of MNEs. The MNEs now emerging from the Third World are likely to be of the North/South or South/South kind.

What, finally are the implications of these speculations for governments? First, it is clear that the industrial nation state is far from dead. Though, in the mid-1980s, most governments are taking a relaxed stance toward MNE activity, it would be unwise to assume that all is well. Economic autonomy is still a widely sought goal; to this extent, there is an inherent conflict between the ways in which individual countries and MNEs view the world. How this conflict is resolved or ameliorated in the later 1980s and 1990s is very likely to be dependent on (1) the costs and benefits of MNE activities, (2) how both home and host governments perceive the impact of these costs and benefits on their national economic and political objectives, and (3) their bargaining power to affect the actions of MNEs or their affiliates so that they can best meet these objectives. My best guess is that, in the absence of war or a collapse of the international financial system, the world will continue along the path it has travelled since 1945 toward "controlled" economic interdependence, but along that path, there will be deviations toward and away from national economic autonomy. For example, in the 1980s, Europe has moved toward a new round of protectionism. This may increase some kinds of international production (e.g., Japanese investment to overcome tariff barriers and other import controls), but it will reduce that kind of multinationalism that aims to take advantage of the international product or process specialization.

One final point. In the future, it may be that countries will find that they have less freedom to be discriminatory or selective in their national policy toward their own or foreign-based MNEs than once they had. Inter alia, this is because of the greater locational flexibility afforded by integration to MNEs. In any event, it is clear from studies of factors influencing the siting of economic activity by MNEs that *general* economic strategies and specific incentives or obstacles pursued by governments act as a much more decisive influence. To attract more foreign investment, efficient and forward-looking macroeconomic and industrial policies, together with the provision of the right kind of educational and technological infrastructure, are likely to prove much more persuasive than short-run incentives such as tax holidays or investment allowances.

At the same time, to benefit fully from both outward and inward direct investment, countries that wish to be part of the new international division of labor in their industrial strategy should give some attention to the ways in which governments should be involved in any restructuring process or provision of aid to indigenous companies. A positive policy of cooperation and understanding between the private sector and the state, similar to that evolved by the Japanese since the 1970s, is the kind of thing I have in mind. Indeed, unless the behavior and operations of MNEs and other foreign-based companies are recognized and reflected in national industrial policy, there are dangers that countries such as China will not gain the benefits from their participation in the world economy that they could and, indeed, should.

Notes

1. Dunning, J. H., and Pearce, R. D., *The World's Largest Industrial Companies, 1962–83* (Aldershot: Gower, 1985).
2. Complete bibliographic references may be found in standard texts such as Caves, Richard E., *Multinational Enterprise and Economic Analysis* (N.Y.: Cambridge University Press, 1982) and the author's writings published elsewhere.
3. For a fuller account of the eclectic paradigm and an examination of its criticisms, see Dunning (1985). In speaking of the theory of international resource allocation, I refer most notably to the Hecksher/Samuelson/Ohlin (HSO) kind.
4. I accept that because of the differing objectives of firms and attitudes of decisionmakers to risk and uncertainty, it may be difficult to fully incorporate strategic variables into the eclectic paradigm. See also Dunning (1985).
5. Again, it is important to identify the exact question one is trying to answer and the perspective from which one is doing so. For example, as far as I am aware, no one has suggested a modification of the theory of the firm to take account of its exporting activities; yet a separate theory of international trade has emerged in the literature, mainly because of the assumption that factor endowments are immobile across national boundaries. Similarly, it may be argued that the need for a separate explanation of international (as opposed to domestic) production must rest primarily on the assumption that at least *some* factor endowments are both immobile and unevenly distributed between countries.

6. As explored by Contractor (1981) and Dunning (1983) when considering the choice between equity and nonequity arrangements of firms for the transfer of technology.

7. In this case, arising at least partly from government fiat or intervention.

8. Except in so far as coordination and entrepreneurship related to coordination can be thought of as resources.

9. In the literature, use is made of the so-called ESP (environment, system, and policy) paradigm to identify ways in which country-specific endogenous variables might influence production decisions of firms (Koopman and Montias, 1971). Here we are primarily concerned with the way in which ESP might affect international market failure.

10. One exception may be trade between neighboring territories.

11. This idea is explored in Dunning and Norman (1985).

12. There are exceptions (e.g., where less well developed countries invest in more developed countries to acquire technology, marketing, and other kinds of knowledge).

13. This point has been taken up by Kojima and Ozawa (1985).

14. For a comparison between the internalization eclectic of the Reading economists and the macroeconomic approach of Kojima, see Buckley (1985).

15. For more details, see Oman, C., *New Forms of International Investment* (Paris: OECD, 1984).

Appendix 1A: World Stock of Direct Investment Abroad by Major Country of Origin in Rank Order, 1983

1A–1

Appendix 1A: World Stock of Direct Investment Abroad by Major Country of Origin in Rank Order, 1983

	Amount ($ billion)					Percentage Distribution					Average Annual Rates of Growth (Percent)			
	1960	1967	1973	1980	1983	1960	1967	1973	1980	1983	1960–67	1967–73	1973–80	1980–83
All countries	66.1	113.9	210.5	511.9	572.8	100.0	100.0	100.0	100.0	100.0	8.1	10.8	13.5	3.8
United States	31.9	56.6	101.3	215.4	227.0	48.3	49.7	48.1	42.1	39.6	8.5	10.2	11.4	1.8
United Kingdom[a]	10.8	17.5	26.9	79.4	95.4	16.3	15.4	12.8	15.5	16.7	7.1	7.4	16.7	6.3
Germany (F.R.)[b]	0.8	3.0	11.9	40.9	40.3	1.2	2.6	5.7	8.0	7.0	20.8	25.8	19.3	-0.5
Netherlands	7.0	11.0	15.8	42.8	36.5	10.6	9.7	7.5	8.4	6.4	6.7	6.2	15.3	-5.2
Japan[c]	0.5	1.5	10.3	19.6	32.2	0.8	1.3	4.9	3.8	5.6	17.0	37.9	9.6	18.0
France	4.1	6.0	8.8	20.8	29.9	6.2	5.3	4.2	4.1	5.2	5.6	6.6	13.1	12.9
Canada[d]	2.5	3.7	7.8	22.1	29.1	3.8	3.3	3.7	4.3	5.1	5.8	13.2	16.0	9.6
Switzerland[e]	2.3	2.5	7.2	23.6	19.8	3.5	2.2	3.4	4.6	3.5	1.2	19.3	18.5	-5.7
Sweden	0.4	1.7	3.0	7.2	10.0	0.6	1.5	1.4	1.4	1.8	23.0	9.9	13.3	11.6
Italy	1.1	2.1	3.2	7.0	9.8	1.7	1.8	1.5	1.4	1.7	9.7	7.3	11.8	11.9
Belgium and Luxembourg	1.3	1.3	2.2	6.2	6.7	2.0	1.1	1.0	1.2	1.2	0.0	9.2	16.0	2.6
South Africa	0[f]	1.9	2.1	5.7	6.5	0[f]	1.7	1.0	1.1	1.1	N.A.	1.7	15.3	4.5
Australia	0.2	0.4	0.5	1.9	3.0	0.3	0.4	0.2	0.4	0.5	10.4	3.8	21.0	16.4
Subtotal	62.9	109.2	201.0	492.6	546.2	95.2	95.9	95.5	96.2	95.4	8.2	10.7	13.7	3.5
Other developed countries	2.5	1.7	3.4	6.0	9.0	3.8	1.5	1.6	1.2	1.6	-5.4	12.2	8.5	14.5
Developing countries	0.7	3.0	6.1	13.3	17.6	1.1	2.6	2.9	2.6	3.1	23.1	12.6	11.8	9.8

Source: For the United States, U.S. Dept. of Commerce, Bureau of Economic Analysis, *Selected Data on U.S. Direct Investment Abroad, 1950–76*, and *Survey of Current Business* (August 1985). For the United Kingdom, Bank of England, *Quarterly Bulletin*. For Germany (F.R.), for 1960–75, "Special statistics" of the Ministry of Economics published in various issues of the *Monthly Report of the Deutsche Bundesbank*; for 1976 onward, "International capital links between enterprises, by country and branch of economic activity," in appendix to the Statistical Supplements to the *Monthly Report of the Deutsche Bundesbank*. For the Netherlands, stock estimates for 1960 and 1967 from J. H. Dunning and J. Stopford, *Multinationals: Company Performance and Global Trends* (London and Basingstoke: Macmillan, 1982), and, for 1973 forward, from OECD, *Recent Trends in International Direct Investment*, based on data compiled by De Nederlandsche Bank. For Japan, for 1960–75, data from the Ministry of Finance; for 1976 onward, direct investment external assets data from the Bank of Japan, *Balance of Payments Monthly* (April issues). For France, stock estimates for 1967 and 1973 from United Nations, *Salient Features and Trends in Foreign Direct Investment* based on H.D. Dragenan, (ed.),

Internationale Direktinvestionen 1973–75, plus or minus cumulative outward direct investment flows for other years' estimates from IMF, *Balance of Payments Statistics*. For Canada, Ministry of Industry, Trade and Commerce, *Statistics Canada*. For Switzerland, Union Bank of Switzerland, *Switzerland in Figures*, and revised, unpublished data for years prior to 1982. For Sweden, stock estimate for 1970 from United Nations, op. cit., based on total assets of majority-owned manufacturing affiliates in Skandinaviska Enskilda Bankens, *Quarterly Review*, no. 2 (1972), plus or minus cumulative outward direct investment flows for other years' estimates from IMF, op. cit. For Italy, appendix to the Bank of Italy, *Annual Report*. For Belgium and Luxembourg, United Nations, op. cit, based on IMF, op. cit. For South Africa, stock estimates through 1982 from South African Reserve Bank, *Quarterly Bulletin*, plus cumulative outward direct investment flows for 1983 from IMF, *op. cit*. For Australia, OECD, *op. cit.*, based on data compiled by the Australian Bureau of Statistics. For other developed countries and developing countries, stock estimates through 1978 from Dunning and Stopford, *op. cit.*, plus cumulative outward direct investment flows for 1979–83 from IMF, *op. cit*, with an adjustment for Kuwait. (See footnote [3] to table 1–2.)

Note: Columns may not add to totals because of rounding.

Data include banking beginning with 1976. Prior to 1979, investment in insurance companies is for the United States only.

a. Beginning with 1979, data include investment by oil companies, insurance companies, and investment in real estate.

b. Beginning with 1976, data are "statistics on levels" as compiled and published by the Deutsche Bundesbank. Data for years prior to 1976 are commonly referred to as "special statistics" published by the Ministry of Economics.

c. Beginning with 1976, data are for direct-investment external assets as compiled and published by the Bank of Japan. Data for years prior to 1976 are "approvals basis data" from the Ministry of Finance.

d. Direct investment abroad by Canadian banks is not included.

e. Data back to 1960 have been revised by the Union Bank of Switzerland to more accurately reflect their estimates, based on sample data, of Swiss direct investment abroad.

f. Included in "Other developed countries."

Appendix IB: MNE Activity in the Early 1980s

Table 1B–1
The Leading Multinational Enterprises

Rank	Name	Nationality	Sector	Sales, 1982 (billion)	Foreign-produced (percent)
1	Exxon	U.S.	Oil	113,197	74
2	Royal Dutch Shell	Netherlands/U.K.	Oil	82,341	60
3	Mobil	U.S.	Oil	68,587	65
4	General Motors	U.S.	Autos	60,026	33
5	Texaco	U.S.	Oil	57,628	67
6	BP	U.K.	Oil	52,231	63
7	Standard (California)	U.S.	Oil	45,229	53
8	Ford	U.S.	Autos	37,067	45
9	IBM	U.S.	Computers	34,364	45
10	Standard (Indiana)	U.S.	Oil	31,304	18
11	ENI	Italy	Oil	30,888	19
12	Gulf	U.S.	Oil	30,025	38
13	General Electric	U.S.	Electrical equipment	26,500	35
14	Unilever	U.K./Netherlands	Soaps, fats, etc.	23,120	39

Table 1B–2
The Fastest-growing Outward Direct Investors

Rank	Country	1983 (1960 = 100)
1	Japan	6,440.0
2	Germany (F.R.)	5,037.5
3	Developing countries	2,514.3
4	Sweden	2,500.0
5	Australia	1,500.0
6	Canada	1,164.0
7	United Kingdom	883.3
8	Switzerland	860.9
9	United States	711.6
10	Netherlands	521.4

Table 1B–3
The Leading Recipient Countries of Foreign Direct Investment, End of 1983

Rank	Country	Value of Inward Capital Stake ($ billion)	Percent of World Capital Stake
1	United States	128.3	23.2
2	Canada	56.6	10.2
3	United Kingdom	50.2	9.1
4	Germany (F.R.)	30.8	5.6
5	France	25.1	4.5
6	Brazil	23.2	4.1
7	Netherlands	17.6	3.2
8	Belgium and Luxembourg	14.5	2.6
9	Switzerland	13.5	2.4

Table 1B–4
The Most Internationalized Industrialized Sectors, 1982

Rank	Sector	Foreign Production as a Percent of All Sales
1	Tobacco products	44.3
2	Pharmaceuticals and consumer chemicals	40.3
3	Petroleum	38.4
4	Building materials	36.5
5	Food products	36.1
6	Office equipment and computers	33.3
7	Rubber products	31.6
8	Industrial chemicals	29.7
9	Automobiles	26.2
10	Drink products	26.2
11	Electronic and electrical appliances	25.7

Appendix Source: Stopford, J., and Dunning, J. H., *Multinationals: Company Performance and Global Trends* (London and Basingstoke: Macmillan 1982); Dunning J. H., and Pearce, R. D., *The Worlds Largest Industrial Enterprises, 1962–83* (Aldershot: Gower, 1985); Dunning, J. H., and Cantwell, J., *IRM Directory of Statistics of International Investment and Production* (London: Macmillan, 1987).

2
Transnational Corporations and World Development: An Evolutionary View

Chen Yin-fang

It is universally acknowledged that the rapid growth and proliferation of transnational corporations since the second World War has had a great influence on the contemporary world economy and on politics. No uniform definition has yet been given to enterprise of this kind in the international forum. Furthermore, opinions are widely divided on the role it plays in world economic development—so much so that scholars with diverse views have made completely contradictory evaluations based on the results of their research. I should like here to contribute my views on the relationship between transnational corporations and world economic development.

The Evolution

The transnational corporation is not a new business organization that emerged only after the second World War. Its postwar operational activities did, however, acquire new characteristics. Since the late 1950s, it has been referred to by various names, such as "multinational corporation," "international corporation," or "global corporation." Starting in 1974, the standardized name of "transnational corporation" found its way into official U.N. documents. A transnational corporation is commonly defined as an enterprise that possesses and controls production or service facilities outside its own country. Such a definition throws light only on the fact that the enterprise organizes transnational operations; it fails to indicate its features and essence.[1] As a result, it cannot serve as a basis for evaluating the role such corporations play in world economic development.

As far as business activities are concerned, enterprises in the developed countries have long been engaged in transnational operations. With the formation of world markets, the advance in science and technology, and the intensification of the division of labor, production and consumption in every country have become international in character. Transnational enterprises

have multiplied day by day, and the business content of transnational operations has become more and more complex and diversified. From simply
exporting commodities and expanding the markets for selling them to trading
patent licences and even to making management contracts with the host
country's government or private entrepreneurs; from setting up commission
agencies and repair and assembly shops abroad to making foreign direct
investment, acquiring existing enterprises or creating new entities in a foreign
country, organizing international production, division of labor, and cooperation, forming extensive overseas management networks, and, ultimately,
establishing what we know as transnational corporations, which are placed
in a monopolistically advantageous position in one or several industries—this
overseas expansion of enterprise has undergone a long period of evolution
through numerous stages of development. Considering the variety of transnational enterprises in the world market, I find it hard to account for the stage
they are at and the capacity they possess merely in terms of their ownership
of overseas production and service facilities. In reality, the management
tactics and the business activities of a highly developed transnational corporation, which has an influence on the world economy and on politics, play a
strikingly different role in world economic development from that of the
ordinary small- and medium-sized firms involved in transnational investment
activities.

Historical conditions are of great significance in the formation and development of transnational corporations. In other words, the international
environment of their time has a close connection with the standard of social
productive force. A transnational corporation is by no means the continuation of the commercial shipping companies of the Middle Ages. It is also
essentially different from the politically privileged and colonially predatory
East India Company in the period of the primitive accumulation of capital.
Modern transnational corporations have resulted from highly developed capitalism. They evolve with the advancement of the world economy. From the
latter part of the nineteenth century onward, large enterprises in Europe and
the United States started to make foreign investments one after another, and
the export of capital became a common practice. With the transition of
laissez-faire capitalism to monopoly capitalism, early transnational corporations took shape. However, at that time, the export of capital was chiefly in
the form of portfolio investment. Direct investment in production accounted
for only a very small proportion of the outflow and was made mostly in
mining and plantations in colonies and dependencies. Only a minority of the
advanced industrial countries made foreign investment in manufacturing.
Not until the eve of the first World War did a very few enterprises form
unified world trusts that controlled capital in billions and had branches,
representative organs, agencies, as well as various kinds of connections, all
over the world.[2] Between the wars, international economic activities were

largely limited by the international cartels, through the formation of which some of the big monopoly enterprises made agreements on prices or sales in order to allocate the world market and maximize their profits. In addition, the Great Depression of 1929–32 had a great influence on these activities. Consequently, the management of most of the early transnational corporations was characterized by local limitation, though these early transnationals' foreign direct investment increased considerably.

After the second World War, great changes took place in the international political and economic circumstances. On the one hand, the postwar technological revolution gave impetus to the rapid development of the world productive force, the enlargement of the objective of labor, the setting up of new industrial sectors, rising labor productivity, and the specialization and internationalization of production. Particularly, the modernization of the means of transportation and communication has relatively shortened space and time, enabling the countries of the world to build closer relationships with one another. With the intensification of the worldwide division of labor, the process of social reproduction in every country has, to various degrees, overstepped national boundaries. On the other hand, world political and economic circumstances and social and economic structures have also undergone great changes. The further concentration of private monopoly capital and the further development of state monopoly capitalism in developed capitalist countries have spurred on and supported the overseas expansion of monopoly enterprises. During the early postwar period, the U.S. transnational corporations were the first to develop rapidly. Starting in the 1960s, the transnationals of Western Europe and Japan also took an active part in overseas expansion. They engaged in fierce monopolistic competition all over the world. Meanwhile, as a result of the collapse of the imperialist colonial system, the suzerain-monopolized markets in the colonies began to open to the world. The Third World countries were struggling for a new international economic order so that they could maintain their national independence and state sovereignty, develop their national economies, and stride forward toward the goals of industrialization and modernization.

It is in these new circumstances of international politics and economy that modern transnational corporations have evolved. As is well known, economy is not the only factor that determines transnational investment in production. There are other factors—political, social, and cultural. Because of the new historical conditions resulting from changes in the environment for international investment as well as from the evolution of the transnational corporations themselves during the course of their adaptation to their objective surroundings, they differ vastly from the early transnational corporations in the direction of their investment, scope of activities, and style and mechanism of management.[3] This fact is acknowledged in numerous research documents.

The Characteristics at an Advanced Stage

Specifically, what are the characteristics of transnational corporations at an advanced stage of transnational operation? It is pointed out in a U.N. report that "a fairly good picture of the situation can frequently be obtained by concentrating on the largest and most important firms, especially those engaged in extractive and manufacturing activities."[4] It is for this reason that scholars usually concentrate on studying the corporate practices of the biggest and most important transnationals. Rich in financial capacity, gigantic in size, and equipped with advanced technology and unique management skills, they have represented the mainstream of the rapid postwar growth and proliferation of transnational corporations. It is their activities that have had a significant influence upon the economic and political development of the modern world. Though entrepreneurs have learned that "corporate multinationalism" is an important philosophy of management, small- and medium-sized enterprises find themselves hard put to practice it.

As a matter of fact, we shall find that each of the "largest and most important" transnational corporations has its own history of growth. In different industries, the program and the style of management are different. If we do away with firm-specific qualities, we shall be able to discover the salient features peculiar to modern transnational enterprises at large:

1. They are either large enterprises or an integrated complex that occupies a monopoly position in one or several sectors. Their basic difference from an ordinary domestic monopoly enterprise lies in the fact that they are internationalized. An enterprise's internationalization not only means that it makes foreign direct investment, sets up branches, organizes international production, and markets through various channels on a global scale, but also signifies that its organization, system of management, procedures of decision-making, and even the personnel employed are all geared to production and trade in a number of countries. Being cosmopolitan and gaining profit from the whole world, their accumulation of capital also bears a global character. It has been said of U.S. business abroad that there is "no country to which it owes more loyalty than any other, nor any country where it feels completely at home."[5] I am afraid this may not be universal. However, it is undoubtedly true that they "see the world as their oyster and judge their performance on a worldwide basis."[6]

2. They implement a global strategy—that is to say, they have both a global strategic aim and a global strategic deployment. The substance of transnational activities is commodity trade, direct investment, and transfer of technology. In order to maximize their profit, the corporations have to plan their production rationally and consider on a global basis the source of raw materials, the employment of labor, the sale of products, and the utilization

of funds. They also have to stress size economy, take advantage of favorable conditions in the host countries and various other regions, and deal with the monopolistic competition of like enterprises in the world market. All this necessitates a combination of commodity trade, direct investment, and the transfer of technology, each interacting upon the other. It also requires the enterprise to make an overall plan while taking into consideration the interests of the whole enterprise and its future development. All transnational corporations have their global strategy despite the wide difference in their industries and their strategic content.

3. *Integration* means close coordination and cooporation within the system of the corporation (parent, branches, and subsidiaries) so that the system becomes an organic whole. The functional departments and organizational forms of transnational corporations may be different, but they must all act upon the principle of centralized decisionmaking and decentralized management. For, to realize its global strategy, the corporation needs unified direction to coordinate its action so as to keep in line with its overall interests. In order to fit in both with the host country's environment for investment and with local market structures, it requires flexible response from its subsidiaries and affiliates. For one thing, they can carry out the parent corporation's strategic plans through hierarchical management planning; for another, they can take risks jointly and share profits and losses through exchange of information and internal transactions. Transnational corporations have diverse types of subsidiaries and affiliates spread all over the world, yet, as a result of integration, they are able to operate under several national governments, like a closely controlled single enterprise located in markets separated by national boundaries.

A transnational corporation characterized by the just-mentioned features and involved in monopolistic competition on the world market with its intangible assets,[7] rich financial capacity, and worldwide business network, has become, to a certain extent, an invisible empire transcending national boundaries. These enterprises can hardly avoid conflicting with national states, and it is not uncommon for a state's sovereignty to be at bay. At home, unemployment is intensified because factories move abroad; domestic investment stagnates owing to the export of capital. These problems have brought censure from a number of public figures. The conflict tends to be more obvious when it is between the corporations' interests and those of the host countries, particularly developing host countries. Many of those countries refer to the corporations as alien agents to extend imperialistic domination and to perpetuate politicoeconomic *dependencia*. Even in developed host countries, some corporate behavior is regarded as a serious infringement upon political independence and even sovereignty itself.[8] The censuring of transnational corporations grew stronger and stronger from the 1960s to the early 1970s. In these circumstances, many countries took such administrative steps against transnational corporation activities as adopting new rules, policies, or guiding principles, and even nationalizing foreign enterprises, so as to maintain their national sovereignty and interests, enhance their capability in dealing with the transnationals, and gear them to their own aims, policies, and priorities of economic development. The United Nations passed a series of resolutions. Among them, in particular, was the Declaration and Programme of Action on the Establishment of a New International Economic Order adopted by the Sixth Special Session of the General Assembly in 1974. It provided the international community with a new fundamental frame of reference for dealing with transnational corporations. In addition, the Charter of Economic Rights and Duties of States emphasized a host country's right to administer and supervise the transnationals within its jurisdiction. On the other hand, transnational corporations, faced with such a grave situation, began to transform their tactics of management and modes of action, to open up a large number of new channels of investment, and, in many cases, to accept their host countries' requirements, such as the renegotiation of their investment agreements. All this proves that an enterprise of this kind is full of flexibility and adaptability and gives the impression that "transnational corporations can play a more constructive role in future world development than in the past."[9] The following section examines what significant changes have taken place since the 1970s.

Changes since the 1970s

The rapid postwar development of transnational corporations is chiefly marked by the increase of foreign direct investment and the remarkable multiplication of corporations themselves as well as their subsidiaries abroad. In 1977, the number of transnationals increased to 10,737, with their subsidiaries adding up to 82,266. The majority of such corporations (2,826) were in the United States. According to another estimate, made by the U.N. Centre on Transnational Corporations on the basis of the statistics reported by various countries, by 1980 there were as many as 100,000 transnational corporation subsidiaries and affiliates throughout the world, while the stock of foreign direct investment of the developed market-economy countries in 1967 was 108 billion. It is reported that at the end of 1983, the amount of world foreign direct investment (chiefly made by transnational corporations) totalled $625 billion, of which 96 percent came from the developed countries, about 3.5 percent from the developing countries, and less than 0.3 percent from socialist states.[10] From the 1960s onward, the annual rate of increase in the developed countries' foreign investment averaged over 10 percent—a rate much higher than those of world industrial production and export trade. It should be noted, however, that, since the 1980s, the pace of increase in foreign direct investment has slowed down. During 1981 and 1983, the investment flowing into the developed market-economy countries decreased by a quarter and that into the developing countries by one-third.[11]

Further significant changes have come to pass in the pattern of investment and the strategies of transnationals. Indications are as follows:

1. As regards patterns of international foreign direct investment, three specific aspects should be noted:

(a) Remarkable changes have taken place in the relative positions of the leading countries making foreign direct investment. In the 1960s, the stock of U.S. transnational corporate foreign investment accounted for more than half that of the world while the stock of Germany (F.R.) and Japanese investment combined made up only 4 percent. With the advent of the 1970s, Germany's (F.R.) and Japan's share increased enormously. The 1980s saw an even more obvious dwindling of U.S. corporate foreign investment, while the continued strengthening of Japanese transnational corporations became one of the major trends of the 1980s. It is estimated that by the early 1980s, investment had been reduced to 40 percent of the world's total, while the U.K.'s totalled 15 percent (the world's second largest), and those of Germany (F.R.) and Japan rose to 9 and 8 percent, respectively.

(b) Changes have also occurred in the distribution of locations for foreign investment. At present, the major locations are in the developed countries, with those in the developing countries constituting a mere quarter. According to a report by the World Bank, since 1965, three-fourths of foreign direct investment has been flowing into the industrial countries and nearly all the rest has been concentrated in the newly industrialized countries and regions, such as Brazil and Mexico in Latin America and Hong Kong and Singapore in South Asia.[12] Of the developed countries that receive foreign investment, the United States heads the list, the stock of foreign direct investment there having totalled $159 billion by 1984.

(c) Changes have also arisen in respect to industries for investment. Traditionally, foreign investment was chiefly in the primary industries of the developing countries, such as agricultural products, extractive minerals, and petroleum. In the early 1970s, foreign investment in the petroleum industry accounted for about 35 percent and, together with investment in plantations, made up nearly half. Meanwhile, investment in manufacturing rose to 30 percent. During the latter part of the 1970s, investment in primary industries declined, whereas investment in manufacturing and services climbed considerably. By 1982, investment by the United States, United Kingdom, Germany (F.R.), and Japan in manufacturing industry had become dominant, amounting, respectively, to 36.6, 42.5, 63.8 and 37.1 percent.

2. From the 1970s onward, big enterprises in a number of newly industrialized developing countries and regions began to make foreign direct investment. In 1980, it is reported, there were already 963 of these corporations, with 1,964 overseas branches and subsidiaries spread out among 125 host countries, with the total volume of investment estimated at $5 to 10 billion, most of it in the manufacturing industry.[13] These firms are characterized by adaptability to small markets, intensive labor, and comparatively low management expenses. They thus have a considerable advantage in the developing countries and are regarded as a challenge to the transnationals of the developed countires.

3. During the 1960s and 1970s, some developing countries endowed with natural resources nationalized the resource-exploiting enterprises invested in by foreign corporations, with the result that transnational corporations had some misgivings about investing in the developing countries. In the latter part of the 1970s, most of the developing countries adopted a policy of utilizing and restricting foreign capital and tried by every means to attract it. As a result, transnational corporate investment tended to increase. But the debt crises that began in 1982 directly affected the amount of capital invested by transnational corporations flowing into the developing countries. In consequence, the amount of capital invested in the developing countries that year was even less than the profit the transnationals remitted out. (The difference in 1984 is estimated at $3.5 billion.)[14]

4. The ways of transnational corporate investment have grown more and more diversified, as is evident from the alterations in ownership policies and nonequity investment. Since the 1970s, entries in the form of joint ventures have multiplied. Some enterprises are jointly operated by the host countries' government or private individuals, others have set up factories in a third country in cooperation with other transnational corporations, and still others, having to comply with the host country's stipulations, have conceded part of their stocks and now share management control with local enterprises or private individuals. In the past decade, what we know as nonequity arrangements have come into fashion all over the world. They include management contracts, productive cooperation, coproduction, comarketing, compensation trade, product sharing, manufacturing, subcontracting, and credit agreements. Though comprehensive statistical data are not yet available, judging from reports coming from various sources, we may conclude that these arrangements have already been extensively used both in economic cooperation between East and West and in investment in developing countries.[15]

5. Great advances have been made in industrial cooperation between the Eastern European socialist states and the developed market-economy countries. It takes such forms as licencing, providing or letting out factories or assembly lines, manufacturing and job contracts, joint production, joint purchases and sales, joint public bidding, and even joint ventures.[16]

6. With the multiplication of transnational corporations' overseas branches and affiliates, their internal transactions have notably increased.[17] Commodity trade is an example. According to the findings of the U.S. Dept. of Commerce, the proportion of trade related to U.S. transnational corporations made up 56.4 percent of the total amount of foreign trade of the United States in 1976; the proportion of exports related to the transnationals accounted for 65.5 percent of total exports and imports 46.0 percent. By 1977, the corresponding proportions increased to 66.7 percent for trade, 81.2 percent for export, and 55.7 percent for imports.[18] These figures not only indicate the important position occupied by transnational corporations in international trade, but also reflect the trend toward the transnational expansion of their commodity sales by way of internal transactions.

7. Competing intensely against each other for a proper share, transnational corporations have from time to time made responses in accordance with the behavior of their competitors. On the other hand, they are capable of colluding with and making use of each other. It is not uncommon for transnational corporations in the same industry to hold each other's shares. As a result of the development of intraindustrial business, their relations have become even more complicated.[19] Controlling prices, output, and outlets for goods through secret consultations has become a common practice. What is more, they have established complex relations on multiple levels through the transfer of patents, the organization of purchases and sales on commission, and the founding of joint ventures. Some of them have even gone so far as to become international groups.

8. In recent years, in both developed and developing countries, attitudes toward transnational corporations have changed and continue to do so. Most developing countries have adopted policies clearly favorable to foreign investment. They offer varied forms of incentives to those firms that are willing to meet their national objectives, though there is controversy about the effects.

This description gives only a brief generalization of the principal changes over the past decade. It is to be pointed out that transnational corporations are not citizens of world, nor are they established by treaty or under an international companies law. Their management activities are subject to influences from all sides, not only from the international political situation, but also from their home countries' policies and from the policies enacted by the host countries. Generally, the government of a transnational corporation's home country is likely to support its corporate foreign expansion, restricting and administering it at times for fear of capital outflow and transfer of technology. There are, of course, some governments that even take advantage of transnational corporations to achieve their diplomatic ends. As for the host countries, things are different in thousands of ways. At present, most countries, developed or developing, have adopted a policy of utilization and restriction in connection with foreign transnational corporations. They simply aim at bringing into full play their positive roles (such as development of production, promotion of export, and transfer of technology), while restricting their negative effect, such as control over the lifeline of their national economy, infringement of their sovereignty, and interference in their internal affairs. The world keeps evolving; the international political and economic situation is ever changing, and the transnational corporations' strategic aims and management tactics are also subject to constant readjustment and alteration. We must take this fact into consideration in commenting on the role transnational corporations have played in world economic development.

Role in World Development

Since world development is so comprehensive a subject, we shall confine our topic to the discussion of physical production, with special attention to Third World economic development. Over the past few decades, there have been extensive arguments about transnational corporations' role in world economic development. Some have considered them one of the most effective engines of development, while others have referred to them as one of the most powerful impediments to Third World development.[20] Those who believed that transnational corporations were benefactors afforded abundant evidence of the benefits they had provided for the economic growth of their developing host countries.[21] Those who argued about their being a curse produced a great deal of proof that the impact of the transnationals on Third World development was negative rather than positive.[22] The debate has shed enough light on both the positive and negative roles of the transnational corporations. Since opinions differ on the facts, which are in reality all available, it is only natural that conclusions should be at variance.

Strictly speaking, the significance of a transnational corporation's role in world economic development lies mainly in the development of production (including the exploitation of natural resources) and the diffusion of technology (including management skills) so as to promote the development of world productive force. From this point of view, we ought to recognize the positive contribution of the transnational corporation. But practice proves that, even if we do so, there still remain a series of problems to be tackled.

According to the experience gained by Third World countries, transnational corporations must be guided by their host country's policies. Mere import substitution or export orientation can bring about harmful effects.[23] An enclave type of economy and growth without development as a result of transnational corporate investment are still less than what the host countries desire. Since the 1960s and 1970s, the transnational corporations of the developed countries have been moving their traditional and labor-intensive industries out of their native lands to the developing countries and territories, where they organize international production (of manufactures in particular) by utilizing local cheap labor and natural resources. These activities have given rise to a new international division of labor in some regions.[24] They have broken up the traditional patterns of international division of labor that the capitalist world used to follow. Consequently, the long-standing role of an outlet for goods and a base for raw materials supply that the developing countries used to play has now been somewhat transformed. In recent years, however, the industrial countries' trade protectionism aimed at restricting the developing countries' exports has reduced their otherwise obtainable export revenues.[25] Not only has this undermined the developing countries' capacity to import and to pay their debts, but it has also exerted a direct influence on the growth of their economy. And while the speedy growth of the Asian and Pacific region has become a popular topic in the world media today, the flow of international capital since the 1970s has been slow to match this trend. Whether transnational corporations can fit in with the tendency still remains to be proved by practice.

Now let us take the diffusion of technology. At present, the world is faced with an upsurge of new technological advances, and science and technology have become the determinants of economic development. The management strategy adopted by the transnational corporations as producers and owners of new technology plays an important part in the future technological development of the world.[26] So far as the developing countries are concerned, they are still lacking, for various reasons, in the capacity to conduct modern scientific research and development. Therefore, they place much emphasis on introducing advanced foreign technology and, at the same time, encouraging foreign investment in industries of new science and technology. As is proved by a great deal of experience, when they transfer their technology, transnational corporations impose a large number of restrictive conditions as well as demand colossal prices. They either adopt a policy of transfer pricing, so that the host countries lose more than they gain, or they spread some truncated technology to make the host countries more technologically dependent on them. Despite all the regulations made by the international community to deal with restrictive business practices, their implementation is poor because there is no open free technology market in the world. At the same time, the transnationals are trying to maintain their dominating position as regards advanced technology. So, in this respect, there is still much room for improvement.

As for the host countries, they should not cherish any illusions. Instead, they should make a realistic appraisal of transnational corporations. It is to be admitted that a transnational corporation is an enterprise aimed at making a profit rather than a charitable institution taking care of social well-being or an agency responsible for economic development. The movement of capital presupposes the gain of surplus value. In making its foreign investment, the transnational corporation is after superprofit—namely, profit exceeding that obtained in its home country. Specifically, an enterprise's decision to invest may aim at expanding its outlet for goods, securing raw materials and natural resources, increasing the growth rate, or improving its efficiency of management. But, in the last analysis, its intention is to maximize its profit. The greater the risks it runs in investment, the more profit it aims for. This rule conforms to the philosophy of enterprise management. In developing their national economies, the Third World countries must mainly rely on themselves and make full use of the favorable conditions provided by the external world. This being the case, they are justified in attracting foreign capital, expanding production, and tapping natural resources on the basis of cost–benefit analysis in order to promote the growth of their own economy.

At present, among the many reasons for the fact that most transnational corporate foreign direct investment is made in developed countries, there are two reasons particularly worthy of our notice. One is that new products and new technology have mushroomed, and markets in developed countries have expanded owing to the postwar development of science and technology; this has made possible a horizontal international division of labor so that monopoly enterprises of the same industries can make the most of their monopolistic advantages in each other's market. The other reason is that said countries are all industrially developed capitalist states, whose investment environment has a great appeal for transnational corporations. That is, they have a rather stable political situation, a relatively perfect legislation, and a fairly good infrastructure. These conditions are not yet available in developing countries. Therefore, it is necessary for the developing host countries to give some preference to foreign enterprises with a view to improving the environment and encouraging them to invest there.

For a developing country, direct investment by a transnational corporation is not necessarily the "agent of industrialization." As a matter of fact, transnational corporations have little interest in investing in most low-income countries. For those in which they are willing to invest, their contributions to economic development to a great extent depend upon their operational strategies and the guiding policies of the host government. In order to promote world economic development and cooperation, mutual understanding and mutual adaptation are what is mostly needed.

As N. T. Wang has pointed out, "it may be of great historical significance to evaluate a transnational corporation's merits and demerits of the past, but we must look forward. From the standpoint of the Third World countries, it is all the more important for them to engage in a search into ways of utilizing foreign capital to promote their own economic development."[27] Sagacious and particularly significant, this argument merits our approval. If between

1960 and 1980, transnational corporations were condemned from all sides, even to the extent of a "storm over the multinationals,"[28] then, from 1980 onward, such a tense situation has been remarkably eased. Looking ahead, though conflict of interest between host countries and transnational corporations is inevitable due to their different aims and social and cultural backgrounds, I am still confident that there will be a broad prospect for their cooperation as long as it is based on the principle of equality and mutual benefit.

Notes

1. Research Section, Institute of Economics, Nankai University. *Transnational Corporations: An analytical study* (Beijing: People's Press, 1978), pp. 12–15 (in Chinese).
2. See Lenin, N.I., "Imperialism is the Highest Stage of Capitalism," *Collections of Lenin's works,* vol. II, p. 790 (in Chinese).
3. *Multinational Corporations in World Development* (New York: United Nations, 1973), chapter II.
4. Ibid., chapter I.
5. Kindleberger, Charles P., *American Business Abroad* (New Haven, Conn.: Yale University Press, 1969), p. 182.
6. Hymer, S., and Rowthorn, R., "Multinational Corporations and International Oligopoly," in *International Corporation* (C. P. Kindleberger, ed.) (Cambridge, Mass.: MIT Press, 1970), p. 58.
7. Caves, Richard E., *Multinational Enterprise and Economic Analysis* (N.Y.: Cambridge University Press, 1982), pp. 3–7.
8. *Multinational Corporations in World Development,* p. 44.
9. *Transnational Corporations in World Development: A Re-examination* (New York: United Nations, 1978), p. 157.
10. Estimates mady by U.N. Centre on Transnational Corporations.
11. *Trends and Issues in Foreign Direct Investment and Related Flows* (New York: United Nations, 1985), p.8.
12. Ibid., p. 76.
13. Wells, Louis T., Jr., *Third World Multinationals* (Cambridge, Mass. MIT Press, 1983), p. 2.
14. *Trends and Issues in Foreign Direct Investment and Related Flows,* p. 34.
15. See, for example, *Transnational Corporations in World Development: Third Survey* (New York: United Nations, 1983), pp. 40–46.
16. *Transnational Corporations in World Development: A Re-examination,* annex 1–3; *Trends and Issues in Foreign Direct Investment and Related Flows,* pp. 41–45.
17. For intrafirm trade and intrafirm technology transfer, see *Transnational Corporations in World Development: Third Survey,* pp. 160–162, 164–166.
18. U.S. Dept. of Commerce, *U.S. Direct Investment Abroad, 1966* (Wash-

ington, D.C.: U.S. Government Printing Office, 1975); *U.S. Direct Investment Abroad, 1977* (Washington, D.C.: U.S. Government Printing Office, 1981).

19. According to the results of the sample investigation into the 430 largest industrial corporations, 22 percent of their sales volume belonged outside the major industries. See Pearce, Robert D., "Industrial Diversification amongst the World's Leading Multinational Enterprises," in *The Growth of International Business* (Mark Casson, ed.) (London: Allen & Unwin, 1983).

20. Ghosh, Pradip K. (ed.), *Multinational Corporations and Third World Development* (Westport, Conn.: Greenwood Press, 1984) Ghadar, Faribort, and Khamabata, Dora (eds.), p. 7.

21. Grub, Phillip D., *The Multinational Enterprise in Transition,* 2nd ed. (Princeton, N.J.: Darwin, 1984), pp. 391–402.

22. See Akinsanya, Adeoye A., *Multinationals in a Changing Environment* (New York: Praeger, 1984).

23. See, for example, Kirkpatrick, C. H., and Nixon, F. I. (eds.), *The Industrialization of Less Developed Countries* (Manchester: Manchester University Press, 1983), pp. 11–44.

24. Fröbel, Heinrichs, J., and Kreye, O., *The New International Division of Labour* (N.Y.: Cambridge University Press, 1980), pp. 1–48.

25. *World Development Report 1985* (Washington, D.C.: World Bank, 1986), p. 37 (Chinese version).

26. "World New Technological Revolution and Its Impact on Various Countries—Summary of Seminar on New Technological Revolution and the World Economy," *World Economy* (December 1985) (in Chinese).

27. Wang, N. T., *Economic Development and Transnational Corporations* (Beijing: Foreign Economy and Trade Press, 1983), p. 71 (in Chinese).

28. *Storm over the Multinationals* is the title of a well-known book by Vernon, R. (Cambridge, Mass: Harvard University Press, 1977).

3
The Theory of Internalization and the Contemporary International Division of Labor

Xian Guoming

Theoretical Background

The transnational corporation (TNC) is an offspring of today's highly developed capitalist system. Since the second World War, and particularly in the late 1950s, the development of the Western monopolistic capitalist economies has impelled a drastic increase in foreign direct investment by various countries. A great number of TNCs came into existence, and there are at present estimated to be about 20,000. Among them, two or three hundred of the largest control most foreign direct investment. They are all dominant monopolistic enterprises in the developed countries. By the end of the 1970s, TNCs were controlling nearly three-fifths of world trade, out of which one-third was conducted within the TNCs themselves. Today, TNC operations are seen in every field of the world economy. Particularly since the mid-1970s, TNCs have made rapid progress in high tech manufacturing sectors and information-intensive service sectors such as finance and insurance. International production by TNCs is becoming more and more important—so much so that TNCs are considered to be by far the most powerful economic institutions newly created by capitalism.[1]

The rapid development of TNCs and their foreign direct investment caught the attention of many Western scholars. They began to study TNCs from evey perspective and their studies were based on a great many theoretical systems. In the early 1960s, an American scholar, Stephen H. Hymer, rejected the traditional theory of international capital movement and, on this basis, first put forward a new explanation of postwar foreign direct investment of U.S. enterprises.[2] Hymer's work has been much criticized and elaborated upon, but it did get the analysis of foreign direct investment off to a fresh start.

The development of Western theories about TNCs between the 1960s and the mid-1980s falls into two phases. The earlier phase is represented by Hymer and Kindleberger's theory of monopolistic advantage and Vernon's product cycle theory, their main object of studying being the foreign direct investment of U.S. enterprises during the period of their rapid postwar foreign expansion. The later phase is represented by Buckley, Casson, and Rugman's theory of internalization and Dunning's eclectic theory of international production, their major concern being directed at the foreign direct investment by TNCs from various countries in the midst of establishing a system of international production. From the point of view of theoretical origin, the two phases borrowed largely from the theory of the firm in Western economies. However, the starting point of their analysis was different in that the theory of monopolistic advantage proceeded from the theory of the firm (particularly the theory of industrial organization), while the product cycle theory made full use of the location theory. So far, of all the just-mentioned theories, the theory of internalization has proved the most influential because it systematically summed up and assimilated the quintessence of previous theories while looking at TNCs' foreign direct investment from a fresh perspective, thus providing a significant basis for the contemporary explanation of the foreign direct investment phenomenon.

This chapter comments on the significance of the theory of internalization and attempts, on this basis, to share with the reader the author's understanding of contemporary TNCs' international investment and division of labor. In addition, it is intended to give a brief outline of the theoretical basis for carrying out an open policy and a policy of introducing foreign investment into the country.

Significance of the Theory

The theory of internalization, which took shape in the middle of the 1970s, was an offspring of the efforts made by Western students of TNCs to establish a so-called general theory of foreign direct investment. They argued that the theories advanced by a variety of schools lacked a uniform theoretical framework, and that they were of little universal significance because they largely took the foreign direct investment of U.S. enterprises as their object of study and often resorted to empirical descriptions rather than abstract positive analysis. They suggested that a general theory of TNCs shuld be established by studying the common characteristics of the various TNCs of the 1970s and assimilating that part of the traditional theories of TNCs concerned with the analysis of the determinants of foreign direct investment. Beginning with the study of the mechanism whereby the TNCs allocated internal resources, Buckley and Casson first advanced the theory of internalization.[3] Then, after a closer study of the relationship between internalization and TNCs' foreign direct investment, Rugman expounded within the analytic structure of this internalization theory the causes of the formation and development of such transnational service enterprises as transnational banks, and created a uniform model involving three choices: export, foreign direct investment, and licencing trade.[4]

In addition, some other scholars reached conclusions similar to the theory of internalization during their separate researches. Magee's appropriability theory, for example, sheds light on the reasons why transfer of technology is carried out within TNCs instead of being licenced.[5] Hood and Young regarded the theory of internalization and the appropriability theory as one and the same when they discussed the issue of the transfer of technology.[6] Analyzing foreign direct investment from a historic point of view, using historic materials in his *A Theory of Multinational Enterprises*, Hennart also arrived at a conclusion essentially similar to the theory of internalization.[7]

Main Contents

When the theory took form, TNCs had long been organizing their international production on a global scale. Why do TNCs open up their internal market through foreign direct investment in order to coordinate their international division of labor, instead of utilizing the existing world market and exchanging products with enterprises of other countries so as to realize the international division of labor among them? That was the analytical starting point of those who studied the theory of internalization. From this point, they made a fresh study of market imperfection and gave an explanation of the determinants of TNCs' foreign direct investment in terms of the relationship between the imperfect market and the efficiency with which the TNCs' allocated their internal resources.

The theory of internalization reexplains the concept of the imperfect market. As a matter of fact, early theories of TNCs (such as the theory of monopolistic advantages put forward by Hymer and Kindleberger) also studied TNCs' foreign direct investment in terms of imperfect markets. But, in the eyes of the scholars of internalization, the early theories laid undue emphasis on the specific forms of imperfect market (such as oligopoly, scale economy, and monopoly of technology), while the theory of internalization on the other hand stresses the general form of imperfect market—namely, market failure and the increase of market transaction costs due to the nature of certain products or to the concentration of monopoly. What is more, this theory places emphasis on the imperfect market for such intermediates as knowledge. Buckley et al. pointed out that, since World War II, developments in research into science and technology have brought about great changes in modern enterprise management, where more and more attention is being paid to sales, research and development, and the management of financial assets. All these activities are dependent on each other, with the intermediates, such as knowledge, as their connector. Generally speaking, an enterprise's coordination of its management calls for a complete set of markets for intermediates. But some of the markets are imperfect, as is indicated by the lack of certain markets for enterprises to exchange their products or by the poor efficiency of operation in some markets that gives rise to an increase in an enterprise's transaction cost on the market. Such a phenomenon is particularly evident in the markets for intellectual products such as information. Imperfect markets make an enterprise unable to use the external markets it faces in order to turn over its intermediates and coordinate its operations and management. Therefore, a profit-maximizing firm must internalize its external markets; that is to say, it must establish its internal markets and coordinate the circulation and allocation of its internal resources by means of its management system so as to prevent imperfect markets from affecting the efficiency of operation. According to Casson, exchanging the ownership of products is the major cause of high transaction costs in external markets.[8] The internalization of markets has avoided the friction of interests resulting from the exchange of ownership and thereby avoided market transaction costs and increased the efficiency of operations for the firms.

Transnational enterprises come into being when internalization extends beyond national boundaries. In other words, according to the theory of internalization, for an enterprise to extend its internalization beyond national boundaries means making foreign direct investment. From this, it follows that the factors driving an enterprise's internalization are the ones that decide its foreign direct investment. Thus, the determinants of foreign direct investment are to prevent imperfect markets from exerting unfavorable influences over an enterprise's efficiency in managing its worldwide operation.

Nevertheless, internalization is not unconditional. On the one hand, it avoids external market transaction costs, increases an enterprise's operating efficiency, and is expected to add to its profit. On the other hand, internalization will also give rise to additional cost, such as the cost of communications, coordination, control, and operating in a foreign environment. Internalization depends on the balance between additional revenue and cost. When the marginal revenue of internalization equals its marginal cost, an enterprise is in a position to be internalized (that is, to make foreign direct investment). Afterwards, however, Casson further proved that since internalization is aimed at avoiding external market transaction cost, an enterprise could expect to achieve its internalization so long as the internalization cost was smaller than the market transaction cost, regardless of the variation in the amount of cost and revenue of internalization.[9]

The theory of internalization places a particular stress on the influence of the imperfect market for such intermediates as knowledge on a transnational enterprise's foreign direct investment. According to the theory, there is the strongest motivation for firms to be internalizers in the market of knowledge. The multinational enterprise can be regarded as the institutional response to the imperfect market of knowledge.[10]

Scholars of internalization have all along been underlining the point that this is a general and long-term theory of TNCs. There are two reasons why it is called a general theory. One is that it can provide an explanation for various types of postwar foreign direct investment, including those made by the enterprises not only of developed nations but also of developing countries. The theory can also account for the formation and development of service TNCs such as transnational banks. The other reason is that the theory of internalization embraces and may even replace to various degrees previous theories of TNCs. Calling the theory a long-term one means that it interprets the patterns of TNCs' growth since World War II. Rugman further expounded the point that the internalization of knowledge would ensure that TNCs could make continuous investments in research and development so that the dynamic character of the foreign direct investment could be maintained.[11]

Main Characteristics

The theory differs from all previous schools of thought in terms of content, form, and approach. Its characteristics may be represented as follows.

First, the interpretation of the determinants of TNCs' foreign direct investment, according to the theory of internalization, differs from all earlier theories, whose object of study was largely confined to the foreign direct investment of U.S. enterprises during their postwar expansion period. What they had in common was that they all considered U.S. enterprises' production abroad to be an extension of and supplement to their production at home, in the belief that their foreign direct investment was aimed at occupying local markets and expelling competitors. When accounting for the determinants of U.S. enterprises' foreign direct investment, the theorists are prone to stress the influence exerted by the oligopolistic structure of industries in the home country or by the change of modes or circumstances of competition in the home or host countries over the enterprises' foreign direct investment. For example, while analyzing U.S. enterprises' foreign direct investment, Hymer et al. argued that the monopolistic advantages of America's enterprises were the determinants of its foreign direct investment. In the meantime, Vernon, proceeding from the changes of the modes of competition, investigated within the model of the product life cycle the timing and location choices facing U.S.

enterprises in their foreign direct investment. Vernon maintained that foreign direct investment is both a substitute for export and a defensive behavior resulting from the alteration of the circumstances of competition at home and abroad.

When the theory of internalization was taking shape, TNCs from various countries vied with one another as they marched forward over the world to organize their production and management on a global scale. Therefore, the theory of internalization was an attempt (1) to epitomize the common characteristics shared by various TNCs in their international operations and (2) to look at the determinants of TNCs' foreign direct investment from the aspect of the way in which the mechanism of cooperation required for its global production and management is formed. The gist of the theory of internalization may be summarized as follows. (1) Postwar technological revolution changed the content and extent of an enterprise's operation and, in particular, the nature or content of the intermediates, whose traditional raw materials and semifinished products are at the same time transformed into information products such as knowledge or technology. (2) Because the external markets lack the mechanism of pricing and exchanging the just mentioned products, there is an increase in transaction costs and a decrease of an enterprise's efficiency in coordinating and managing its production on a global scale. Consequently, the enterprise has no alternative but to internalize its external market (that is, to make foreign direct investment and build up a system of allocating its resources within its own organization). It is thus clear that the theory of internalization attempts to interpret the determinants of foreign direct investment in terms of the conflicts between external markets and the mechanism for allocating and coordinating internal resources within an enterprise in a time of technological revolution. An interpretation of this kind obviously varies from the early theories of TNCs.

The theory of internalization still places emphasis on interpreting the determinants of TNCs' foreign direct investment in terms of monopoly and technological advantages. But it differs from other theories in that (unlike Hymer et al., who proceeded directly from the structure of the oligopolistic market as they explained the determinants of foreign direct investment) this theory provides an interpretation for the impact of monopoly on an enterprise's foreign direct investment on the basis of the influences over an enterprise's operation exerted by the structure of monopoly market or the behavior of the bilateral monopoly. According to Buckley et al., the bilateral concentration of monopoly might place a limit on the efficiency of coordinating an enterprise's management by means of the market mechanism, and give rise to an increase of market transaction costs. The monopolistic nature of technology merely intensifies the buyer's uncertainties and adds to the contract costs, with the result that the enterprise is impelled to overcome the effect of buyers' uncertainties on its operation by way of internalization of foreign direct investment. Therefore, the theory of internalization devotes much attention to the monopoly factor merely because it is regarded as a factor in increasing market transaction costs for intellectual products—a factor that has only an indirect influence on an enterprise's foreign direct investment. In their analysis of the influence of technological advantages on TNCs' foreign direct investment, Hymer et al. stressed the point that it was the monopoly of technology that enabled U.S. enterprises to have an advantage over local enterprises. The theory of internalization, on the other hand, underlines the special properties of technological products and the conflicts between the flow of such products and the conventional mechanism of external market transaction. In other words, the nature of a technological product may result in an imperfect external market, which, in its turn, will cause TNCs to make foreign direct investment. In short, the theory of internalization has brought various determinants of TNCs' foreign direct investment into line with the concept of the imperfect market and has described them as exercising an indirect effect upon TNCs' foreign direct investment by affecting market transaction costs.

Second, the theory of internalization takes TNCs as an institutional response to an imperfect world market. Therefore, in the theory, the focus of the research has been shifted from the foreign direct investment itself to the institutions that make the investment decision. This shows another remarkable characteristic intrinsic in the theory of internalization. In fact, the theory regards TNCs as a special case of a diversified firm and foreign direct investment as nothing more than a means whereby TNCs build up internal markets within their system of international division of labor or, rather, as a result of TNCs' institutional transformation due to their efforts to overcome the imperfection of the external market. For this reason, the theory of internalization has to give a new explanation of the nature of TNCs. In this respect, Coase and associates have provided scholars of internalization with an important means of analysis by advancing a new theory of the firm. During the 1930s, Coase made a study of the scale and nature of the firm. He believed that it was imperfect markets, that started the rise of transaction costs and thereby forced enterprises to internalize their external markets while building up internal ones so as to prevent the transaction costs in the external market from affecting the enterprises' operations. On the basis of this argument, Coase regarded the firm as a new type of an enterprise organization form by which the firm tried to realize its internalization.[12] Scholars of internalization have incorporated and improved upon Coase's insights. They used the concept of transaction costs and internalization to throw light on the fact that it was the development of an enterprise's operational content and scale, coupled with its conflicts with the mechanism of external markets, that caused TNCs to build up internal markets by making foreign direct investment and to coordinate their operational activities in the world by virtue of their managerial system. As far as their institutional form is concerned, it is but a means or a tool in the hands of the transnational enterprises from developed countries in organizing their internal international division of labor. Thus, according to the theory of internalization, an explanation of the formation of such a specific enterprise organization of international division of labor as TNCs is a prerequisite for an explanation of contemporary TNC foreign direct investment. Only on this basis can a rational explanation be given of the behavior of foreign direct investment.

Third, the theory of internalization still follows the framework of traditional microeconomic analyses, as is evident in the fact that (1) this theory accepts the traditional assumption of microeconomic theory that the firm is apt to maximize its profit and (2) proceeding from the behavior of the individual firm, it interprets the influences of the imperfect market on TNCs' foreign direct investment by way of a comparative cost–benefit analysis. But, in its explanation of the imperfect market, it introduces the Coasean Theorem, and redefines the nature and content of imperfect markets as the failure of the external market mechanism and the market transaction costs entailed thereby. It is precisely because of this transaction cost that TNCs make foreign direct investment. For this reason, we may safely assert that the analytical instruments of traditional microeconomic theory constitute the framework of the theory of internalization, while the new theory of the firm advanced by Coase makes up the content. The internalization approach is the result of combining traditional microeconomic theory with the new theory of the firm. Consequently, the theory of internalization is capable of utilizing the approach of microeconomic positive analysis to explain contemporary TNCs' behavior in making foreign direct investment while establishing their system of international division of labor, and it is thus convincing.

Last, the theory of internalization is also characterized by consistency in its emphasis on the point that it is a general theory of TNCs.[13] To some extent, this characteristic is determined by the two qualities just mentioned. Indeed, compared with all other schools of thought, this one is able to abstract the most common factor from the determinants of TNCs' foreign direct investment in order to give a general explanation of the said investment activities. The most common factor is simply the general form of imperfect market. In the author's opinion, this is no more than the conflict between the mechanism of the external market and the mechanism of coordinating the international division of labor among contemporary TNCs. Of course, proceeding from this factor, we can expect to expound the behavior of foreign direct investment by contemporary TNCs of all countries, all types, and all trades. Does this necessarily mean that this theory is the only explanation that can substitute for all other theories? That question is still open to discussion.

Brief Comments

The theory of internalization has made a great contribution to the West's theory of international capital movement, which may be roughly divided into two phases: the early phase being that of pre-Hymerian neoclassical theory and the later one that started by Hymer's theory of international investment. The neoclassical theory of international capital movement interpreted that movement in terms of the Heckscher-Ohlin model. It argues that the cause of international capital movement is the difference in interest rates among various countries, and that this discrepancy depends on the relative abundance of capital stock in the countries. In fact, the neoclassical theory is a study of the international movement of financial capital only and, thus, is incapable of accounting for the postwar international movement of direct investment. It was Hymer who ushered in a new phase in the theory of international capital movement. Together with Kindleberger, he made a distinction between financial capital and foreign direct investment, indicating that it was the difference in profit rather than interest that determined foreign direct investment.[14] Hymer et al. gave emphasis to their study of the reasons why TNCs were able to create larger profit than the local enterprises (that is to say, why the former had various advantages over the latter). But Hymer's observation lacked a uniform framework of analysis and a uniform theory. For instance, he interpreted the origin of TNCs' monopolistic advantages only in terms of such imperfect markets as oligopoly. But, as it merely gives an account of the necessary conditions for TNCs' foreign direct investment, this interpretation is not enough to explain their motivation in making the investment. For this reason, Hymer needed to find full conditions for TNCs' foreign direct investment in the tariff barriers erected by the host country's government (that is, to make it clear that the enterprises' motive in making foreign direct investment was to occupy markets by getting around the tariff barriers). Another example of the defects in Hymer's theory is the undue stress it lays on the various specific forms of imperfect market, which may keep altering with different times and places. Such being the case, Hymer's theory strikes us as fluid. In other words, it is always subject to expansion by the inclusion of new forms of the imperfect market. What is more, Hymer et al. studied the foreign investment behavior of U.S. enterprises only at the time when they felt most eager to expand overseas. Therefore, it is difficult for this theory to interpret international direct investment made when the system of international production of TNCs was taking shape.

    The theory of internalization is an attempt to overcome these defects. Proceeding from the formation of the mechanism of allocating TNCs' internal resources, it probes into the influence of the external market on the efficiency of the allocation of internal resources so as to shed light on the determinants of TNCs' foreign direct investment. In addition, so far as the theoretical system is concerned, the theory of internalization has to some extent inherited the analytic approach peculiar to traditional microeconomic theory and, in so doing, has established a relatively unified and complete system of theoretical analysis. We are justified in saying that the emergence of the theory of internalization marked the maturity of the theory of international capital movement of the West, both in form and in content. Unlike the neoclassical theory of international capital movement and Hymer and Kindleberger's position, the theory of internalization takes account of the contributing factors in initiating foreign direct investment from the basis of the unification of the foreign direct investment with the present pattern of the international division of labor, with TNCs as the main actors. Therefore, it provides a more satisfactory explanation of the factors that decide contemporary foreign direct investment. This is one of the major reasons why it has won prompt and extensive approval.

But the theory of internalization also has its limitations. It is itself too much confined to the framework of the traditional microeconomic positive analysis and is not yet freed from the influence exerted by Hymer's analysis of the behavior of foreign direct investment. The limitations of the theory manifest themselves chiefly in the fact that, in examining TNCs' foreign direct investment only from the standpoint of enterprise organization, it fails to make a macroeconomic analysis, namely, an analysis of the determinants of TNC foreign direct investment based on the world economic environment in which contemporary transnational enterprises undertake their international production and division of labor. The scholars of internalization may well have been aware of this qualification, for they tried either to enlarge the concept of internalization cost, embracing as many as possible of the determinants of an enterprise's internalization, or to evade it and replace it by simple term of transaction cost.[15] The substitution of transaction costs for all the factors affecting TNCs' foreign direct investment oversimplified the theory. In reality, it is impossible for transaction costs to cover all the determinants of foreign direct investment. Take, for example, the factors of location. The theory of internalization itself neglects the choice of space, or location, for TNCs' foreign direct investment. This neglect somewhat contradicts its point of departure—namely, the mechanism of allocating an enterprise's internal resources. This incongruity undeniably constitutes a serious drawback to the theory. In fact, a great number of factors of location affect not only the cost or benefit of internalization and the orientation of foreign direct investment movement, but also the TNCs' motivation in making their foreign direct investment. Laying undue emphasis on the general form of imperfect market and the analysis of transaction costs, the theory of internalization has difficulty in incorporating the analysis of the factor of location into its own analytical framework, and this undoubtedly weakens its significance of analysis and prediction. On the other hand, whether the theory of foreign direct investment should include the analysis of the location factor depends on how we look at foreign direct investment itself. In the theory of internalization, foreign direct investment is considered to be a means whereby TNCs expand the internalization of their market beyond their national boundary. In other words, it is a means by which TNCs build up their internal markets. Therefore, according to the theory, foreign direct investment equals the behavior of internalization. Regarded thus, the attention of the theory must be focused on the imperfection of markets and the rise of transaction costs. But foreign direct investment is a process of TNCs' international production shifting in space and of TNCs' establishment of an international division of labor and international production system. From this point of view, the factors of a host country's location naturally become an important determinant affecting TNCs' foreign direct investment. Of these factors, some enter directly into the process of TNCs' international production as inputs, while others serve as external conditions for the TNCs' operations and have an influence on the efficiency of their operation.

In contemporary Western theoretical study of international capital movement, there appears a tendency to combine macro- and microeconomic analysis. A view of the evolution of the theory of international investment shows that the pre-Hymerian neoclassical theory of international capital movement is, so to speak, a macroeconomic analysis, for it uses the Heckscher-Ohlin model to interpret international financial capital movement. Microeconomic analysis started with Hymer, who employed the theory of industrial organization to explain the impact of technological advantages on U.S. enterprises' foreign direct investment. Hymer's approach had a great influence on the later researchers. But, beginning with the 1970s, a great number of scholars devoted their attention to explaining TNCs' foreign direct investment using macroeconomic analysis. Kojima, a Japanese scholar, began to make conscious use of Heckscher-Ohlin's theory of international resource allocation in his interpretation of the influence that the advantages of comparative costs of various countries exerted upon TNCs' foreign direct investment.[16] This tendency is particularly remarkable in Dunning's eclectic theory of international production. Dunning made a great effort to analyze the origin of the competitive advantages of the enterprises in various countries, the motivation of internalization, and the location characteristics found in the international production carried out by enterprises of all countries. [17] The studies made by these scholars shed light on a tendency; that is, the behavior of contemporary TNCs' foreign investment tends to be affected not only by microeconomic factors but also by macro ones. Theoretically, therefore, the behavior of TNCs' foreign direct investment should be studied on the basis of combined micro- and macroeconomic analysis.

The Contemporary International Division of Labor

By interpreting the contemporary TNCs' foreign direct investment on the basis of the mechanism of TNCs' internal resource allocation, the theory of internalization expounds the characteristics of contemporary international division of labor and provides an important theoretical inspiration for our study of contemporary TNCs.

After the second World War, the changes in the world political and economic environment gave rise to the growth of TNCs in developed countries.

First, the postwar technological revolution made rapid progress. Technical innovation became fundamental to monopolistic enterprises in developed countries in their efforts to maintain and expand their market powers. They were obliged to invest profusely in research and development. The monopolistic nature of technological products came to determine the monopolistic enterprises' absorption and utilization of the products within themselves. This tendency intensified the enterprises' foreign economic expansion by way of foreign direct investment. The interaction between postwar technological development and monopolistic competition reinforced the trend of foreign direct investment by the monopolistic enterprises of all developed countries.

Second, the development of the technological revolution gave impetus to the division of labor, coordination, and professional production among the world's enterprises. The internationalization of production gained speed. International production and division of labor in the form of transnational operation became more and more popular. TNCs appeared as the chief organizers and promoters of international division of labor. At the same time, TNCs became typical international monopolistic institutions and their international production became the basis for maintaining and expanding their international monopoly. As TNCs evolved from domestic enterprises to international monopolistic enterprises, the need to maintain and expand their international production and monopoly turned out to be the determinant of TNCs' foreign or international direct investment.

Third, the contemporary international division of labor presents a number of new characteristics, evidenced, in the main, in the fact that the basis for international division of labor has undergone changes as the natures of the intermediate products to be exchanged among enterprises have altered. The traditional division of labor based on natural resources has by and large given way to a division based on the relative advantages brought about by modern scientific and technological development. The resulting shocks to the concept of market have brought about changes in the institutional form of division of labor. The establishment of internal markets has gradually taken the place of the departmental or industrial division of labor based on external markets.

The destruction of the mechanism of market pricing has changed the coordinative mechanism of international division of labor. As a result, the international division of labor coordinated automatically by the mechanism of market pricing has been weakened and replaced by one that is coordinated by the internal managerial system of TNCs. The characteristics show that the relative advantages of technological development have turned into the basis for international division of labor, and the major form that such a division takes is one within enterprises. The growth of monopolistic enterprises in developed countries has made it possible for the division of labor to extend beyond national boundaries. Foreign direct investment is instrumental in bringing about the evolution of the division of labor from domestic into international, while TNCs are the institutional form of such division.

Fourth, the contemporary international division of labor, with TNCs as its backbone, has greatly spurred the development of the world economy. The change of market mechanism has helped to avoid instability and the interference that the world market is prone to, and it has promoted production in all countries. Dividing labor internationally, in accordance with the law of comparative advantages, TNCs have enhanced the efficiency of allocating world resources and brought about a great advance in the productive force of all countries. The contemporary form of international division of labor has accelerated the exchange of technological information and, in a sense, promoted the technological development of all countries.

Fifth, with this advance in the contemporary international division of labor, economic relations among various countries are growing closer and closer. The present world economy tends to be increasingly open. A closed economy is unable to change the backward economic conditions in developing countries. Adopting an open policy and taking an active part in the international division of labor has proved an efficient means of developing their economies. China is a socialist state and, at the same time, a developing country. Therefore, it is a long-time basic national policy for China to open to the world, absorb foreign investment, and participate in the contemporary international division of labor.

Notes

1. Dunning, J. H., *International Production and the Multinational Enterprise* (London: Allen & Unwin, 1981).

2. Hymer, S. H., *The International Operations of National Firms* (Lexington, Mass.: Lexington Books, 1976).

3. Buckley, P. J., and Casson, M., *The Future of the Multinational Enterprise* (London: Macmillan, 1976).

4. Rugman, A. M., *Inside the Multinationals* (London: Croom Helm, 1981).

5. Magee, S. P., "Information and the Multinational Corporation: An Appropriability theory of Direct Foreign Investment," in *The New International Economic Order* (J. N. Bhagwati, ed.) (Cambridge, Mass.: MIT Press, 1977).

6. Hood, N., and Young, S., *The Economics of Multinational Enterprise* (London: Allen & Unwin, 1979).

7. Hennart, J. F., *A Theory of Multinational Enterprise* (Ann Arbor: University of Michigan Press, 1982).

8. Casson, M., "Preface" in Rugman, op. cit.

9. Ibid.

10. Rugman, op. cit.

11. Ibid.

12. Coase, R. H., "The Nature of the Firm," *Economica* (New Series), vol. 4 (1937): 386–405.

13. Buckley and Casson, op. cit.

14. Kindleberger, C. P., *American Business Abroad* (New Haven, Conn.: Yale University Press, 1969).

15. Casson, M., *Alternatives to the Multinational Enterprise* (London: Macmillan, 1979).

16. Kojima, K., *Direct Foreign Investment: A Japanese Model of Multinational Business Operations* (London: Croom Helm, 1978).

17. Dunning, op. cit.

4
Orientations and Organization of Transnational Corporations

Jack N. Behrman

T ransnationals encompass a variety of activities located overseas, complementing the activities of the headquarters company in order to achieve the corporate objectives. Most transnational corporations (TNCs) engage in a variety of activities oriented to different market objectives, and these in turn lead to different locational strategies and organizational structures—all reflecting the international strategy. All TNCs seek a high degree of flexibility and mobility so that they can respond to changes in national and international markets.

All privately owned and many state-owned TNCs are market-driven in the formation of their strategies, and locational decisions respond to market pulls with sufficient fluidity to permit shifts with market changes. Rigidities in organizational structures hinder rapid responses to competitive markets. Given the size of transnational companies and the desires of host governments, headquarters companies have to fight continuously to overcome tendencies toward bureaucratization of the organization and the demands of host governments for permanence and certainty in local operations. Host governments tend to impose a variety of "performance requirements" that rigidify the international activities of TNCs, making their strategies less responsive to market changes. Different company orientations and organizational structures seek to increase the company's ability to remain competitively mobile.

Orientations of TNCs

TNCs have three major orientations (with subcategories) reflecting their strategies and affecting their negotiating positions. The three major orientations can be classified as "resource seeking," "market seeking," and "efficiency seeking."

1. The *resource seeking* activity leads to investment overseas in a location that supplies a key production factor, which will make the TNC more competitive in markets it already serves. The TNC is already competitive in that market and does not have to find or penetrate it, but simply produce more competitively through lower-cost resources.

2. The *market seeker* looks for investment in a new market or in a market now served by exports that are being cut off through government action or competitive pressure.

3. The *efficiency seeker* is looking for the least-cost method of production around the world so as to serve more competitively markets that it has already entered or can enter only through lower-cost production. The efficiency seeker wants a high degree of mobility of production and specialization among affiliates.

A more detailed assessment of each of these orientations will help to explain the locational strategies of TNCs and their organizational structures.

Resource Seekers

The international activities of companies based on a search for new and cheaper factors of production tend to be focused on natural resources and human resources. Capital, management, and technology are readily mobile across international boundaries. They do not have to be tied to any company, though a company may be the generating source, giving it a special ability to move them internationally. It is the mobility of these three factors that makes it possible to search for the less mobile resources of minerals and labor in different international locations. The searches for natural or human resources differ considerably in their impact on corporate strategies.

There are similarities between the two in that they are generally tied to existing operations of the parent company, which has already established its presence in attractive markets. It is simply trying to become more competitive and profitable. It may be seeking means of expansion through price reduction or means of maintaining its markets in its home country, in the face of foreign competition from cheaper sources. Such pressure may force it to seek a location of production similar to those of its competitors in order to reduce costs. Or, it may simply be seeking an additional source of supply in the face of rapid depletion of existing natural resources or in the face of rising labor costs at home.

For both types, the criteria for a decision as to location arise from within the parent company, which will seek a location compatible with its market objectives—either in the home country or in its established worldwide markets. The criteria generally lean to least-cost with necessary quality; not only is proximity of supply important, but so is regularity of supply with established quality.

The management style of the foreign affiliate using or developing the low-cost resource will generally accord with that of the parent company, so that it can know what the affiliate's costs are likely to be and can be assured of the needed supplies. (The extent of transmission of the parent's management style to the affiliate will depend on the relationships of ownership and control, which are discussed later.)

The differences in orientations of the two types of resource seekers arise from the fact that the location in the case of the natural-resource seeker is fairly well fixed, according to the location of the resources themselves—mineral, agricultural, or water. Once the investment is made, it becomes more immobile, since significant capital and equipment have been committed, as well as costs incurred in moving management and preparing technology for transfer. The higher such costs, the less mobile becomes that particular activity. On the other hand, the human-resource activity remains highly mobile in that the investment tends to require relatively little capital equipment and quite specific transfers of technology plus minor managerial transfers; local management can eventually take over, and the technology transfers diminish. Given that rapid start-up is feasible for a human-resource activity, it is feasible to close one down and open a similar activity elsewhere if costs or government regulations become too oppressive.

A quite different resource-seeking activity is that which creates a tie to a foreign research and development (R&D) capability. The need to be abreast of technological developments in major regions of the world and the fact that several countries are at the frontier of science make it desirable for many companies to establish ties with R&D units overseas. Various options exist: these ties may be made between completely independent companies through a cooperative R&D arrangement; a technological joint-venture may be set up; the R&D cooperation may be subsumed under a regular joint-venture agreement; an R&D capability may be bought with the purchase of an existing company; or a new R&D group may be established drawing on local talent. Host governments like such ties if the result is new technologies in the host country; but, if any new technology is merely sent to the foreign parent, it sees the result as a "brain-drain."

Market Seekers

The companies seeking new markets—or seeking to stay in ones that are being closed by government regulations or strong competitive pressure—are willing to invest directly in the foreign market or to offer a local company a licence. In each, the TNC might supply technology, management, and capital, though usually only technology is supplied in a licencing agreement.

The decision criteria for investment in that host country come largely from the availability of resources (capital, management, and technology) to be transferred abroad, the prospects of market growth, and the access to local resources so as to reduce imports of materials and components. The fact that the TNC is being induced by the government to invest locally is probably itself a reflection of scarcity of foreign exchange, so that the new investment must save on foreign exchange through substituting for imports and not significantly relying on imported parts or materials. If the market is sufficiently sophisticated so that it will grow into the larger product line of the parent, if it is sufficiently large so that increases in scale of production and sales can be achieved with a standard product line, or if the location can become a production base for a regional market as yet untapped—if any substantial potential growth exists—there is an attraction to invest or at least to licence and gain a production foothold. But, the decision will be made among existing investment opportunities (*not* through a comparison of all potential markets around the world) or against a threshold concept of potential profitability. If the parent company has ample capital, managerial, and technical resources, it will use the threshold decision criterion, attempting to determine whether the investment has a potential return above a minimum figure; and, if it does, the TNC will proceed. (There are, of course, a number of other criteria affecting the decision, but I cannot go into all of them in this chapter.) If the parent's resources are not sufficient for all opportunities, the decision will then be based on relative attractiveness in terms of the longer-range profit potential, including the security of that return and the political risks likely to be faced.

Since this type of investment in the host country is for the purpose of serving the local national market, the criteria for the operations and the management style will arise from within the host country. It is unlikely that the parent will insist that the foreign affiliate be managed in precisely the same way as the parent itself, given that the culture, consumer tastes, distribution system, advertising media, workers' orientations, and government relations may all be quite different. It may insist on similarity in production processes and financial controls, but most of the rest of managerial decisions will be left to local determination.

Efficiency Seekers

The efficiency seeker faces opportunities to serve relatively open international markets with standardized products—that is, the same products are desired in the various markets. The same markets will be served by a number of highly competitive international enterprises, each of which is attempting to distinguish its product from the others, largely based on technological characteristics. Since the markets are already well developed and each company is seeking simply to enhance its position therein, the method of doing so most readily is through production efficiency. (Advertising can gain a quick short-term advantage, but it is likely to be met by similar success on the part of competitors.) Repair and maintenance service is also a critical element in competitive strength, but this is itself a substantial cost reduction for the customer, who obtains repair promptly and effectively, minimizing downtime on the equipment.

The location decision, therefore, is based essentially on the ability to achieve high quality and low cost through melding production facilities in various parts of the world across national boundaries. The world may be seen as a single market, or as groups of regional markets, served more efficiently from several different agglomerations of production facilities within a TNC that do not compete with each other but each of which can supplement production in others as needed to meet variations in demand. A given production location will be more attractive if there is a substantial domestic market that can be served locally, providing a base of large production runs and reducing the cost of its product or components; production for export then aids cost reduction. Development of a local demand for the TNCs full product line provides a market for production of other TNC affiliates, thereby balancing imports and exports and reducing any drain on foreign exchange.

The management style of activities tied together in this way tends to move toward a worldwide style, not reflecting any one country wholly, but more similar to the style of the parent company than to any of the others. To date, no TNC has achieved a wholly nonnational management style, combining the various styles of its major affiliates. In fact, no TNC has even become significantly multinational in its ownership or its board of directors. The "global corporation" is still far from view, given the government restrictions that isolate markets.

Activities of Transnationals

These orientations of TNCs give rise to distinct production and commercial activities that influence their organizational structures.

The *natural-resource seekers* develop mineral, agricultural, forestry, and water resources. The *human-resource seekers* are found in branch-plant manufacturing, which produces a given component or carries out a given phase of production (such as cut-and-sew operations in textile manufacturing). Human-resource seekers are also investors in commercial activities that are close to the market and require local personnel in order to carry out the functions.

In this category we find the major mineral companies—Utah International, Cerro de Pasco, Rio Tinto Zinc, Amax, the leading petroleum companies, tea and rubber plantations, and other agri-industrial producers (such as Unilever). In the labor-seeking group, we find textile, electronics, and other companies that establish facilities to carry out isolated stages of production or manufacture of components.

One finds these activities located worldwide, for resources and agricultural opportunities exist in virtually every country, and labor is attractive in each according to levels of productivity and wages. Consequently, we see investment among these types of companies shifting location as new resources are discovered and as labor rates and productivity change. The shifts will be more or less rapid in response to changes in market tastes, government pressures, and technological discoveries.

The *market seekers* tend to be found in such service activities as banking, retailing, insurance, consulting, tourism, accounting, law, construction and entertainment, plus a variety of industrial manufacturing areas that are tied for competitive or regulatory reasons to serving the local market. Since the production of a service is often required close to the customer, competitors from distant locations are not particularly feared. But in manufacturing, if local costs are relatively high, some protection must be given the foreign investor to induce the commitments of capital, management, and technology required for local production.

Within this group, we find the international hotel chains (Hilton, Intercontinental, Sheraton, Holiday Inns), the worldwide banks, the large U.S. accounting firms, many consulting firms and construction companies (Fluor, Bechtel, Lummes); the manufacturing companies are numerous (Coca-Cola, Pepsi-Cola, Ford, Fiat, Dow, Du Pont, Siemens, Ciba-Geigy, Unilever), including large and small TNCs. Each of these has located production in a foreign country for the purpose of serving that market with minimal imports or exports.

The activities of the *efficiency seekers* are marked by production of high technology products with low transport costs and standardized qualities, leading to economies of scale in production and marketing. In order to serve worldwide markets, they must have low barriers to trade and to movements of capital. With these characteristics, they can and do seek to serve worldwide or regional markets from multiple production locations through an integration of component and assembly activities. Not all companies can engage in this kind of activity—it is very difficult for mineral companies to do so or for service sectors to be set up in this fashion. In fact, few if any companies are wholly oriented to this activity, though major segments of IBM, Singer, Ford-Europe, Du Pont, GM, Dow, ITT, Philips, ICI, and others are operating in this fashion. TNCs based in the United States and European countries have moved in this direction, but those from Japan are still largely of the resource-seeker and market-seeker types. The major Japanese companies have yet to meld their international affiliates into a network of production and distribution; most are still tied to the home market and that of the country in which the affiliate has been set up.

Further, the efficiency seeker, facing fairly stringent government regulations in developing countries, has found it feasible to set up integrated affiliates principally only among North American and European countries, with some slight inclusion of affiliates in Japan. The developing countries have, for reasons of national policy, largely excluded themselves from participation in this type of activity. Yet, it is the most efficient and most challenging in terms of future industrial development.

Given the differential development of major regions of the world—North America and Europe, Latin America, South Asia and Africa, and the Far East and Middle East—some of the efficiency seekers are moving to orient themselves regionally by setting up self-contained production capabilities among Europe, the Middle East, and Africa; throughout North America and Europe; or tying Latin America to either North America or Europe, depending on the location of the parent company. As of the mid-1980s, much of Latin America, Africa, South Asia, and Southeast Asia are served only from locally oriented affiliates, which will become increasingly tied to their regional brothers and sisters as regional markets are opened up.

Organization and Ownership

The orientations and activities of the different types of companies lead to different organizational structures and patterns of ownership and control. What governments want in this regard is not always achievable, simply because companies have different objectives and capabilities, given the market orientations and production capabilities just outlined.

The *resource seekers,* being suppliers of materials or components to the parent company, have generally been set up in such a way that they are guided by or run out of a division of the parent company which needs that particular product or component as an input. The mineral producer or agricultural affiliate supplies product with regular schedules, quantities, and qualities as needed by the parent. To have this input, the natural-resource affiliate does not have to be owned completely by the parent company; it is sufficient if there is a guaranteed supply at acceptable quality and price. Most transnationals consider that the guarantee is less certain than what is desired if they do not have significant ownership. However, long-term contracts have substituted successfully in many instances, and joint ventures are readily accepted in natural-resource affiliates. In fact, anything from zero ownership and long-term contracts to 100 percent ownership, including a variety of joint ventures or 50/50 arrangements, are found in these activities. Any can work out satisfactorily if there is goodwill and assured supply.

But the affiliate producing high tech components is usually tightly integrated with the parent company; thus, an electronic component will be manufactured or assembled and tested abroad and then returned to the division of the parent needing it; this division controls the schedules and qualities coming from the foreign affiliate. This divisional unit is likely to be far down the organizational structure of the TNC and will seldom show up on the published organization chart of the company. The parent has very tight control over the schedule of production, supply, and quality in order to be able to rely on it for further manufacturing.

Ownership patterns in the human-resource affiliates vary, however, according to the significance of the technology component in the arrangement. Thus, if the activity is cut-and-sew operation in the textile industry, it is not so important to have that affiliate owned 100 percent by the parent; in fact, that same operation may be performed by the affiliate for other companies on similar products with no conflict of interest. In this case, the arrangement is simply a manufacturing contract wherein a local company guarantees to supply a particular operation to a foreign company on a regular basis. The TNC may own part of the affiliate or not, extend a manufacturing licence only, or permit local sale by the licensee as well.

However, when the affiliate has been set up to use a particular technology developed by the parent company, there is much more likelihood that it will be tied tightly to the parent through 100 percent ownership. This is particularly the case when a component is being produced abroad that will be used directly in the further production of the final product by the parent.

Where the arrangement leads to a final product in the foreign country, the ownership relations can vary from zero plus a licencing agreement to joint ventures of various sorts with licencing agreements having different provisions from a straight licencing arrangement. Since the market is the parent company itself, the ties between the affiliate and the parent in terms of marketing, pricing, production, quality control, and technology are all quite tight and bent toward the interests of the parent. Consequently, if such an activity is set up on a joint venture basis, there are likely to be a number of conflicts over the product line, direction of marketing, financing, R&D activities, personnel, and external relations since the interests of the parties in these functional activities are likely to be different. It is the history of such ventures that they are frequently bought out by one of the parties to eliminate these conflicts.

For both the human- and the natural-resource affiliate, the most comfortable arrangement for the parent is 100 percent ownership, but it will accept less than that under commercial, economic, or political pressures.

The organization of the *market-seeker* activity reflects the fact that the foreign affiliates are very little integrated with the parent or among themselves. Since they are strongly oriented to the local market and are generally relatively high cost, they cannot sell effectively outside of their national borders. This orientation marks these affiliates for operation principally in the developing countries, though they also exist in some advanced countries reflecting the international strategy of the parent. For example, Unilever is less integrated worldwide than is Du Pont, simply because of a managerial decision as to the strategy of the company regarding ownership and control. Unilever prefers a looser network of control among its affiliates, giving each of them a fairly high level of responsibility in their own national markets. Du Pont, on the other hand, provides for a higher degree of coordination among the parent and the affiliates related to each industrial division of the company.

At the extreme, the affiliates of market seekers can be highly independent of both the parent and each other, so that managerial control over the major functional decisions is left in local hands. Such a company becomes a local activity in everything but name, capital supply, and technology; it, therefore, satisfies almost every desired goal of the host government in a developing country (except exports). The pattern of government requirements suggests that this is not adequately understood, since governments continue to insist on joint ventures for these kinds of activities, despite the fact that joint ventures are not likely to produce more favorable economic results and will generate conflicts of interest. Given the fact that there is little integration of activities across national boundaries, however, the market-seeker TNC can accept joint venture partners of various types without doing damage to its overall strategy. The parent company can do this so long as there is no insistence on exporting from the local affiliate, which would immediately run into conflicts with the marketing activities of other affiliates or the parent itself.

The organizational structure of the market seeker has historically been one in which the transnational has a large domestic operation in the home country and satellites in various foreign countries owned and controlled by an international division within the transnational. Thus, there is a clear separation between parent company activities and activities of affiliates, with assistance from the domestic company and the home country in terms of technology and possibly capital and some managerial support. Apart from some guidance from the international division in the parent company, affiliates can be left fairly independent. Such activities are principally import-substitution–oriented and have been well received for this reason in many developing countries. Their agony in the past decade or so over the inflow of foreign direct investment has frequently been misdirected to perceived problems with foreign ownership and control, based on a misunderstanding of the different orientations and operations of TNCs.

The foreign affiliate that has been set up to achieve international *efficiency* through cost reduction is generally tightly integrated with the activities of other affiliates and with the parent company. This is done in order to achieve specialization within the company itself (comparable to the specialization that was supposed to have been achieved under free trade, but that has been prohibited by government interventions and the lack of competitive markets).

In order to achieve a rationalization of product lines through specialization in production of finished products, components, and assembly operation, the parent company requires a high degree of control over financing, marketing, pricing, production schedules, quality control and assurance, purchases of materials, technology employed, and even the external relations of the various affiliates. R&D activities will seldom be decentralized save for exceptional circumstances, but personnel activities are likely to be decentralized in order not to raise conflicts over differential wage levels and benefits in the various national economies.

Given this high degree of integration and centralization, companies with this orientation have found it most desirable to own the foreign affiliates 100 percent. Any minority shareholding raises conflict over the rates of expansion and capital contribution, the rate of earnings, the payout of dividends, the product line, the pattern of exports, local purchases, and even government relations. Such TNCs simply find it too time-consuming and inefficient to try to meld joint venture affiliates across national boundaries into an integrated whole. Therefore, when joint ventures are accepted into such a structure, they are set up with quite specific tasks that are not readily accomplished by any of the other affiliates. This limitation will itself gradually create conflicts that are likely to be removed through a 100 percent buyout at a later date.

The advantage of the integrated, centralized organization, which frequently leads to a complex organizational structure of a matrix type, is its high flexibility, permitting shifts of the location of production within existing affiliates, shifts in production schedules, shifts in technology employed and production processes, and shifts in capital resources to make the most efficient use of all resources committed to the corporate objectives.

Implications for Government Policy

There are two major implications for government policy in dealing with TNCs and their foreign affiliates. One is the negotiating strength of the TNC in the initiation stages of forming any new venture; the other is the impact on the host country in terms of its integration into world markets.

Negotiating Strength

The negotiating strengths of the various types of TNCs differ significantly among themselves and over time for each of them.

The *natural-resource seeker* faces what is called the "obsolescing bargain," which means that it has a very strong bargaining position before it has made any investment (though this may be weakened if there are a number of companies competing from the same opportunities in the host country), but, once the investment has been made, it has fewer options in facing any further pressure from the host government. The more funds it has invested, the larger the capital equipment and technological assistance, the more it has weakened its current bargaining power. This situation requires that the investing company make as equitable a bargain as it can so that it is treated well and the government also considers that its share is adequate, so that it does not change tht terms of reference on the transnational investor.

The *human-resource seeker* has a strong bargaining position virtually throughout the lifetime of its investment simply because it is employing workers who otherwise would not be as well employed, if at all, and it brings in foreign exchange through the sale of the component (at least to the amount of the value added). Though no new markets are developed, there is a gradual growth of technological capability in the host country, which it deems desirable along with the other contributions. Further, given the mobility of this type of investment, the government has very little opportunity to put pressure on the investor for more favorable contributions; it will simply go to the next best offer from another country.

The negotiating strength of the *market seeker* is also high at the beginning and gradually dissipates, except for the fact that a TNC's investment in any one country may be relatively small in comparison to total worldwide investment. And there are no serious damages to other operations of the company if an affiliate in one country is expropriated or pressed by the host government to change its operations. The negotiation continues to be a bilateral one over a very specific activity in the host country, and the host country does not gain a great deal by forcing the foreign investor out or reducing its ownership or control. There may be some prestige gains from doing so, but there are also some losses in the contribution from the foreign investor (who will be less interested now in the development of that affiliate) if forced into a joint venture position. There is, therefore, a continuing bilateral negotiation of more or less equal parties over the activities of a market-seeker affiliate. Each may gain or lose if the terms of reference are changed. Though it may appear to the government that it can gain by forcing exports from an affiliate that was not set up to provide them, the TNC parent has other ways of recouping some of its losses, and, to prevent this rebalancing, the government would have to incur the cost of substantial surveillance and control. To move in that direction would signal to potential foreign investors that receptivity was not high, and the costs to the government are likely to be substantial but hidden.

The negotiating strength of an *efficiency seeker* is probably at its highest in the initial stages of the formation of the agreement, for there appear to be a number of contributions that the company can make, including foreign exchange earning or at least a balancing of exchange costs and revenues. It also brings technology, capital, management, and an international reputation that is desired by the host country. This bargaining strength with governments will diminish to the extent that the investment becomes fixed and the relationship between affiliates gets locked in. The interruption of supply from one affiliate to another can be quite damaging; for this reason, some of the efficiency seekers have set up alternative sources of supply so that they cannot be pushed to the wall in subsequent negotiations with governments. The ability of the transnational to adjust production locations and schedules among affiliates introduces some mobility, options, and, therefore, bargaining power vis-à-vis any one host government. Further, there is enough exchange of information among governments and through the United Nations that any special deal with one government would raise the question of establishment of a precedent that would be claimed by other governments. Therefore, the transnational that has extensive integrated activities around the world will be very careful in its negotiation with any one government not to affect its worldwide activities adversely.

International Integration

One of the objectives of host countries is to achieve a foothold in international markets through expanding their exports; at the same time, they frequently wish to reduce balance of payments deficits and foreign exchange drains by substituting for imports; and they seek local ownership as a counter to charges of exploitation. The different transnational orientations have different impacts on these objectives.

Foreign affiliates of both types of *resource seekers* are likely to be net gainers of foreign exchange, though this may not occur in the first years. A substantial amount of equipment has to be imported, particularly for the natural-resource seeker, though much of this can be financed by the capital contributions of the foreign company. Throughout subsequent operations, however, there should be a value added that provides a net gain in foreign exchange since the market is abroad.

For the *market-seeker* affiliate, the primary objective is to develop the domestic market of the host country, which may have been served by imports previously or not served at all. If there was an importation of the total product previously, the new production is likely to reduce the foreign exchange drain significantly over the years, though initially there will be a substantial import of capital equipment and even some materials or components until local suppliers have been developed. This, of course, is the objective of the "import-substitution" strategy of development. If there were no previous imports, however, the new investment may still produce a drain of foreign exchange through imports of materials, components, or equipment until local suppliers have been developed, though they themselves may increase the import drain. Ultimately, however, the import-substitution strategy raises import requirements—though not necessarily to the previous level—through the mere growth of total demand the income elasticity of demand for imports.

The *efficiency seeker* is the affiliate most able to balance import and export demand through its integration of affiliates and its centralized decisionmaking. However, to do this requires 100 percent ownership leading to full parental control of the activities; otherwise, conflicts of interest are likely to cause it to make trade-offs that are not wholly beneficial to the host country. In order to achieve that control and to avoid joint venture requirements such as those imposed by India, Spain, and Brazil, transnational companies have been willing to guarantee a fairly high level of exports through their worldwide affiliates, thereby benefiting the host country. However, the market development is through the international company and would be lost if the company were pushed out by the host country's government.

In sum, different activities of the transnational companies offer different benefits to the host country and require different trade-offs. It is not feasible to treat them the same way under government regulations or negotiations and at the same time gain the major contributions that each can bring. This is one reason why codes of conduct are inappropriate if they become very specific and why government regulations frequently bring results opposite to those desired. Effective and mutually beneficial operations can be achieved only by a thorough understanding of the purposes of the venture on the part of all parties, with a clear understanding as to how it is to be organized, how decisions are to be made, and how the affiliate is to be operated.

5
Knowledge-processing Technologies and the Global Strategies of Transnational Corporations: Issues for Developing Countries

Edward M. Roche

The Age of Microelectronics

It is expected that by 1990, in the developed countries, "everyone" will have a personal computer with a capacity of 1 to 10 million instructions per second (MIPS), equipped with 1 to 5 megabytes of memory and having 70 to 500 megabytes of disc space storage. To accomplish this goal, the obsolescence of technology will intensify. Product life cycles are about 2 years; in other words, any product more than two years old is obsolete.[1] The exponential growth of price/performance capabilities of microelectronics has meant that each year it is possible to purchase approximately 20 percent more computing capacity with the same amount of money. Microprocessor execution speeds have continued to increase rapidly, from 2 MIPS in 1985, to an expected 10–20 MIPS by 1990. The various types of memory devices, particularly random access memories, have been making very rapid progress at the technological level. Given a constant cost, the density and capacity are doubling annually. Given a constant density, the costs are halving annually. In addition to the greatly reduced costs, the miniaturization of semiconductors results in lower power consumption and the development of portable and sophisticated equipment. For magnetic media (which are used primarily for bulk storage of records), given a constant cost, the density of storage has been doubling annually. The price per megabyte of storage has declined from $25 in 1985 to $13 in 1987 and is expected to be only $5 in 1990, if not sooner. The development of very small magnetic discs is now close to a cost floor, and optical media are beginning to emerge as an alternative technology to magnetic media. Optical storage still faces a "read-write" problem (it is still primarily "read" only), but it does hold forth the promise of the development of massive archives. At the microcomputer level, the Intel 386 microprocessor and the Motorola 68020 microprocessor will shortly accelerate the evolution from 4-bit to 8-bit to 16-bit (currently most popular) to "true"

32-bit multitasking processors. These microprocessors will provide many new capabilities, such as multitasking, larger memory addresses, and higher processing speeds. The sophistication of graphics capabilities will greatly increase as a result.

At the level of telecommunications, the next step will see the emergence of the integrated services digital network (ISDN). This system, when it emerges, will have great potential for yielding the generalized effects of standardization found in any technology. The marketplace for different vendors of information technology will greatly increase. This will result in accelerated price erosion and competition. The general standardization will make possible accelerated linkages between different applications and systems. There are a few problem areas in international development of the ISDN, but the mid-1980s forecast holds that its effect will begin to be felt in the short to medium term. It will greatly simplify the continued introduction of value-added networks (VANs) at both the domestic and international levels.[2]

During the early phases of computerization, little communication was needed. Computers required entire rooms, used vast amounts of electricity, were cumbersome to operate, were terribly expensive, and actually did little. They were associated with a "cult of programmer" and "cult of the operator," the elite few who could understand the mysterious doings behind the sealed glass walls surrounding the mammoth giants of technology, which today seem behind the times and almost laughable.

The physical and architectural configurations of computer installations have changed greatly. Control of the central computer installation has weakened. The creation of remote batch technology has made it possible for greater numbers of persons to have access to computer technology. Telecommunications lines have extended the reach of the central computer throughout the corporation and into society as a whole.

Information Technology and Transnational Corporations

The technological revolution taking place in microelectronics and telecommunications is shaping the international strategies of transnational corporations. Those rationalizations of business operations made possible through the use of information technology, which started within the transnationals' own organizational structure, have gradually spread out into society as a whole, particularly at the international level. The glut of available technology is making it possible for these corporations to put onto the market international information-intensive goods and services, many of which were in the past protected by parastatal organizations behind a wall of national sovereigny. A conflict has emerged between the nation state and its internal information systems and those of transnational corporations. There are many barriers hindering the rapid expansion of international information-intensive services, but these barriers will break down if they follow the pattern established in the past after the first emergence of international telecommunications systems. The issues this raises for developing countries, apart from questions of national sovereignty, involve investment trajectories in technology, industrial policies for internal development, emphasis on high technology in education and training, and the general question of the challenge to parastatal organizations posed by the emergence of new international information-intensive services.

Transnational corporations are economic entities that have evolved over time from the days of large-scale state trading in force during the imperialist era of the fifteenth and sixteenth centuries, up to the 1800s. Primarily a European invention, these forms of economic enterprise were responsible not only for carrying out basic economic transactions, but also for helping in the inforcement of the regulations and laws foisted upon some developing countries by the imperial powers.[3]

The transnational corporations of today are vastly different from those existing in the early years of the twentieth and late years of the nineteenth century. However, in spite of these differences, there are fundamental similarities in the control and channelling of information that make today's organizations similar to those of the past. Understanding the role of information technology in the control and operation of the vast economic systems presented by transnational organizations is the key to comprehending the role of technology as a vital element of economic control and rational use of resources.

International trade has been inextricably linked with international communications systems, first based on the transportation of messages by fast ship, and then gradually based on linkages of international telegraphic systems, which until the second World War were almost completely controlled by the United Kingdom. These systems for the international transmission of control data by large, internationally operating economic enterprises have shifted from the use of telegraph and telex to use of the computer and transborder data flow linkages of knowledge and information-processing computer-based applications. As European expansion took place, international communications systems were installed to serve as a command and control system for commerce. Resources could be located, identified, and gradually brought into the world trading system. Exotic plants, minerals, and other resources discovered in this era were made part of the European system. This early stage of the transnational corporation could be called one of informational expansionism.

It is true that during the initial phases of European imperialist ventures in the fifteenth and sixteenth centuries, the risks were great and there was no effective and systematic means of global communication. Once distant resources had been located and were needed in a steady supply, the system of global communications, albeit primitive, became crucial to the success of the system of trade relations. Political news of diplomatic importance; reports from wars; historical, cultural, and scientific data—all these types of information composed the substance of this early stage of international communications. But it was the economic advantages to be gained from an effective international system of resource control that powered the internal combustion of the system.[4] As European civilization expanded, it was communications that made possible effective material and political coordination.

Large complex economic organizations, such as transnational corporations, have intensified their use of information technology in many different locations. Branch offices of the transnationals in different countries (such as those in Europe or the Far East) have been given separate computer installations. Large computer suppliers have built up worldwide systems of distribution, service, and sales. In the early stages, many computers were leased, and their interconnections with the telephone and telegraph systems of host countries were minimal.

International telecommunications have improved, through such major steps as agreements on international direct dialing, increases in total international capacity, development of communications satellites in the early 1960s, stabilization of rates, protected arrangements for state-promoted universal service, and improvements in reliability and overall capacity.

The headquarters of large transnational corporations have developed the capability to receive highly detailed reports concerning their operations overseas. These regular electronic reports are vital to efficient business operations. For the best understanding of the transnational corporation's use of knowledge-processing technologies, particularly with regard to the powers of nation states, it is useful to examine how transnational corporations had their beginnings in international communications networks.

The general trend is for more and more of the bureaucratic functions within transnational corporations to be absorbed into the computer system. These technologies are used primarily to automate functions that were carried out before through paper-based manual systems. Although this automation of bureaucratic functions has yet to produce any significant decrease in the number of persons employed as bureaucrats, it has greatly increased the amount of work that can be done and has perhaps prevented a rapid rise in the number of information workers that would theoretically have been necessary if computerization had never taken place.

According to Max Weber the structure of large bureaucratic organizations is similar to a pyramid: orders are given at the top and are carried out subsequently in greater levels of detail by a highly specialized and trained cadre of workers.[5] It follows, therefore, that, assuming that the underlying structure of the organization is unchanged, the first effect of computerization is to increase the throughput of information and thus to speed up the pace of decisonmaking. Utilization of information technology in transnational corporations is subject to various effects that are dependent upon the *velocity* and the *structuring* of information. The relationships at the departmental level between workers, the information they use, and the information technology they have access to is one class of analysis. A second level of analysis involves the study of informational and structural relationships between the departments themselves. A third level of analysis examines the structural relationship between the organization as a whole and its environment.

It is typical for the flow of information between departments to follow a logical sequence determined by the nature of the organization and the specific product or service being offered. Most transnationals today use a hierarchical model resembling a pyramid as their underlying fundamental structure. In traditional business theory, this hierarchical structure shows the "chain of command" that is followed as management decides the steps to take and the functions to process in the organization as a whole. The availability of interdepartmental channels of communication is weakening the traditional functioning of the chain of command. Horizontal communication is taking the place of vertical communication.

There is a parallel relationship between the electronic structure and flow of interdepartmental information and emerging pressures for change of the hierarchical nature of transnationals. First, with the increasing complexity of organizations, flows of information controlled through the top levels (or center) of the organization have slowed down. This has raised the pressure on individual departments to set up their own informal "back-door" channels of communication, linking one department with another on an informal basis and yet accomplishing the needed task without contact with the top levels of the hierarchy (which are sluggish). The second catalyst is the emergence of departmental computing and shared multiuser systems, such as minicomputers, operating at the departmental level.

In general, information technology allows traditional forms of bureaucratic control to be gradually weakened and undermined by electronic flows of information that can exist only with the help of the information technology system. Eventually, depending on the velocity of interdepartmental communications, the functional relationships of the departments may appear to be merged from the point of view of the top controlling circles. One eventual result would be a complete elimination of the vertical communications channels.

The greatest acceleration in information speed takes place when information technology is used to substitute for paper-based systems—the type of information system most frequently found in developing countries. As the velocity of information reaches greater speeds, the functional relationships between departments tend to blur. The information velocity may reach such great speeds that, for all practical purposes, it becomes real time. When this occurs, the individuality of the departments linked together through the electronic information system is blurred and departments tend to act as one unit. In order to save on human resources, departments are merged into one another and the information system is changed accordingly. Technological solutions adopted in order to merge information technology with preexisting hierarchical structures of the classical Weberian mold have reinforced the rigidity of those structures but at the same time have provided the vehicle for the substantial transformation of working patterns. This has occurred in phases.

The phases of computerization for transnational corporations can be defined as a function both of the amount of high-level management attention being devoted to problems, issues, and investments in information technology and of the degree of actual centralization or decentralization in the system's architecture.[6] For purposes of simplification, these phases can be called, respectively, early years, discovery, neglect, and rediscovery.

Phase	Period	Business Utilization
I	Early years	Little business use
II	Discovery	High-priority item
III	Neglect	Uncontrolled growth Management neglect
IV	Rediscovery	Strategic use

As the table shows, in contrast to the neglect phase (in which responsibility for information technology was delegated to lower levels of management) in the subsequent rediscovery phase, top management resumes charge of the deployment of information technology.

The decentralization taking place is a reflection of the large amount of information technology available. On an international scale, the development of computerization in transnational corporations lags behind the development of headquarters organizations in originating countries. It is a question of scale. The degree of decentralization for transnationals was always much greater than for domestic corporations. They always lacked the close coordination with central authority and the management control present in other organizations. As top management turns attention to the development of strategic information technology applications for their computer organizations, they will also turn increasingly toward the global picture as an axis of competition. In all but a few protected industries, the viability of a strategic plan will be judged by its ability to operate successfully on a global basis. It is this connection between the global strategies of transnational corporations and their utilization of information technology that is at the heart of developments for the medium term. It is possible to divide the stages of computerization roughly into decades: the 1960s, the 1970s, the 1980s, and the 1990s. Each stage is marked by a specific type of relationship between the formal hierarchical structure of an organization and its underlying technological linkages.[7]

Within complex organizations, departments are linked into various chains of cause and effect that together in sequential form constitute the linear processes of discrete functions. When analyzing each departmental unit using the input/output technique, it is possible to calculate the amount of value added created by subtracting the inputs used from the outputs created.[8]

Already in the United States, there are a few examples where entirely new organizations, with new functions, have been designed completely from scratch, based primarily on the type of underlying computer technology being used.[9] These organizations do not have to suffer through the evolutionary process of destabilizing automation. They do not have to cope with the dilemma that, in most cases, when more computers are introduced, there is a temporary decrease in productivity, and that this drag on productivity may continue for one or two years. There is some indication that destabilizing automation is less frequently a problem in small organizations of fewer than 250 employees.[10]

In the same way that information technology is being used to link together different departments of corporations, it is being used to link together different units of transnational corporations at the international level. A transnational corporation operating an international computer communications system has a variety of computer applications. The information-processing environment may vary from country to country, but there are many basic functions and characteristics of knowledge technologies that hold true at the international level. Many data communications programs, operating systems, or general financial and personnel applications may perform the same functions, regardless of the country in which they are operating.

The development and emergence of international computer-communications systems may be complicated by the variety of applications installed in various countries. Each knowledge-processing center has a variety of applications resident at its site. Each country has a specific environment that tends to change the nature of the applications used. Some applications are the same in different country environments. Some applications are linked together from one country to another. Linkages between the applications resident in different data processing centers can span from one country to another.

The Nation State on the Defensive

During the early 1970s, concerns were raised regarding the security of data about individuals. Countries entered into international negotiations to attempt to work out some type of arrangement that would both protect the individual and not inhibit international trade.

During these negotiations, many issues were raised that tended to broaden the issue of international computer networking beyond concern for the privacy of data on individuals being carried internationally through computers. Questions about national sovereignty, protectionism, cultural integrity, and taxation of data came to the fore. Although the initial concerns were privacy and confidentiality, the scope of negotiations expanded to include all transborder data flows of information.

Critics of information technology have contended that computers and telecommunications systems are tools to reestablish colonial-type relationships between the developed nations and the rest of the world.[11] These fears and concerns have contributed to the erection of barriers against the international diffusion of knowledge-processing technologies. It is a reflection of an open debate about the true effects of computers: are they a force for maintaining a frightening control over economies and societies or are they a labor-saving technology that will help to liberate both white collar and blue collar workers from boring and meaningless work and promote a new age of enlightenment through the global flow of information?

The barriers encountered internationally may be explained from two sources. First, some barriers have been in place all along, but have been "discovered" as pressures from the utilization of information technology have become greater. Second, they flow from the realization that the public bureaucracies in developing countries, which are unable to cope with international competition, must either be protected by the state or allowed to wither away, with all of the consequences to the fundamentals of nation-state power that would result.

If the world's global economy is taken as a whole, it is easy to demonstrate the efficiencies that could be gained in development if nationally imposed barriers were erased. This is an old problem in international politics. It shows itself at many levels within international society. Each state attempts to maximize its advantage against all other countries and, in so doing, acts in what it perceives to be its own interest. In the area of knowledge-processing technologies, countries have a variety of policies designed to protect their interests. Other limitations may be imposed by external forces. For example, a country's balance of payments situation may necessitate the careful screening of applications for spending scarce foreign currency. This juggling of national priorities (whose selection and prioritization is forced upon the sometimes reluctant state policy machinery) may result in a reduced status for information technology. This type of prioritization is easily understandable: poverty, hunger, housing, health, electricity, and other areas of concern may have greater priority since they are assumed to be preconditions for the "information society."

Types of Barriers

The various types of barriers used by nation states to implement their priorities for the utilization (or avoidance) of information technologies can be classified as *technical, regulatory, trade protectionist, bureaucratic inertia, national sovereignty,* and *industrial policy.* These categories provide a system for basic analysis of the dynamics of nation-state inhibitions against information technologies.

Technical. The physical infrastructure lies at the most fundamental level of any international data communications system of the type that supports knowledge-processing technologies. It is at this level that technical regulations and controls can either promote or inhibit the growth of knowledge-processing technologies. The interconnection of data communications equipment to national and international networks is the focus of technical barriers. The types of plugs used, the types of "protocols" or "languages" of communication, may vary. Each variance denies the benefits of standardization, and not only complicates the planning and implementation of these networks but also raises the costs of having linked knowledge-processing systems. Technical standards may also be used as an excuse by some nation states to veil other intentions, such as aiming to keep out foreign equipment. In those cases where national technical standards are established and inforced by a nationalized or state-controlled parastatal organization, standards may be used to put an honest face on activities designed to protect the very monopolies responsible for compliance with the proposed technical standards.

Regulatory. The regulations governing the interconnection of computers across international borders can be a significant barrier to efficient operations. Sometimes, there are outright prohibitions against operating certain given classes of information technology within certain states, and these regulations are not exclusively the preserve of the host state but may originate with the headquarters state as well.[12] In addition to controls over international flows of information and data, there may be ancillary controls over the import and export of equipment. Even in cases where the importation of equipment needed in a business is not expressly prohibited, it may be that the bureaucratic machinery will take an inordinate amount of time making decisions. The economic impact of these delays in deliberation—the amount of time between when a decision or ruling is asked for and when it is actually made—is seldom calculated, but the delays cost someone money and may be responsible for much of the lag in economic development in many situations. (China is reported to have many problems in this category.)

Trade Protectionist. Every nation state has an industrial policy, either by plan or by default. In the centrally planned economies, there is a conscious effort on the part of the state to formulate industrial policy. These national plans are built around the idea that various types of controls can be used to guide economic development along a path that reflects the optimum benefit for society.[13] In the area of foreign trade, the importation and exportation of technology can be guided to reflect the same set of concerns. Diffusion of information technologies can take place as a result of industrial policies that are using as one of their tools control over the importation of products. The secondary consequences of this type of state action may be as follows:

Internationally operating organizations may be denied the benefits of technology.

Inefficiencies may result as organizations are forced to utilize less than technologically optimum knowledge-processing systems.

Entire lines of economic activity may be cut off as a result of the lack of enabling technologies upon which they are dependent. This is particularly important with information-based activities.

Trade friction may spill over into other sectors.

Bureaucratic Inertia. Since all forms of economic and social organization require a significant amount of information control, they require bureaucracies to carry out that control. Bureaucracies are an inescapable fact of life, although there are few known methodologies that can even begin to approximate their contribution to economic development and society. Many critics would argue that bureaucracies are unnecessary and do little more than hinder the operations of dynamic sectors of society. Others point out that without some type of informational organization of society, as exemplified by bureaucracy, the economy and its supporting society would quickly slip into chaos and anarchy. In terms of the international diffusion of information technologies, particularly through the conduit of transnational corporations, the bureaucratic organization of states can play a significant role in either a positive or a negative direction. Bureaucratic controls can be used to accomplish objectives in a very indirect manner. Delays, fines, fees, excessive requests for information, secrecy, obfuscation, and other techniques can damage economic operations significantly. The greatest delays caused by bureaucratic organizations may take place when there is no institutional machinery to handle a new technological development or service. There may be a complete lack of understanding on the part of the regulating bureaucracy as to the details and real significance of the different options being proposed by the transnational organization. Economic and social consequences are difficult to anticipate for a bureaucracy with no prior experience in the new area. In terms of new information-based services, there may be a complete lack of understanding. Furthermore, the types of services proposed may pose a conflict with the old, established bureaucracies of the host nation state. The postal and telegraphic services, for example, may be threatened by electronic mail. They will fight for the continuation of a system that guarantees them monopolistic revenues. In doing so, they will argue that, should their monopolistic position not be preserved, foreign economic organizations will usurp the revenues that would normally remain in the country. This type of argument is difficult to defeat. It may be extremely difficult, if not impossible, in these circumstances, to introduce new information-based services or new knowledge-processing technologies.

National Sovereignty. In its most brutal and comprehensive form, "national sovereignty" means that, within their borders, states can do whatever they please. They may reject or accept technology. They may control, tax, inhibit, encourage, or sometimes even steal technology entering their borders. They may take a somewhat neutral stand. But, regardless of the particulars of the environment, some type of policy will certainly exist. In terms of transnational corporations and their use of knowledge-processing technologies, the nation state may use controls over technology to change the nature of business for the transnational. Various surveys have shown this area to be one of significant conflict between developed and developing countries. It is particularly evident in the GATT negotiations on trade in services. Since information-based services are included in the definitions, these ongoing international negotiations will change the role of national sovereignty arguments in the regulation of knowledge-processing–technology diffusion and utilization. Until such time as new agreements are reached, however, the argument of national sovereignty will continue to be the final word for justifying state actions that cannot be rationalized in any other way.

Industrial Policy. A coherent industrial policy for the information technology and communications sectors may constitute a general strategy in which some protection may be progressively conferred on ever more sophisticated knowledge-processing technologies as they come to be produced by the nation state's enterprises. This type of strategy may be called *technologically incrementalist infant-industry protection*.[14] Technologies that are not produced in the state are not controlled. Once production starts, however, the aim of achieving a world-class competitive position by reaching economies of scale in manufacturing the given product is boosted by prohibition or strict licencing aimed at curbing the importation of competing products. Theoretically, the price of the domestic product, once it is successfully produced, will drop below the average world-market price, thus eliminating the need for further protection since consumers tend to buy the cheaper product of comparable quality. This type of activity on the part of the nation state can inhibit the efficient absorption of technology severely because there is almost certainly a delay between the availability of knowledge-processing technologies and the development of national technologies that take its place.

In summary, there are many barriers that nation states may impose that have the effect of inhibiting the efficient absorption of information technologies. These barriers can be imposed for a variety of reasons and may not in all cases be totally intentional on the part of the nation state. Regulations, bureaucratic inertia, justifications of national sovereignty, state planning efforts and the accompanying industrial policies, the need for control of foreign currency allocations, and other reasons may all conspire to inhibit information technologies.

The Microelectronic Revolution—Choices for Developing Countries

Information technology and the way in which it is used by transnational corporations present both problems and opportunities for developing countries. On the one hand, there are important benefits to be gained from allowing technological diffusion, particularly in the area of knowledge-processing technologies. On the other hand, if the use of these proprietary technologies by transnational corporations results in advantages that cannot be duplicated in the developing country, and if those advantages are used to its detriment,[15] then the developing country faces a difficult choice in weighing benefits against problems.[16]

The fundamental problem is that developing countries, including those in East Asia (with the exception of Japan), are behind the developed nations in the development of the services sector of their economies. Many are overly dependent on heavy industry, light assembly, or natural-resources exploitation, and have weak infrastructures in telecommunications. The services sector of many economies is the most information-intensive. According to statistics released by the World Bank, most of the developing countries of East Asia and the Pacific are behind the developed countries in two important criteria: their GNP per capita and the amount of their GDP devoted to the service sectors. Figure 5–1 compares GNP per capita to percentage of GDP in services of developed countries and the East Asian and Pacific countries. In the figure, China is located at the lower left corner of the countries represented.

This would seem to indicate that China's prospects for the quick absorption of knowledge-processing technologies may be quite small for two reasons:

Figure 5–1. GNP per Capita versus Percentage of GDP in Services for Developed and East Asian Countries

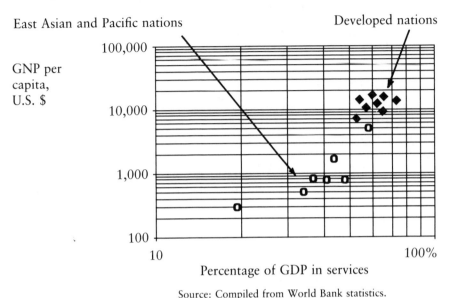

Source: Compiled from World Bank statistics.

The amount of GNP per capita would suggest that other national development priorities besides knowledge-processing technologies would get more attention.

The active service sector of the economy is not developed enough to quickly absorb new ways of handling information.

The development of knowledge-processing technologies, although no doubt a great priority in many developing countries, is extremely capital-intensive. Large amounts of resources are required for each succeeding generation of microelectronic technology, particularly semiconductors. In addition, the human resources capable of effectively producing the technologies are becoming scarcer. Infusions of capital alone are not adequate. Nor can the building of a wall of protectionism around national industries stand for long against the need to acquire technology and know-how from outside. On the other hand, to allow completely free trade and transfer of technology risks the complete abandonment of efforts to develop a nationally based skills structure.[17]

What can a developing country do? It is caught in a cycle of ever-increasing needs for capital and resources that it cannot allocate without damaging other investment priorities. At the same time, it faces the international competition of transnationals, many of which are well equipped with sophisticated technologies.

There are two fundamental issues that must be faced: scarcity of human resources and investment priorities in equipment.

Human Resources

As countries make strides to absorb knowledge-processing technologies, it is important to plan for a great general increase in the skills required for the new age of information-processing–oriented economic sectors. The educational institutions must plan for the challenges ahead. Although much public policy in developing countries is based on the notion that the costs and corresponding investments in information technologies will increase constantly as development takes place, what is less well known is that the cost of the human-resources component of the knowledge-processing sector is going to grow proportionally more.

The cost of the amount of effort required to manage the software in computers, such as through programming, is going to grow more than that of the equipment itself. It is not expected that this trend will diminish until the impact of fifth-generation languages makes possible complete intermediation between the end user and the computer. Programming costs have been increasing more rapidly than hardware costs, the former is expected to rise from an index of $2.50 to $12.00 between 1985 and 1995 and the latter from $0.50 to $1.00 in the same period. The estimated costs for programming will increase more than for hardware. Since the bulk of programming and software costs is dependent on the availability of trained human labor, each developing country has to surmount a large learning curve before it can adequately master knowledge-processing technologies.[18] The implications for education and technical training are that planners must anticipate spending more and more resources in this area as knowledge-processing technologies are diffused into the society. The amount of resources spent in this area will exceed that for the purchase of the equipment.

Investment Decisions—Price versus Quality

Another implication of the revolution in microelectronics for developing nations involves the constant need to examine carefully the trade-offs between price and quality in available technology. Many nations are in the process of giving priority in their imports to technology that is not the most up-to-date. Their argument is that the most modern technologies are not needed because the factor endowments differ so radically between developed and developing countries.[19]

In the area of telecommunications, many developing countries are facing the need to upgrade their installed systems or to build new systems to cope with rapidly growing urban populations. Since the old Stowager switch analog configurations are much cheaper (according to the initial purchase price) than new digital systems, and since the use of copper wiring is much easier than the use of new fiber optics or digital-based systems, many developing countries have been moving toward the use of the older-generation technologies. They miss the opportunity to leapfrog from old technologies to new. More disturbing, the great amount of training of scarce human resources taking place must be in areas that will not be useful for the future, since they are essentially outdated before training is begun. This appears to be the case in China.

There are, naturally, certain savings and rationalizations gained from taking the approach of old and proven technologies, but, if the human costs and the maintenance implications are considered, this route is rarely the most optimum. To make the conscious choice to lock a country's technology path into an outdated route may save money in the short term but is actually borrowing from the future potential for technological development.

The International Response to Technological Change

Technological change has opened the door to new possibilities for transnational corporations to build international computer communications networks. The development of international network has, in turn, influenced the type of institutional governing arrangements appropriate for efficient regulation. Many institutions are in need of change. Since technologies have changed much faster than institutional capabilities and relational structures, the institutional frame has collapsed into a crisis marked by conflict between differing interest groups on an international scale. When the international governing regime was stable, technology was moving very slowly. As technological progress accelerated, many national postal, telephone, and telegraph administrations were forced to make various exceptions, on a sector-by-sector basis, for international dedicated networks. As microelectronics continued to revolutionize technological possibilities, conflicts ensued and private international networks began to spring up. The capabilities of very large scale integration (VLSI) will continue to increase the pressure on international institutional arrangements until such time as a complete reshaping takes place. The relationships between the available technologies and the type of international networks developed would suggest that the international system is in need of new institutional arrangements.

The types of institutional arrangements governing international utilization of information technology, the rapid progress in the fundamental characteristics of the underlying technologies (particularly microelectronics), and the response of international users in their utilization of available services and technologies are by no means independent of one another. It is expected that, as a result of the changes being brought about by the radical improvements in microelectronics, the international arrangements governing computer networking will reach a crisis and then transform themselves completely. They cannot currently handle the changes in technologies, and matters can only become worse under the present institutional arrangements.

Notes

1. For developing countries with capabilities of importation, but with limited internal capacity, the rapid fall in prices of electronic computer equipment means that it will take less time to wait for technology to become cheap enough to import. Because of the reduced product life cycle, it is less and less likely that equipment brought in as used equipment will be out of working order. The active life cycle and reliability of this equipment exceeds by a good margin the two-year product cycle. Although most products become obsolete, they may well remain in working order.

2. Value added networks are telecommunications networks that perform advanced functions (such as protocol conversion, voice recognition, voice synthesis, and data processing) in addition to the standard point-to-point functions performed by the traditional telecommunications network system.

3. In China, of course, the transnational organizations of the nineteenth century created and inforced many regulations that were later revised. China has rejected the influence of TNCs in the past, but now seems to realize their importance in the transfer of technology and in helping the development process. China's current problem seems to lie in attempting to extract benefits from TNCs without allowing much profit to accrue to them.

4. Roche, Edward M., "From Sending a Runner to Sending a Telex: A History of Modern Communications," in *World Progress through International Telecommunications: A Salute to the International Telecommunications Union* (New York: United Nations Association of the U.S.A., Inc., 1980).

5. Weber, Max, *Economy and Society: An Outline of Interpretive Sociology* (G. Roth and C. Wittich, eds.) (Berkeley: University of California Press, 1978).

6. The *early years* of computing were characterized by a lack of concern on the part of management. Eventually, this concern started to increase, but the cost of computers was very high, and only the largest organizations could seriously contemplate an acquisition study. Gradually, the cost of computers began to improve as a function of their capabilities, and management began to take an interest.

The discovery phase of computing was when top management in various companies was actively engaged in studying the possible uses of computers in their firms. It was during this phase that computers, aided by the 360 family of IBM, began to be widely accepted into the marketplace. The cost of computers at this time was very high, rating along with expenditures for major capital equipment in most organizations. A result of this high cost was a very high degree of top-management attention to the problem of costs. As computers were accepted into the fabric of large organizations, top management shifted its concerns elsewhere.

The neglect phase of computerization was the result. Computers were accepted by organizations, but only in the back areas. Directors of computer centers tended to be technically oriented or of an accounting mentality—not the fabric from which the top management of a corporation is made. At the same time, the size of computer installations began to grow. International networks were linked up. The penetration of information technology into the organization of the corporation continued to intensify. Top management tended to delegate authority and command over computer resoruces farther and farther down the organization's line of command. Computer people were rarely thought of as being of "line management" quality. During this phase, the dynamics of technology were such that computers began to spread rapidly throughout the organization. This was when the personal computer arrived and when the terminals from large computers existed almost everywhere there was a way to link into the telephone network. The neglect phase of computerization ended approximately in 1982.

As of 1986, we are in the *rediscovery* phase of top management relationships with information technology. Top management, looking to the famous example of the American Hospital Supply Company, have learned that there is a strategic relationship between information technology and market share. In virtually every major corporation throughout the developed world, high-level strategic planning sessions are being conducted to determine how information technology can be used as a competitive weapon. In every sector—manufacturing, finance, insurance, banking, transportation, food, retail, distribution, publishing—this rediscovery phase is pointing to the development of new applications for the utilization of information technology. Although each sector has unique aspects that distinguish its uses of information technology, in every sector there is an underlying pattern revealing a heightened awareness on the part of top management.

7. The 1960s stage of utilization was dominated by the large central processing unit (CPU) located at headquarters. This period is traditionally called the *era of centralization*. The 1970s stage of utilization saw two developments; first, the expansion of the reach of the central organization's CPU farther out into the corporation; and, second, the emergence of departmental systems linking users. During this phase, the vast majority of end users were not involved with information technology. The 1980s stage of utilization has included several developments. CPU central systems have continued their thrust into different parts of the corporation. New types of communications have proliferated, including linkages between the CPU and various departmental minicomputers, as well as communications linkages between departmental systems. The amount of overlapping between departmental systems has increased. Finally, the departmental systems, primarily minicomputers, have penetrated substantially into the traditional domain of the CPU systems. In the 1990s stage of utilization, the vast majority of end users will have access, either to processing services from the CPU central systems as they continue to expand, or from the various departmental minicomputer systems as they continue to expand. End user groups will provide the same opportunities for rationalization as links between departments.

8. Basic departmental value added (VA) can be calculated by outputs minus inputs (O-I). Since various departments are linked together into productive causation

chains, their total value added is approximately the sum of the value added amounts for each department.

9. The Battery March Company of Boston, Massachusetts, engaged primarily in equities portfolio management.

10. See Strassmann, Paul A., *Information Payoff: The Transformation of Work in the Electronic Age* (New York: Free Press, 1985). (Observation is based on conversations with Mr. Strassmann.)

11. These writers include Samir Amin, Herbert Schiller, and Mohammad Bedjaoui.

12. Brazil prohibits various levels of equipment, and much equipment from the United States cannot be exported to Communist countries.

13. The problem is that no bureaucracy is efficient enough to actually "plan" an economy. The effort is simply too complex. Delays are endless, statistical information is inaccurate, and innovation is crushed. These problems seem to have been recognized somewhat in Soviet reforms of the late 1980s.

14. See Roche, Edward M., "South Korea's Informatics Race," in *AGORA: Informatics in a Changing World*, vol. 9 (Rome: Intergovernmental Bureau for Informatics, 1984), pp. 12–14.

15. The use of the term *detriment* is not meant to include profit making by transnational corporations from their activities in developing countries (since this is the foundation of their participation in the local economy) except for rare or inopportune circumstances.

16. In the area of services (such as banking, insurance, telecommunications, and other financial sectors), there is little doubt that the state-protected economic organizations of most developing countries could not hold up against the strength of the active transnationals, should protective barriers be removed. They would be severely damaged if completely free trade in this area were allowed. Even in the case of a developed Western European country, the Netherlands, the national leading banks have been severely challenged by large foreign banks plying more advanced information and telecommunications technologies making it possible to provide very sophisticated customized global cash management systems to the customer base. Without the ability to provide such sophisicated information-technology–based services, the national banks lost market share. It is quite clear, therefore, that, should a great wave of liberalization of these heretofore protected parastatal sectors take place, the impact of the strong transnational organizations, largely owed to their sophisticated use of information technology, would pose a serious challenge. If the challenge went unanswered major social and economic dislocations might result in some countries in some sectors.

17. This is the classical problem of protectionism in high technology. It is exemplified very strongly by Brazilian informatics policy.

18. It is unrealistic to think that most developing countries will ever be able to catch up.

19. For example, countries with a surplus of oil are unlikely to place a high premium on imports of equipment or goods that save energy. Similarly, countries having a surplus of labor are unlikely to place much priority on the importation of goods that cut down on the labor component of production—technologies such as robotics.

6
The World Crisis and Transnational Corporations

Jun Nishikawa

The international environment for overseas private investment is rapidly changing. In spite of the devaluation of the dollar, higher U.S. interest rates keep a large flow of capital pouring into the United States from other parts of the world. In Europe, stagflation is still dominant and the unemployment rate is around 10 percent. In Japan, where automation and robotization have been aggressively practiced in recent years, the unemployment rate, despite the small recovery in the economy, was nearly 3 percent as of December 1985, the highest rate in a quarter of a century. Developing countries are suffering an increasing burden of external debt. Many people in Africa and Asia are starving, and the poorest countries are undergoing a food crisis. On the other hand, the arms race between the big powers has been intensifying and world military expenditures now amount to $1 trillion—one-twelfth of total world GNP. The world crisis seems to have been exerting pressure on the lower sectors of the population in both the developed and the developing countries. The superpowers—and the ruling class of each country who are their allies—are trying to contain the revolt of the oppressed and exploited through increasing militarization and promoting a chauvinist nationalism as well as a wasteful, consumption-oriented life-style in every part of the world. This chapter analyzes the relationship between the world crisis and the transnational corporations (TNCs). First, I shall examine the progress of TNCs in the world economy and, second, the relationship between TNCs and the deepening world crisis. Third, I shall compare Japan's TNCs with those of the United States. Fourth, I shall look at the conflicts between TNCs and the host and home countries. After examining these points, we shall be able to see what measures the popular and workers' movements could take in order to control TNCs and construct a more harmonious world order in the place of the present one, which is subject to constant and successive crises.

The Progress of TNCs in the World Economy

Overseas private direct investment has been increasing steadily since 1960, when the total accumulated amount was $66.7 billion. By 1980, it had reached $523.6 billion—a sevenfold increase in twenty years. This growth rate corresponds more or less to that of world GNP during the same period. In 1981, total production of the world TNC network was estimated at $2.741 billion or 22 percent of world GNP.[1] The largest investor is the United States, which controls 41 percent of the total overseas investment. In 1980, Japan ranked fifth after the United States, the United Kingdom, the Netherlands, and Germany (F.R.). In recent years, TNCs originating in developing countries have increased their investment, but their share is still only 2.7 percent of the total accumulated investment.

This huge investment and the transnational network of production are controlled, according to a Harvard Business School Survey, by some 10,000 big corporations, of which the United States accounts for 21 percent and Germany (F.R.) and the U.K. 14 percent each. Japanese TNCs are estimated to number 572. (When the Japanese Ministry of International Trade and Industry—MITI—made a survey in 1983, it received 1,367 replies from home countries.)[2] Only 364 TNCs (3.5 percent of the total) originate in developing countries. The growth of the international oligopolistic structure of transnational enterprise, which is dominated by a small number of huge companies originating in the Northern countries, is clearly visible.

Which countries are the recipients of international investment? In 1980, 71 percent of the recipients of foreign investment were developed countries and the share of the developing countries was 27 percent. Western Europe, the United States, and Canada are the major recipients. In recent years, mutual investment between the developed countries has increased considerably and the share of investment going to developed countries has been increasing. Japan has also invested heavily in the United States and the European Community, but it remains a very small recipient of foreign investment (figure 6–1). This is why Japan is accused by other OECD countries of closing the door to investment.

This, then, is the general position of TNCs in the world economy. Let us now examine the relationship between their activities and the crisis in the capitalist economy.

TNCs' Activities and the World Crisis

To what extent are TNCs and transnational banks responsible for the world crisis? First, these huge corporations cannot accumulate profits earned in the domestic field as they would become the object either of a progressive corporate tax or of distribution by government and labor unions. These profits would

Figure 6–1. Investment between Japan, the E.C., and the United States as of 1984 (billions of U.S. $)

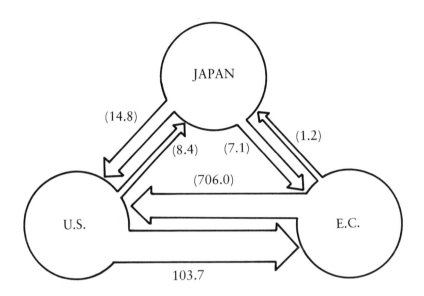

Source: Ministry of International Trade and Industry, *Tsūshō Hakusho* (White Paper on Trade), 1986 edition.

also become surplus capital equipment that might decrease the rate of profit. In major capitalist countries, the share of overseas investment in total fixed capital formation has been increasing since the 1960s. From 1960–62 to 1978–80, its share increased in the United States from 3 to 4.7 percent; in the United Kingdom from 5.0 to 7.6 percent; in Germany (F.R.), from 1.0 to 2.5 percent; and in Japan from 0.5 to 0.8 percent. The total OECD average during this period ranged from 2.1 to 2.9 percent (table 6–1). This decrease in domestic investment, together with the administrative price that monopolistic and oligopolistic firms have been imposing on consumers, is one of the reasons for the stagflation that has hit capitalist economies since the 1970s.[3] Of course, some newly industrializing regions and countries have benefited from the shift of investment. However, the profit-oriented distribution of resources on a worldwide scale has increased the disparities between nations and regions.

Second, transnational firms and banks today handle huge resources in Eurocurrencies or Eurodollars. The Eurocurrencies market was estimated to contain some $2 trillion in 1983, 70 percent of which were Eurodollars (the other 30 percent being composed of other OECD currencies, such as the

Table 6–1
The Share of Overseas Direct Investment in Domestic Fixed Capital Formation, 1960–80
(*Percent*)

	1960–62	1972–74	1978–80
OECD total	2.1	2.7	2.9
United States	3.0	4.0	4.7
Canada	0.9	2.3	4.6
United Kingdom	5.0	9.0	7.6
Germany (F.R.)	1.0	2.2	2.5
France	2.2	1.3	1.9
Sweden	1.1	3.0	1.4
Japan	0.5	1.1	0.8

Source: Organization for Economic Co-operation and Development.

pound, mark, and yen. To use these funds profitably, firms often speculate on fluctuations in the exchange rate of national currencies, which accelerates a currency crisis. In the course of the 1970s, international banks lent huge sums of money to developing countries that needed funds for the accelerated industrialization that is one of the origins of today's debt crisis. By the end of 1983, half of the $602 billion external public debt of the developing countries was owed to the private sector at a high interest rate. In 1987 the developing countries pay 22 percent of their total export income as debt servicing: in 1970, this was still 10 percent.[4]

Third, these big businesses have recently been promoting automation/rationalization investment in their home countries in order to establish a new form of international division of labor. As of 1982, nearly 60,000 robots (servo-controlled and non–servo-controlled point-to-point) were in operation in the developed countries (table 6–2), and the manual part of the production tends to be assigned to developing countries with cheap labor. (The finishing of semiconductor chips is one example.) Together with the

Table 6–2
Robot Installations in Selected Countries, 1983
(*number*)

Japan	41,265
United States	9,400
Germany (F.R.)	4,800
France	2,010
Italy	2,000
United Kingdom	1,953
Canada	1,953
Sweden	1,900
Belgium	514

Source: Robot Institute of America.

transfer of a part of the production system abroad, this increasing automa-tion/rationalization diminishes employment in the developed countries.[5] In the developing countries, the new international division of labor certainly increases employment, to some extent. However, transfer of technology is difficult to achieve since the developing countries are regarded merely as suppliers of low-cost labor. Thus, the income gap between North and South increases while the number of unemployed people in both parts of the world grows.

Fourth, as these firms expand their operations networks in the world, they become keen on the "stabilization" of the world political situation. A large proportion of them have become the basis for a rapidly growing mili-tary-industrial complex that promotes a worldwide militarization of the economy. This militarization of the economy gives them two advantages: one is an increase in military power, designed to protect their overseas assets, and the other is an increase in unproductive government expenditure, which gives them an outlet for their increasing production. However, the use of limited resources on unproductive military expenditure further deepens the world-wide crisis.[6]

Of course, the origin of the current crisis of the capitalist world is complex. We cannot attribute it entirely to the growth and development of TNC activities. The decay of the old international division of labor that originated in colonial times, followed by the drive for a New International Economic Order accompanied by the reevaluation of prices for raw materials and fuels, is one contributing factor. The shift of the industrial structure from the older to the newer part of the world is another, as is the financial crisis being undergone by developed welfare-oriented governments. Changes in the mind and behavior of people no longer controlled by the production system (examples being frequent absenteeism and strikes in Europe) may also be partially responsible.

TNCs are not independent factors for change. Rather, they develop their activities according to changing international circumstances and thus give effect to the change. However, this very behavior by TNCs in turn accelerates the crisis in the capitalist world system. To understand this, we shall examine the difference in the behavior of U.S. and Japanese TNCs.

Comparison of U.S. and Japanese TNCs

Historically speaking, U.S. transnationals began overseas investment in Eu-rope in the 1960s, thinking to benefit by penetrating the large market that would be formed by EEC integration. However, in the 1970s, U.S. investment in Asia and Latin America increased considerably. This shift of investment included industries manufacturing electrical machinery, transportation equipment, and textiles, all of which involve labor-intensive production; food and chemical industries, which were seeking locations with a resource supply; and resource-development industries. The move was an offshore transnationalization that took advantage of production factors. This move was itself a response to increasing exports from Japan, Europe, and the newly industrializing countries.

However, when U.S. firms began to move into the Third World, there were immediate repercussions for Japanese enterprises, which maintained a large percentage of trade with the developing countries. Japanese enterprises, especially those involving labor-intensive production, inevitably moved into the developing countries in order to defend their markets there and maintain their exports to the U.S. market. This move corresponded to the rising demand for the New International Economic Order (NIEO) and the promotion of industrialization as well as the establishment of the sovereignty of developing countries over their natural resources.

After the 1960s, when import-substitution industrialization was promoted by the developing nations and Japanese labor-intensive and knockdown industries established their plants in the developing parts of the world (in Asia, in particular), heavy and chemical industries that primarily process raw materials and hydrocarbons began, in the 1970s, to establish joint venture enterprises in the developing countries. This not only corresponded exactly to the NIEO move in this period but also to the increasing problems of pollution in Japan resulting from high economic growth. (In 1976, pollution-prevention investment constituted as much as 19 percent of the total private investment.)[7]

Thus, the securing of the market, cheap labor force, convenient location of plants, and resource development are invariable motives for the transnationalization of firms. However, let us look at the difference between U.S. and Japanese investment more closely.

First, in both countries, the investment has been made by big oligopolistic firms. In the United States, the top-ranked 200 giant companies account for 80 percent of total overseas assets. In Japan, the big enterprises with capital of more than 100 million yen accounted for 73 percent of total parent companies in 1982 and their share has been increasing steadily. (In 1973, their share was 67 percent.)[8] However, in the case of Japan, a large investment project is generally carried out by one of the six big enterprise groups (Mitsubishi, Sumitomo, Mitsui, Daiichi-Kangin, Fuyō, or Sanwa). These six groups control three-quarters of the total sales of big enterprises, the shares of which are traded in the First Section of the Tokyo Stock Exchange.

There is competition among enterprise groups, but when one of them sets up subsidiaries, the rest become an extension of Japan's oligopolistic industrial structure.

Second, until March 1984, 32 percent of Japan's total authorized investment was destined for the manufacturing sector. In recent years, the share of the tertiary sector in investment in the developed countries has increased considerably and has reached 49 percent of the total investment. The structure of investment by sector is more or less the same as in the United States. However, as regards geographic distribution, the developing countries account for 53 percent. In the case of U.S. investment, 73 percent went to the developed countries in 1980. Dependence on the Third World is still strong in Japanese investment. This means that Japan's investment has followed its trade pattern rather than having been motivated independently.

Third, U.S. transnationals have developed a global strategy and are extending specialization within the enterprise across national boundaries. Japanese enterprises are strikingly behind in this respect; most of them limit their transnationalization to one other nation or to import-substitution levels. In 1982, among manufacturing subsidiaries, 74 percent of the products were sold in the local market. Japanese subsidiaries generally make a profit: in 1982, the ratio of profits to total sales amounted to 0.5 percent (domestic firms earned 0.7 percent). The ratio of profit to total capital in the manufacturing industry was 3.0 percent. Forty-three percent of all subsidiaries distributed a dividend and the average rate of dividend for these subsidiaries amounted to 9.8 percent.[9] However, besides dividends, home companies receive benefits in the form of royalties or fees. At the same time, subsidiaries serve either as suppliers of cheap and stable raw materials or as exclusive outlets for their products. This is why the financial accounts of subsidiaries are not of primary importance for home companies. The subsidiaries tend to be considered useful appendices to the trade network of home companies. This is why many Japanese home companies are satisfied with having subsidiaries only on a bilateral basis, since they are not necessarily concerned with developing a multinational strategy.

Fourth, U.S. TNCs frequently insist on retaining 100 percent of a subsidiary's stock. If this is not the case, obstacles to multinational strategy will develop. There also seems to be a fear of information being leaked to competitors. However, Japanese companies commonly form joint ventures with local capital. Moreover, while U.S. companies are normally averse to joint ventures with government capital, Japanese enterprises often actively enter into such arrangements with the local government. In this sense, this is an aspect in which Japanese transnationals cooperate with the move for the New International Economic Order. However, at the same time, Japanese firms are often accused of being reluctant to promote transfer of technology, which is one important area of NIEO.[10] This reluctance or indifference derives from the fact that Japanese firms tend to consider their subsidiaries only as appendices to home production and not as indispensable links in their multinational strategy.

We have examined the characteristics of U.S. and Japanese TNCs and grasped their differences. Let us now consider the problems of conflicts between TNCs and national sovereignty.

Conflicts between TNCs and Host and Home Countries

Overseas investment by productive enterprises serves to equalize somewhat the inequalities in the availability of production factors among countries. It may also serve as a useful instrument for the transfer of technology. For this reason, developing nations, which were largely cautious about TNCs in the initial stage of overseas investment, changed their attitude and expected TNCs to cooperate in their industrialization and in closing the North–South gaps.[11]

However, inherent contradictions may be perceived between the behavior of TNCs and national sovereignty.

First, theoretically speaking, transnationalization means that an enterprise extends its internal division of labor across the national border. It does not necessarily guarantee coincidence with priorities in national goals. One country may want to develop engine manufacturing in automobile production, as this would have spillover effects for other industries. But it may be assigned only the assembly part or body-press part of the production line. This is why the ASEAN car project of the Ford Motor Company failed. From the point of view of management, the ultimate decisionmaking on worldwide production and sales generally takes place at the headquarters in the mother country. The regional headquarters, located in the regional center cities, are in charge of the formulation of regional plans coordinated with the worldwide plan. The regional offices try to maintain a feedback system to the decisionmaking of the home headquarters. However, the local factory or office rarely intervenes in this hierarchical decision-making system. This system certainly guarantees the optimum distribution of resources according to the needs of the enterprise, but it does not guarantee the optimum use of local resources.[12]

Second, TNCs widely practice so-called transfer pricing and try to maximize their profit. In Thailand, a Japanese jute company set up a subsidiary in order to export jute sacks under cost. The parts and raw materials exported by a home company to a subsidiary may also be priced over the normal export price. Further, these companies may use subsidiaries in Hong Kong, Singapore, Panama, or even the Bahamas, where tax is lower than in other countries ("tax havens"), to accumulate benefits there and avoid taxation in both the home and host countries. Every year, the Japanese Taxation Office discloses a number of examples of tax avoidance by Japanese companies using subsidiaries abroad.

Third, the restrictive business practices often adopted by TNCs may harm a country's economic objectives. Even if a country wanted to promote an export to a wider market, the export could not be promoted if a TNC attributed the export outlet to some other country in accordance with the worldwide strategy.[13] If a country wished to use local resources in industrial production, such localization would be difficult if materials continued to be imported from abroad. In addition, huge capital transfers by TNCs and transnational banks could have a detrimental effect on a government's financial policy. Of course, governments, exercising various policies such as indigenization or localization of enterprise, seek to control the behavior of TNCs, but real control seems to be difficult.

Fourth, since TNCs often consider subsidiaries as simple local appendices, many conflicts may arise not only between a TNC and a government, but also between a TNC and a labor movement, or people in general.

In 1977, the Japanese MITI made a survey of conflicts between Japanese enterprises and developing host countries between 1974 and 1976.[14] According to this survey, the major conflicts were related most often to labor problems (28 percent), followed by environmental problems (19 percent) and problems of management goals (15 percent). Since the problems of management goals are related to the business practices just mentioned, we will look at the first two sources of conflict.

Labor problems arise from such causes as an oppressive stance by Japanese management toward workers (e.g., a refusal to allow the formation of unions or collective bargaining, the encouragement of a house union), the imposition of Japanese methods that fail to consider local customs, or the refusal to grant promotion to local employees (the language problem often being given as the pretext).

Labor problems are often related to the violation of human and social rights by employers. It was recently reported in Indonesia that a Japanese textile factory practiced a medical inspection when hiring female workers that included a "virginity" examination. What most often becomes a problem is that Japanese enterprises tend to be on their guard against labor disputes, frequently request "government assistance" from autocratic political powers, and obstruct the growth of the rights of workers and labor unions.

Conflicts between TNCs and labor unions are not restricted to labor movements in host countries. For labor unions of home countries as well, overseas investment must constitute a problem of surplus transfer (which could be distributed to home workers) or of the decrease of bargaining power on the part of the trade union movement. In the case of Japan, the trade union movement should work toward the generalization of fair labor standards or the recommendations of the International Labor Organization (ILO) on work conditions at both domestic and overseas factory sites, since backwardness in this regard strengthens the violations of human and social rights by Japanese enterprises that are so widely seen in many parts of the world.

Other problems of human rights violations are related to environmental pollution. This involves pollution from industrial wastes, failure to carry out reforestation and environmental conservation measures, tanker accidents, and the destruction of the ecological system and the living environment. Numerous examples can be cited: the construction of an aluminum plant in Asahan, Sumatra, caused soil erosion as well as water pollution; an iron sintering plant with a yearly output of 5 million tons displaced many local residents and caused water and air pollution; destruction of forests in the Philippines and Indonesia has led to inundation and drought problems; water pollution was caused by synthetic soap containing phosphorous that was manufactured by two Japanese soap companies in Thailand. It was reported that Japanese agricultural chemical companies in Southeast Asia produce the organic chlorines BHC and DDT, whose manufacture is prohibited in Japan. We may recall that, up to 1983, officially recognized pollution victims in Japan totalled 85,265, while 9,086 died. Japanese enterprises are repeating this sad experience in Asia.

Thus, labor conflicts and environmental problems (two major reasons for TNC conflicts in the Third World) originate in Japanese business practices that disregard human rights and dignity, both in Japan and abroad. However, in the developing countries, this disregard takes a cruder form than in the home country.

These four points of conflict between TNCs and a nation's sovereignty and rights are valid in both host and home countries. That is why TNCs practice widespread corruption and bribery, offering "political funds" to the ruling party and class. In Japan, the ruling conservative party is largely financed by these big businesses.

In the developing countries, TNCs often become linked with autocratic political power in order to repress popular and labor movements. We know that when Marshal Thanom Kitchkachorn was expelled from Thailand, his wife was a member of the board of directors of some thirty Japanese companies. Furthermore, as overseas assets have increased, big businesses have become promoters of militarization. The military-industrial complex is the major agent in today's accelerated arms race. Businesses also have an interest in rapidly exporting obsolete arms to the developing countries. In this way, big oligopolistic businesses tend to harm democracy and peace in every part of the world.

Prospects for Controlling TNCs

There are several levels at which to control the activities of TNCs. First, at the international level, the United Nations Commission on Transnational Corporations has since the mid-1970s been discussing the Code of Conduct on Transnational Corporations.[15] The code emphasizes respect for national sovereignty, human rights and basic freedoms, and the social and cultural values of each nation as well as the prevention of corruption and bribery. Where the economic, financial, and social aspects of TNCs are concerned, it stresses the importance of decentralization of the decision-making process, respect for balance of payments problems, the prevention of transfer pricing and tax evasion, the prohibition of restrictive business practices, the promotion of technology transfer, and the protection of consumers and the environment. Concerning the information aspect, it institutes measures for the disclosure of information. Regarding the relationship with the state, the code guarantees fair treatment between TNCs and local enterprises and protects TNCs against unfair nationalization.

Last, it provides for international cooperation in the execution of these measures and the monitoring of the implementation of the code by the United Nations Centre on Transnational Corporations.

This type of international code or guideline was already promulgated by the OECD in 1976[16] and, if the United Nations were to establish an international code, it would be useful as every nation's guideline for the control of TNCs. However, the discussion so far demonstrates the difficulty of reaching a consensus of governments on the code since, in a time of world depression and crisis, there are always governments that hope for better business by welcoming TNCs. At the same time, in recent years, TNCs originating in newly industrializing countries have been increasing in number, and this seems to be another reason for the difficulty in establishing a uniform code.

At the national and local levels, governments always possess various legal means of controlling TNC activities. In Japan in 1977, as a result of speculative activities developed by big businesses at the time of an oil crisis, the Diet adopted a strengthened version of the Antimonopoly Law, although it was somewhat mutilated by the ruling conservative party. In 1981, the New Banking Act, requiring the disclosure of fiscal documents, was passed by the Diet. In 1985, the Employment Equalization Law was adopted and the Environmental Assessment Law is currently being discussed. Though there are problems with these laws, there is no doubt that they were a result of growing popular opposition to the progressive economic concentration and domination by big enterprises occurring in Japan.

At the local level, several prefectures have already instituted the Disclosure of Information Act, the Environmental Assessment Act, or the Plan for the Promotion of the Status of Women. In the United States, the Unitary Tax Act (which counts all the profits of both parent companies and subsidiaries as the basis for tax calculation, and which has been adopted by a number of states) is a serious blow to the transfer-pricing system practiced by TNCs. It would be more pragmatic to strengthen the various measures for controlling

TNCs at the local level, where the inhabitants are faced with TNC activities daily, and then to extend them to the national and international levels.

At the labor level, to prevent arbitrary domination by big enterprise over workers across the border, the exchange of information among trade unions and the unionization of all workers is necessary. In particular, the trade unions should monitor unfair labor practices in both home and host countries and should try to improve the labor conditions of all workers across the border by extending ILO treaties and recommendations on work conditions and international labor standards. In the future, it is conceivable that all the trade unions relating to the same industry or company might negotiate with the TNC headquarters. To strengthen workers' unity, international solidarity among trade union movements is primordial. The trade union movement should, at the same time, try to work out an alternative plan for the distribution of resources on the international level. The common training of labor leaders in both the developed and the developing countries could be a first step in this direction.

At the level of the citizen's daily life, it is important to retain an autonomous life-style, one that is unaffected by aggressive TNC advertising. In Japan, with the growth of transnational food-processing companies, the restriction on food additives has been relaxed. In 1983, 11 chemical additives were added to the existing 347 artificial additives, and the use of 13 additives was further relaxed.[17] This is an effort by food-processing transnationals to develop their activities abroad as well as to import processed food from the United States. The food-processing transnationals are growing at the expense of people's health and life. We know that milk powder manufactured by transnationals has caused the death from diarrhea of numerous babies in the developing countries. In Japan, 48 percent of daily food expenditures went to processed food in 1965 and, by 1982, this percentage had increased to 55 percent. If we do not establish autonomy over our lives, our diet will be controlled by profit-seeking big businesses at the expense of our own health. If we do not change our life-style, which is currently heavily affected by transnational companies, we will be transformed into mere purchasing machines. In order to establish autonomy over our lives, popular movements and participation by the people are important for activating local and regional communities. At the same time, workers' movements aimed at controlling their own lives in the company and the industry are also important. By accumulating experience in self-management, we may be able to prepare a framework for a new society in which human beings control enterprise, which is a social institution, instead of vice versa.

We have seen that transnational and multinational big enterprises can grow rapidly, even in a time of world depression and crisis. In a sense, TNCs are one of the factors that accelerate the crisis in the capitalist world market. TNC activities affect a nation's sovereignty and the life of its people. Nevertheless, TNCs are not uncontrollable demons. Many steps and measures have been taken to establish the control of nations and peoples over TNC activities. In order to establish really effective control over TNCs, however, the key factors seem to be solidarity among workers and popular participation.

Notes

1. Stopford, J. M., and Dunning, J. H., *Multinationals: Company Performance and Global Trends* (London: Macmillan, 1985).

2. Ministry of International Trade and Industry (MITI), *Wagakuni Kigyō no Kaigai Jigyō Katsudo. Dai 12/13 Kai Chosa* (Overseas Activities of Japanese Enterprise: 12/13th Survey), 1984.

3. Barnet, R.J., and Müller, R.E., *Global Reach* (New York: Simon and Schuster, 1974), was one of the first studies to raise this problem.

4. See Nishikawa, J., "Daisan Sekai kara mita Ruiseki Saimu Mondai" (Accumulated Debt Issues from the Third World), *Ekonomisto,* Tokyo, December 18, 1984.

5. This is particularly the case in European countries.

6. See Nishikawa, J., "Military Expenditure and Economic Growth: The Case of Japan," report made at a seminar of the International Economic Association on military expenditure and economic growth, UNESCO, Paris, July 1982.

7. In fact, an MITI White Paper explains one of the reasons for government support of private overseas investment as follows: "This is to alleviate the burdens on domestic resources such as land and water, environment and social capital." (MITI, *Sangyō Kōzō no Chōki Bizion [Long-Term Vision of Industrial Structure], 1975), p. 317.*

8. See Nishikawa, J., *Sekai Keizai wo Miru Me* (How to See the World Economy) (Tokyo: Nihon Hoso Kyokai, 1984).

9. MITI, *Wagakuni Kigyō no Kaigai, Jigyō Katsudo,* Annex, tables 34, 36, 38, 40.

10. This point was frequently raised by local governments and joint venture partners when the author made a survey of small- and medium-scale enterprises in ASEAN countries on behalf of the Asian Productivity Organization in July-August 1984.

11. This change can be seen in three reports published by the United Nations Centre on Transnational Corporations: *Multinational Corporations in World Development* (1973), *Transnational Corporations in World Development: A Re-examination* (1978), and *Transnational Corporations in World Development: Third Survey* (1983).

12. Hymer, S., *Multinational Operations of National Firms: A Study of Direct Foreign Investment* (Cambridge, Mass.: MIT Press, 1976).

13. United Nations Centre on Transnational Corporations, *Transnational Corporations in World Development: Third Survey,* p. 158.

14. MITI, *Wagakuni Kigyō no Kaigai Jigyō Katudō,* 1977 Survey, table 91.

15. Report of the Intergovernmental Working Group on a Code of Conduct on its 15th, 16th and 17th Sessions (E/C.10/1982/6, annex).

16. Organisation for Economic Cooperation and Development, *Guidelines for Multinational Enterprise* (1976), *International Investment and Multinational Enterprises* (1984).

17. See Nishikawa, J., *Shokuryō* (Food) (Tokyo: Iwanami-Shoten, 1984), chapter 6.

Part II
National and International Policies and Experiences

7

U.S. Policies toward Transnationals

Stefan H. Robock

U.S. policies toward transnationals are rather simple to explain. They are based on the economic philosophy that free-market forces should determine the direction of capital flows throughout the world to maximize economic efficiency. An official U.S. policy statement on international direct investment, issued in 1983, states as follows:

> International direct investment plays a vital and expanding role in the world economy. To ensure its maximum contribution to both global and domestic economic well-being, the United States believes that international direct investment flows should be determined by private market forces and should receive non-discriminatory treatment consistent with the national treatment principle.[1]

The Free-Market Ideology

This free-market policy appears both to overseas direct investment by U.S. enterprises and direct investment in the United States by foreign enterprises. The United States has no national ministry or federal department that exercises general control over either inbound or outbound direct investment. Thus, the policy might be labelled an "open door" or a "no-door" policy—although there are a few exceptions that I will mention shortly. At the international level, the United States has taken specific multilateral and bilateral steps to help liberalize international investment flows and to support the concept of national treatment: namely, that foreign investors should be treated no less favorably than domestic enterprises in like situations.

An exception to the open door policy for overseas direct investment by U.S. firms relates to national security considerations. The export of certain advanced technology products and scientific information that have a potential for military use requires a licence issued by the U.S. Dept. of Commerce, working in cooperation with the Dept. of Defense and the Dept. of State. Although the control program applies specifically to exports, in effect it restricts the establishment of foreign production facilities for "sensitive" national security products.

The U.S. open door policies are not passive, but include affirmative steps to encourage international direct investment flows. Because political risk has often been a major deterrent for overseas investment in certain countries, the U.S. government has long had a political risk insurance program. Also, U.S. tax policies have encouraged overseas investment by permitting U.S. firms to receive a credit against U.S. taxes for taxes paid to foreign governments.

In cooperation with other governments, the United States has supported such multilateral agencies as the World Bank's International Center for the Settlement of Investment Disputes (ICSID) and the Multilateral Investment Guarantee Agency (MIGA), designed to spur investment capital flows into developing countries by issuing guarantees against noncommercial risks. MIGA is also expected to disseminate information on investment opportunities and provide technical assistance and advice to member governments seeking to attract foreign investment.

The United States accepted and adheres to the Guidelines for Multinational Enterprises adopted by the Organisation for Economic Cooperation and Development (OECD) and it has pressed in the GATT for reductions in barriers to foreign investments such as performance requirements. In the area of technology, the United States has encouraged adherence to the Paris Convention for the Protection of Industrial Property Rights, reflecting its conviction that the lack of adequate protection for intellectual and property rights (such as patents and trademarks) is a major disincentive to investment in many types of manufacturing facilities and to the transfer of technology.

As for inbound investment, the U.S. official statement of its policy is as follows:

> The United States has consistently welcomed foreign direct investment in this country. Such investment provides substantial benefits to the United States. Therefore, the United States fosters a domestic economic climate which is conducive to investment. We provide foreign investors fair, equitable, and non-discriminatory treatment under our laws and regulations. We maintain exceptions to such treatment only as are necessary to protect our security and related interests which are consistent with our international legal obligations.[2]

The exceptions to the inbound open door policy are federal restrictions on foreign investment in certain sectors of the economy having a fiduciary character, relating to national security, or involving the exploitation of some natural resources. The important sectors affected include radio communications, nuclear energy, hydroelectric power, mining on government-owned lands, domestic air transport, and coastwise and inland shipping. In addition, some state (provincial) governments impose restrictions on foreign investments in banking, insurance, and land ownership.[3]

Except in the proscribed areas, foreign firms investing in the United States do not have to secure permission from any government agency, nor do they have to register their investments with the government. As the executive of a French company that invested in the United States explained, "The U.S. really has a no-door policy. In every other foreign country we have had to go through a door to request permission to invest. In the United States, we could never find the door."

Ideology Coinciding with Pragmatism

The open door policy of the United States, although solidly based on a free-market economic ideology, also has a pragmatic dimension. After the end of the second World War, U.S. firms were in an especially advantageous position for expanding internationally. They had accumulated financial resources and developed new technologies during the war. They were not constrained by controls over dollar outflows. Furthermore, the U.S. government wanted to encourage foreign direct investment as an aid to European and Japanese economic reconstruction and as a form of assistance to the developing countries. It was not surprising, therefore, that during the early postwar period, U.S. transnationals were the dominant overseas investors and the multinationalization of business through direct investment was viewed as an exclusively U.S. phenomenon.

Until the early 1970s, the United States was not a major host country for foreign direct investment. In 1973, for example, the total stock of foreign direct investment in the United States was $21 billion, whereas overseas investment by U.S. firms was about five times as large—$101 billion. If the United States had imposed new restrictions on inbound investment, a cynic might have observed that foreign countries would be encouraged to retaliate and impose more restrictions on U.S. investment abroad. In such a move and countermove, U.S. overseas investors would have the most to lose.

Every country has elements opposed to foreign investment. Some opposition arises from xenophobic or philosophic motives. Other opposition may reflect the desire of domestic business firms for protection from foreign competition. In the past, these elements in the United States were not strong enough to influence the U.S. government to impose controls on inbound investment. As of 1985, however, the situation changed dramatically. From a ratio of 1 to 5 in 1973, foreign investment stock in the United States had become almost as large as U.S. investment stock overseas—$183 billion inbound as compared to $233 billion outbound. With such a different balance between the interests of outbound investors and those who feel the impact of inbound foreign investment, it may be easier in the future for opponents of inbound investment to get political support for control measures. But this is a speculation rather than a forecast.

The Global Setting

Given the open door and free-market philosophy of the U.S. government, one must look beyond the government-policy level to understand U.S. patterns of overseas direct investment. The motive force is the decisionmaking of private enterprises. An examination of past direct investment patterns, therefore, should help to identify the behavior patterns of the U.S. transnationals.[4] Also, as U.S. firms are competing for foreign investment opportunities with non-U.S. transnationals, the U.S. patterns must be placed in a global setting.

As mentioned previously, in the immediate postwar period, U.S. firms had relatively little competition and dominated the global direct investment situation. But, since the late 1960s, the business firms of Western Europe and Japan have become active overseas investors and have increased their foreign direct investments at a much faster rate than U.S. firms. In 1967, U.S. firms accounted for about half of the total world stock of foreign direct investment, as shown in appendix 1A. Because of the faster rate of expansion by non-U.S. firms, the U.S. *share* of the total had fallen to 35 percent in 1984. From 1967 to 1981, U.S. overseas investment stock quadrupled. Over the same period, German overseas direct investment increased by a factor of 15 and Japanese investment by a factor of 25, as reflected in appendix 1A.

It is not surprising that countries such as the United States and Canada that had not been devastated by the second World War emerged as the dominant investor countries during the immediate postwar period. In Western Europe and Japan, most business firms were concentrating on domestic reconstruction. Furthermore, these countries had serious shortages of foreign exchange and were restricting the outflow of capital through rigid controls. In addition, German and Japanese investors had lost their investment abroad through war-related expropriations and felt that the risks involved in foreign direct investment were high.

During the late 1960s, the investment activity of Western European and Japanese firms began to revive as government restraints on capital outflow were eased. Also, Japanese and European enterprises had achieved phenomenal growth in size, managerial capability, and access to resources, all of which supported international expansion. In addition, the technology balance had shifted with the success of European and Japanese firms in closing the well-publicized postwar technology gap.

Another important factor in the early 1970s was the devaluation of the dollar, which for many industries made foreign direct investment a more economic way than exports to serve the U.S. market—thus, the dramatic increase in the attraction of the United States as a host country for foreign direct investment. In the 1980–81 period, for example, almost 40 percent of the new flows of foreign direct investment went to the United States as host country.

Overall U.S. Direct Investment Patterns

Within this global setting, what has been the geographic pattern and industry mix of U.S. overseas direct investment and how have these patterns varied over the years? These patterns, as shown in greater detail in tables 7–1 through 7–4, can be summarized as follows:

Rate of Expansion. The growth rate of U.S. overseas investment was remarkably steady over the three decades from 1950 to 1980, averaging an annual growth rate of 10 percent over the 30-year period. (See table 7–1.) From 1980 to 1985, however, U.S. overseas direct investment increased at an annual rate of less than 2 percent.

Geographic and Industry Patterns. Although the rate of expansion was steady over most of the postwar period, the geographic patterns and the industry mix varied greatly. These patterns can be characterized for different time periods as follows:

- *1950–57: the petroleum boom years; investment in Canada.* By 1957, petroleum accounted for 36 percent of total U.S. overseas investment. (See table 7–2.) As a recipient of large investments in petroleum, manufacturing, and other sectors, Canada became the host to more than one-third of total U.S. overseas direct investment. During the period, the

Table 7–1
Average Annual Percent Change, 1950–85

	Total	Petroleum	Manufacturing	Other
1950–57	11.4	15.3	11.0	8.9
1957–66	8.2	5.0	11.1	8.3
1966–74	10.0	5.8	12.0	10.4
1974–80	11.8	14.0	10.3	12.5
1980–85	1.7	4.5	1.4	0.5

Source: U.S. Dept. of Commerce.

Table 7–2
U.S. Direct Investment Position Abroad by Industry, Year End, 1950–84

Industry	1950	1957	1966	1974	1980	1984
(*$ billion and percent*)						
All industries						
(billions of dollars)	$ 11.8	$ 25.4	$ 51.8	$110.1	$213.5	$233.2
	100	100	100	100	100	100
Petroleum	29	36	27	19	22	27
Mining and smelting	10	9	8	5	3	3
Manufacturing	32	32	40	47	42	40
Chemicals and allied products	4	5	7	9	9	9
Machinery	7	7	10	13	11	11
Machinery, except electrical	4	4	6	—	8	7
Electrical machinery	3	3	4	—	3	4
Transportation equipment	4	5	8	7	6	5
Food products	4	3	3	4	4	4
Primary and fabricated metals	3	4	3	3	3	2
Other manufacturing	10	8	9	10	9	9
Paper and allied products	3	3	2	—	—	—
Rubber and miscellaneous plastics	2	2	2	—	—	—
Other	5	4	5	—	—	—
Transportation, communication and						
public utilities	12	8	4	3	2[a]	—
Trade	6	7	8	10	12	13
Finance and insurance	4	4	9	11	13	12
Other (including agriculture)	7	5	4	4	4[a]	5

Source: U.S. Dept. of Commerce.
Note: Columns may not add to totals because of rounding.
[a] Data from 1979.

share invested in the developing countries—mainly Latin America—dropped from 49 to 41 percent. (See table 7–3.)

• *1957–74: expansion in Europe; obsolescing resource investment.* In response to the formation of the European Common Market in 1958 and the European Free Trade Association in 1960, the expansion of U.S. overseas investment occurred largely in Western Europe. The share of U.S. total overseas investment in Europe increased from 16 percent in 1957 to 41 percent in 1974. (See table 7–3.) The investments in Europe were largely in manufacturing facilities. Thus, the manufacturing share of total U.S. overseas investment increased from 32 to 47 percent over those years. (See table 7–2.)

This geographic shift was at the expense of Canada and the developing countries. Considerable disinvestment in the resource areas of petroleum and mining occurred due to expropriations by many developing countries in the Middle East, North Africa, and Latin America. Thus, the share of total investment in the resource industries dropped sharply (as shown in table 7–2) and the share of total investment in the devel-

Table 7–3
U.S. Direct Investment Position Abroad By Area, Year-end, 1950–55

(*$ billion and percent*)	1950	1957	1966	1974	1980	1985
(billions of dollars)	$ 11.8	$ 25.4	$ 51.8	$110.1	$213.5	$233.2
All areas	100	100	100	100	100	100
Developed countries	48	55	68	75	74	74
Canada	30	35	30	26	21	20
Europe	15	16	32	41	45	46
Other	3	4	6	9	8	8
Developing countries	49	41	27	18	25	24
Latin America	39	32	19	18	18	13
Other	10	9	8	—[a]	7	11
International and unallocated	3	4	5	7	2	1

Source: U.S. Dept. of Commerce.
Note: Columns may not add to totals because of rounding.
a. Disinvestment in Middle East.

oping countries declined from 41 percent in 1957 to only 18 percent in 1974. (See table 7–3.)

- *1974–80: saturation of Europe; the newly industrializing countries; the rise of service industries.* Beginning in 1974, the flow of new investment to Western Europe slowed considerably and the U.S. share in Canada actually declined. Concurrently, investments in the developing countries accelerated, with big increases occurring in several of the newly industrializing countries (NICs) of Asia. (See table 7–3.) In particular, relatively large amounts of U.S. direct investment were to Singapore, Taiwan, and Hong Kong.

  On a global basis, the rapidly expanding sectors for U.S. overseas investment were in the service areas such as finance, banking, insurance, and trade. (See table 7–2.)

- *1980–85: a pause in U.S. overseas investment.* Since 1980, the outflow of U.S. direct investment has been small. (See table 7–1.) This stagnation has resulted from slow economic growth in the developed countries and the related debt crisis in many developing countries. As growth rates in the U.S. continued to be relatively attractive, the principal increases in foreign direct investment were those of non-U.S. transnationals expanding in the United States.

Sectoral Patterns of U.S. Overseas Investments

To understand better the patterns of U.S. overseas investments, it is helpful to examine past trends by industry sector. These can be classified according to investment motivation as (1) resource seekers, (2) market seekers, and (3) production-efficiency seekers.

Resource Seekers

U.S. transnationals have long been major overseas investors in the area of petroleum exploration, refining, and distribution. The geography of new investments in petroleum exploration, however, has been shifting. From 1946 to 1950, the big push was in the Persian Gulf. During the 1950s, the main buildup in petroleum investment was in Canada and Venezuela. But during the 1960s and 1970s, as many host countries assumed national ownership and control over petroleum investment, the share of U.S. total overseas investment in petroleum projects declined sharply. Canada did not nationalize the petroleum industry, but through forced divestment was able to reduce greatly the degree of foreign ownership in this area.

By 1985, the trend for nationalizing foreign investments in petroleum seems to have run its course, and several host countries have become more receptive to foreign direct investment in petroleum. Also, many countries have negotiated new types of foreign participation agreements that give the host countries greater control. At present, the principal countries that welcome foreign direct investment in petroleum are the United Kingdom and Norway in the North Sea, Indonesia, Peru, Colombia, Canada, and China. The major constraint on new investment in this area has been the sharp drop in the international price for petroleum. At $10–15 a barrel, fewer areas are attractive than when petroleum was selling for $30 a barrel.

Foreign direct investment in other resource areas such as mining and forestry has declined in importance for U.S. firms. One reason has been the slow growth in recent years of world demand in these sectors. Another reason is that many countries can secure the technology and technical skills needed in these areas for their own national industries.

Market Seekers

Overseas investment by U.S. firms in manufacturing industries that supplied local markets was the most rapid growth area during the 1960s and 1970s. The major market-oriented industries for overseas investment have been machinery, chemicals, transportation equipment, and food products. (See table 7–4.) Investment in the machinery industry, particularly for office and computing machines, has continued to be strong. Investment in electric and electronic equipment has also been expanding, although a significant share has been the offshore production of electronic components in developing countries but not for local markets.

Table 7–4
U.S. Investment Overseas in Manufacturing by Industry, 1950–84

	1950	1957	1966	1974	1980	1982	1984
($ billion and percent)							
All industries (billions of dollars)	$ 3.8	$ 8.3	$ 20.7	$ 51.2	$ 89.1	$ 83.5	$ 93.0
	100.0	100.0	100.0	100.0	100.0	100.0	100.0
Machinery	22.1	20.7	24.3	27.3	26.2	25.4	26.7
Other than electrical	11.0	11.6	15.6	—	18.0	16.6	17.3
Electrical	10.1	9.1	8.7	—	8.2	8.8	9.4
Chemicals	13.4	17.2	18.5	19.9	21.4	22.0	22.6
Transportation equipment	12.7	15.0	18.9	15.2	13.9	13.4	11.9
Primary and fabricated metals	10.0	11.7	7.0	6.7	7.1	6.6	6.7
Food products	12.6	9.0	8.5	8.5	9.3	9.0	10.3
Other	30.3	26.3	22.8	22.4	22.2	23.6	21.8
Paper & allied products	9.9	9.0	6.3	N.A.	N.A.	5.0	N.A.
Rubber products	4.8	5.0	3.9	N.A.	N.A.	2.6	N.A.
Instruments and related products	—	—	—	—	—	6.1	N.A.

Source: U.S. Dept. of Commerce.
Note: Columns may not add to totals because of rounding.
N.A. = Not available.

U.S. overseas investments in chemical and allied products have been increasing in importance consistently over the past three decades. (See table 7–4.) This category includes industrial chemicals, drugs, toilet goods, and agricultural chemicals. Investments in the production of transportation equipment (motor vehicles) have declined in importance since the mid-1960s, reflecting the loss of competitiveness by the U.S. automobile industry. An important industry in the food category is beverages, such as Coca-Cola and Pepsi-Cola. Instruments and related products account for about one-fourth of the direct investment summarized in the "other" category.

Production-Efficiency Seekers

These types of investments are difficult to separate in the official statistics. They represent the attraction of low-cost labor in many developing countries for producing such items as textiles, apparel, and electronic components more efficiently than in the home country of the transnational. Such investments have been expanding in recent years and are significant for a number of Asian and Latin American countries. Yet they still represent a relatively small part of the total U.S. overseas investment. In many cases, foreign firms can "source" in low-cost labor areas by purchasing from local firms without making a direct investment in the local companies.

The largest concentration of "sourcing" investments as of 1985 was in

Singapore—about $1 billion of investment. This was about the same as total U.S. direct investment in Switzerland.

Attracting U.S. Foreign Direct Investment

A key question for the Chinese may be how to attract more foreign direct investment. In my view, this will depend mainly on the economic, political, policy, and administrative situations in China.

As I have outlined, U.S. government policies do not constrain overseas direct investment by U.S. firms except in certain technology areas related to national defense considerations. In the area of international trade, the United States does impose tariffs and quotas on some imports. These trade policies could deter some overseas direct investments from producing goods such as textiles and apparel for the U.S. market. But, because U.S. firms are usually buyers and importers rather than foreign producers of these products, the main impact of these policies is on trade rather than direct investment.

In the absence of government controls, U.S. overseas direct investment will depend on the decisions of individual U.S. enterprises. These enterprises may be resource seekers, market seekers, or production-efficiency seekers. But in all cases, the overseas investment must have the prospect of being profitable to the enterprise. This simple point must be emphasized. The United States has practically no government-owned enterprises and the continued existence of U.S. enterprises depends on their being profitable.

As shown by historic investment patterns, U.S. firms have long been active overseas investors in resource projects. In the future, U.S. firms are likely to continue to be resource-seeking overseas investors. But the amount and location of such investments will depend on the international demand and price situation, the resource attractiveness of specific areas for production, and the kind of arrangements offered by host countries.

The greatest number of potential foreign investors in China would be attracted to China as market seekers. A necessary condition for such market seekers would be the ability to repatriate some of their profits in hard currency. If a project is successful and the local market keeps growing, the foreign firm will most likely reinvest a major share of its profits for expansion rather than withdraw its profits from the country. Nevertheless, it is crucial for the foreign enterprise to know that it can repatriate profits even though the firm is likely to choose not to do so.

Requiring market seekers to do some exporting, to earn foreign exchange needed for importing components and services and for profit repatriation, may solve the foreign exchange problem in some cases. If the foreign enterprise can produce components in China that it can supply to its other foreign affiliates or parent company, this may be easier than having to sell China-produced goods to unaffiliated buyers in other countries. Also, if the market seeker is producing goods previously being imported, the savings in foreign exchange might be allocated, at least in part, to resolving the foreign exchange availability problem.

In some cases, government officials should probably take a long-term view and recognize that what is initially an import-substituting industry, if properly selected, can eventually become an exporting industry.[5] A number of countries, including Japan, Brazil, and the United States, have given so-called infant industries protection and access to the local market. Over time, the protection was steadily reduced as the infants became mature and the industries were able to improve their efficiency and expand their scale of operations to achieve economies of scale. The removal of protection was important to put competitive pressures on the local industry, and before too long, the import-substituting industries became internationally competitive and significant earners of foreign exchange. The toy industry in Japan and, more recently, the automobile industry in Brazil are cases in point. In the case of the Brazilian automobile industry, the process required about 20 years.

In all cases, a necessary condition for attracting foreign direct investment is stability and certainty in agreements made with host governments. It is well known that foreign firms need to have an understanding of the political, economic, and cultural environments of host countries. It is less often recognized that host countries need to have an understanding of how the transnationals operate.[6] In particular, foreign firms are concerned that agreements that have been laboriously negotiated should be implemented expeditiously and without unilateral changes being made by the host country.

To summarize, U.S. government policies toward foreign direct investment in China are positive rather than a constraint. The United States adheres to a free-market philosophy for investment and has an open door for both outbound and inbound direct investment. The crucial task for host countries that want to attract U.S. overseas investment is to develop economic attractiveness, efficient policies, and administrative machinery that make investment opportunities profitable.

Notes

1. U.S. Dept. of Commerce, *International Direct Investment* (Washington, D.C.: U.S. Government Printing Office, August 1984), p. 85.

2. Ibid., p. 87.

3. U.S. Dept. of Commerce, *Foreign Direct Investment in the United States, Volume 1* (Washington, D.C.: U.S. Government Printing Office, April 1976), pp. 141–55.

4. See Robock, Stefan H., "The Rise and Decline of U.S. International Business,"

in *The Multinational Enterprise in Transition* 2nd ed. (Philip D. Grub, Fariborz Ghadar, and Dara Khamabata, eds.) (Princeton, N.J.: Darwin, 1984), pp. 38–49.

5. See Robock, Stefan H., "Industrialization Through Import Substitution or Export Industries: A False Dichotomy," in *Industrial Organization and Economic Development* (Jesse W. Markham and Gustav F. Papenek, eds.) (Boston: Houghton Mifflin, 1970), pp. 350–65.

6. See Robock, Stefan H., and Simonds, Kenneth, *International Business and Multinational Enterprises,* 3rd ed. (Homewood, Ill.: Richard D. Irwin, 1983).

8
Indian Foreign Investment Policies

Anant R. Negandhi

T he purpose of this chapter is to examine recent changes in Indian
foreign investment policies. To provide a perspective on these
changes, I will first briefly describe the origin of Indian policies,
followed by the rationale for changes in these policies.

More specifically, the chapter will analyze the following aspects of Indian
foreign investment policies:

The origin of the Indian investment policies;

The rationale for inviting and encouraging private foreign investment in
India;

The amount, sources, and types of existing foreign investments in India;

A change in policies in 1973;

Implications of restrictive Indian foreign investment policies; and

Recent changes in Indian foreign investment policies.

Rationale for Foreign Investment

It has long been realized that the needs of developing countries for capital for
generating industrial and economic development are so huge that no single
source can satisfy them. In addition to loans and grants from industrialized
countries as well as domestic saving and outside borrowing, private foreign
investment will be needed to achieve the goal of industrialization of the less
developed countries.

Some 30 years ago, this realization was underscored by the Rockefeller
Foundation: "The capital needs of less developed countries are so huge,
relative to their resources, that rapid economic growth can be achieved only

if local saving and public foreign investment are supplemented by an increasing inflow of private foreign investment."[1]

Among others, Rostow,[2] Mikesell,[3] Behrman,[4] Lewis,[5] and McMillan, Gonzales, and Erickson[6] have stressed the role and potential of foreign private investment in promoting economic development in underdeveloped countries. They all argue that such investment not only adds to the capital resources of the host nations but that it is also the chief mechanism through which the managerial and technical skills of advanced nations are made available to less developed countries.

Governments of many developing countries have realized the role that the private foreign investor can play in their economic development efforts. The late G.L. Mehta (former ambassador of India to the United States) expressed the sentiments of many leaders of developing countries when he said:

> The justification of foreign private enterprise lies not only in the compulsions of our foreign exchange problem but our needs of securing advanced technical and managerial know-how. . . . Trade in capital and know-how takes place among advanced countries and even among countries which have no capital or foreign exchange shortages. . . . I would, therefore say . . . foreign investment would be advantageous to us. . . . We are a part of the community of nations and should not seek to close our doors to winds of knowledge and skills from abroad.[7]

China's recent open door policy clearly reflects this concern.

Indian Private Foreign Investment Policy

Foreign investment in India dates back to the arrival of the East India Company from the United Kingdom in the seventeenth century. Initially, foreign investment, mainly from the United Kingdom, was in the form of loans to the government, construction of railroads and other public utilities, tea and coffee plantations, and agriculture-based industries such as cotton and jute. It was only after the first World War that industries attracted foreign investors significantly. For example, the inflow of British capital, which was only $30 million in 1913–14, increased to a level of $58 million in 1921 and $72 million in 1922. Between the two World Wars, investment flowed into a number of consumer industries such as cigarettes, matches, rubber, tires, paints, chemicals, paper, cement, textiles, leather, and sugar. During the second World War, the government encouraged the setting up of new industries in India both to replace imports and to support the war effort. It was during this period that foreign investment was diversified and channelled into light engineering industries as well as general-purpose workshops, the chemical industry, and the oil sector—all oriented toward defense.

By 1948, foreign private investment in India was estimated to be around Rs. 2.5 billion (one U.S. dollar = 12.50 Indian Rs. as of September 30, 1986), of which 21 percent was in the manufacturing industries, 16 percent in agriculture, 4 percent in mining, 27 percent in trading, and 14 percent in banking. Within the manufacturing sector, more than 50 percent of the foreign capital was invested in the jute, cotton, and rubber industries and around 10 percent in iron and steel and other hardware industries. It was against this background that India's industrial policy was announced soon after independence on April 6, 1948. A new Industrial Policy Resolution was adopted on April 30, 1956. This 1956 policy resolution continues to guide India's industrial policy today though it was modified in 1970, 1973, 1977, 1980, and 1985 to make it responsive and receptive to the changing needs of technology for the modernization and growth of industry.[8]

The Industrial Policy of 1956

The Industrial Policy of 1956 divides industries into three categories. The first category includes all such heavy and basic industries as arms and ammunition, atomic energy, iron and steel castings, mineral oils, aircraft, telephones and telephone cables, and electricity. In this group of industries, only the state may begin new undertakings. However, existing private industries in this group have been allowed to expand.

The second category covers industries in which both the government and private enterprise may start new undertakings. Specific industries are: aluminum; ferroalloys and steels; antibiotics; fertilizers; synthetic rubber; chemical pulp; sea and road transport; dyestuffs; and plastics.

The third category is a catchall covering all remaining and undesignated industries. It includes all consumer goods industries. The group is left open to private enterprise, but the government also may enter the field at any time.[9] Only in the second and third categories were foreign investors allowed to invest.

The guiding principles of the foreign investment policy derived from the 1956 Industrial Policy Resolution were:

All undertakings—Indian or foreign—must conform to the general requirements of the government's industrial policy.

Foreign enterprises would be treated on a par with Indian enterprises.

Foreign enterprises would have freedom to remit profits and repatriate capital, subject to foreign exchange considerations.

If foreign enterprises were compulsorily acquired, compensation would be paid on a fair and equitable basis.

As a rule, the major interest, ownership, and effective control of an undertaking should be in Indian hands.[10]

Further Tightening of Restrictive Measures in 1973

The 1956 policy was intended to govern the entry of fresh foreign investment into India in the future, but it was silent on the regulation of existing foreign private investment in Indian industry. It was only in 1973 that legislative measures were taken to cope with the problem posed by the existing foreign-owned companies. This was done by amending the Foreign Exchange Regulation Act (FERA), which regulated the entry into the country and channelled the growth of existing foreign investment. Until then, foreign companies had continued to grow, expand, and diversify their activities in their own ways.[11]

Essentially, the FERA Act of 1973 required all foreign companies, existing and new, to reduce foreign equity to 40 percent, unless the firms provided sophisticated technology not yet available in India, were in priority sectors as defined by the Indian government, or exported 60 percent or more of their production. The departure of IBM and Coca-Cola from India in 1978 was mainly due to the implementation of this act. Salient features of the current foreign investment policy are given in appendix 8A.

Foreign Investment Trends. The total number of foreign collaborative undertakings in India is approximately 6,000, while total foreign capital investment in India is approximately US $3.0 billion. Table 8–1 provides the number of collaborations and capital investment approved in the period from 1971 to 1984. Table 8–2 shows the sources of foreign capital in India.

Technology Policy. The basic objectives of the new technology policy are the development of an indigenous technology, as well as the efficient absorption and adaptation of imported technology appropriate to national priorities and resources. Its aims are to:

Attain technological competence and self-reliance in order to reduce vulnerability, particularly in strategic and critical areas, by making the maximum use of indigenous resources;

Table 8–1
Foreign Private Investment in India through Collaborations Approved, 1971–1984

	Number of Collaborations			Foreign Investment (Rs. million)
	Total	Technical	Technical cum Financial	
1971	245	199	46	58.4
1972	257	220	37	62.2
1973	265	231	34	28.2
1974	359	304	55	67.1
1975	271	231	40	32.1
1976	277	238	39	72.7
1977	267	240	27	40.0
1978	307	263	44	94.1
1979	267	235	32	56.4
1980	526	453	73	89.2
1981	389	232	57	108.7
1982	590	477	113	628.1
1983	673	544	129	618.7
1984	752	601	151	1130.0

Source: *Partners in Progress, 1960–1985*, New Delhi, India: Indian Investment Center, 1985).

Provide the maximum gainful and satisfying employment to all strata of society, with emphasis on the employment of women and the weaker sections of society;

Use traditional skills and capabilities, making them commercially competitive;

Ensure the correct mix between mass production technologies and production by the masses;

Table 8–2
Sources of Foreign Capital in India as Percentage of Total Investment, September 1985

Total	100.0
United Kingdom	21.2
United States	19.7
Germany (F.R.)	18.0
Japan	8.7
Switzerland	5.8
France	5.0
Italy	3.9
Others	17.1

Source: *India and Japan: A Retrospect and Prospects for Bilateral and Economic Cooperation* (New Delhi: Indian Investment Center, 1985), pp. 58–59.

Ensure maximum development with minimum capital outlay;

Identify obsolescence in technology currently in use and arrange for the modernization of both equipment and technology;

Develop technologies that are internationally competitive, particularly those with export potential;

Improve production speedily through greater efficiency and fuller utilization of existing capabilities, and enhance the quality and reliability of performance and output;

Reduce demands on energy, particularly energy from nonrenewable sources;

Ensure harmony with the environment, preserve the ecological balance, and improve the quality of the habitat; and

Recycle waste material and make full utilization of by-products.[12]

Restrictive Foreign Investment Policy and the Strategy of Self-Reliance. Generally speaking, Indian foreign investment policy is regarded as restrictive in business and government circles. Owing to various restrictive measures, foreign investment in India has been minimal as compared to countries such as Brazil, Mexico, South Korea, and Singapore. The rationale for a restrictive policy is the Indian government's stress on self-reliance. This philosophy can easily be discerned from the technology policy just outlined.

Implications of the Restrictive Foreign Investment Policy

The restrictive policy is a two-edged sword. It fosters indigenous development, but it also creates stagnation in technological development. In addition, it encourages a monopolist tendency and a lethargic attitude and behavior on the part of existing enterprises. A resultant sellers' market taxes the consumer, who is forced to pay higher prices for poorer quality goods. Such market conditions are rampant not only in India but in many other developing countries where competition and imports are restricted. I will briefly examine some contrasting results of India's restrictive foreign investment policy.

Indigenous Development and Growth of Technology. Since independence in 1947, India has made rapid strides in different sectors of the economy through the process of planned economic development strategies. The agricultural sector has undergone a revolutionary change. The production of food grains increased from 51 million tons in 1950–51 to 152 million tons in 1983–84. India not only has achieved self-sufficiency in food grains and agricultural raw materials but is now exporting sizable amounts.

Broad-Based and Diversified Industrial Development. In the field of industrial production, with the accent on basic, heavy, and machine-building industries, a firm foundation has been laid for a modern and diversified industrial structure, resulting in a significant change in the pattern of industrial production from traditional to nontraditional items. The country has now achieved near self-sufficiency in the manufacture of consumer goods, while most of its requirements for machinery and equipment are also met by the local industry.

The diversification of India's industrial production has resulted in a significant change in the composition of its foreign trade. India has ceased to be an exporter of agricultural and other primary products and has emerged as a large exporter of manufactured products, which include not only consumer durables such as refrigerators, air conditioners, bicycles, sewing machines, and electric fans, but also sophisticated capital equipment such as cement and sugar plants, textile machinery, thermal power plants, blast furnaces, chemicals, and pharmaceuticals. Manufactured products now constitute over 50 percent of India's total exports. Indian manufactured goods are exported not only to the developing countries but to a large number of developed countries as well.

Development of Science and Technology. Apart from building up a modern and diversified industrial structure, India has also made significant progress in developing capabilities for design and process know-how. Although, in the initial stages, it had to depend mainly on the import of technology from the developed countries, a great deal of attention has also been paid to the development of science and technology within the country. About 1,300 research and development institutions, employing over a million persons, are working under the central and state governments. Nearly 3,000 patents developed by Indian nationals are being commercially exploited. The National Research and Development Corporation (NRDC), which licences the patents of processes developed by the government-owned and -controlled institutions in the country, has so far licenced more than 1,000 processes, half of which have been commercialized. Some of these have been licenced to users in other countries. The total value of goods produced from the processes licenced by NRDC has risen from Rs. 3 million in 1960–61 to Rs. 1,200 million in 1983.[13]

In 1987 the *Asian Wall Street Journal* reported "Foreign Companies Create a High-Tech Haven in Bangalore [India]." Many major computer and electronics companies (such as Texas Instruments, Hewlett-Packard, Data General, N.V. Philips, I.M. Erickson, and Telefon AB) have been attracted to Bangalore to take advantage of highly skilled Indian scientists and technicians. All these companies are coming to India to serve the world market. Besides the multinationals, an increasing number of U.S.-educated Indians who had been working in Silicon Valley are returning home to set up computer companies.

In a reversal of the traditional technology-transfer role, many companies in Bangalore are now providing needed software technology to the industrialized countries. For example, PSI recently helped to design and develop a specialized computer for a Japanese company, the Software Consultant Corporation.[14]

Development of Brain Power. India can boast the following achievements in the development of human skills and technical institutions:

Total scientific and technical personnel: 2.5 million

Industrial training institutes: over 160,000 annual admissions

150 engineering colleges with annual admissions of over 25,000

80 postgraduate engineering and technical colleges with annual admissions of over 6,000

100 universities and 4,000 colleges with 3 million students

1.25 million engineering degree holders

Polytechnic institutes for diploma courses

30 institutions offering management courses

R&D work carried out in over 900 organizations employing one million persons

Mandatory training in all industrial establishments to impart technical skills

Selling Technology Overseas. Another measure of achievement is the outflow of Indian technology and investment overseas. As of January 1, 1985, Indian companies had established approximately 237 joint ventures in 38 countries. Breakdowns of the Indian joint ventures abroad by country and industry are given in tables 8–3 and 8–4.

Indian joint ventures abroad cover a very wide spectrum of industrial products, ranging from consumer goods to heavy engineering products. These items include textiles, light engineering goods, iron and steel products, auto-

Table 8–3
Indian Joint Ventures Abroad by Country, January 1, 1985

Region and Country	Total	In Production	Under Implementation
South Asia			
Subtotal	38	17	21
Bangladesh	1	1	—
Nepal	11	2	9
Sri Lanka	26	14	12
West Asia			
Subtotal	23	16	7
Bahrain	2	1	1
Kuwait	2	1	1
Oman	2	2	—
Saudi Arabia	8	3	5
U.A.E.	9	9	—
Africa			
Subtotal	48	27	21
Botswana	1	1	—
Egypt	2	—	2
Kenya	13	9	4
Liberia	1	—	1
Mauritius	3	2	1
Nigeria	23	14	9
Senegal	1	—	1
Seychelles	1	—	1
Tanzania	1	—	1
Uganda	1	1	—
Zambia	1	—	1
Europe			
Subtotal	26	16	10
Cyprus	1	—	1
Germany (F.R.)	2	2	—
France	1	1	—
Gibraltar	1	1	—
Greece	2	—	2
Netherlands	1	1	—
Switzerland	2	1	1
U.K.	15	9	6
Yugoslavia	1	1	—
Oceania			
Subtotal	4	3	1
Australia	1	1	—
Fiji	1	1	—
Tonga	1	1	—
Solomon Islands	1	—	1
America			
Subtotal	12	11	1
U.S.	12	11	1
*Total	237	159	78

Source: *Partners in Progress* (New Delhi: Indian Investment Center, 1985).
Note: Columns may not add to totals because of rounding.

Table 8–4
Indian Joint Ventures Abroad by Industry, January 1, 1985

Industry	Total	In Production	Under Implementation
Light engineering	39	30	9
Chemical and Pharmaceuticals	31	15	16
Textile and allied products	21	19	2
Oil seed crushing and palm oil refining	10	9	1
Iron and steel products	9	8	1
Pulp and paper	4	3	1
Glass and glass products	5	4	1
Food products	1	—	1
Commercial vehicles	3	1	2
Leather and rubber products	6	3	3
Cement products	2	1	1
Other and manufacturing	16	9	7
Trading and marketing	21	17	4
Hotels and restaurants	26	16	10
Engineering contracts and construction	11	5	6
Consultancies	10	5	5
Other nonmanufacturing	22	14	8
Total	237	159	78

Source: *Partners in Progress* (New Delhi: Indian Investment Center, 1985).

mobile ancillaries, machine tools, hand tools, instruments, commercial vehicles, scooters, heavy engineering projects, nonferrous metal products, chemicals and pharmaceuticals, plastic products, cement, glass and glassware, pulp and paper, sugar, processed foods, confectionery, beverages, oilseed crushing and refining, hardboard, mosaic tiles, rubber products, leather products, cables and conductors, electronics, hotels and restaurants, consultancy, and construction projects.

Project export is another form of transfer of technology. Indian enterprises have successfully completed a large number of projects in diverse fields in such developing countries as Libya, Kuwait, the United Arab Emirates, Iraq, Nigeria, Tanzania, Mauritius, Thailand, and Malaysia. The areas covered include power plants, sugar, textiles, cement, paper and pulp, metallurgical and engineering and chemical and pharmaceutical plants. These undertakings have been set up by Indian enterprises in the face of stiff competition. Many of them have been financed by international institutions such as the World Bank and Asian Development Bank.[15]

To sum up, the positive impact of the restrictive Indian foreign investment policy is rather impressive. In other words, as Sanjay Lall's comparative study of multinationals from developing countries shows:

India's inward-looking, protectionist, self-reliant strategy has given it a strong and diversified base in many manufacturing technologies. . . . Whatever the other effects of inward-looking, protectionist industrialization strategy, there is little doubt that they foster technological capabilities over a broad range of industries.[16]

The Negative Impact. On the other hand, the restrictive foreign investment policy not only has created monopolistic market conditions in India, but also has brought about stagnation in technological development. Furthermore, it has created vast inefficiencies in existing enterprises. To quote Sanjay Lall again:

> Large areas of Indian industry lag behind world frontiers in technology . . . managerial and marketing skills are not developed . . . large areas of industry remain high-cost and technologically backward by world standards. Export growth is significantly restricted.[17]

A recent study of the impact of technology conducted by the Economic and Scientific Foundation in New Delhi shows that, considering the requirements, the import of technology into India is insignificant. For example, India's payments for technology during 1976–77 were only U.S. $67 million as compared to U.S. $272 million by Brazil, $101 million by Argentina, $167 million by Mexico, $866 million by Germany (F.R.), $821 million by France, and $72 million by Japan. Besides the 5,500 collaboration agreements concluded between 1957 and 1979, technology payments were less than one percent of the world's total payments during 1976–77. India's share in international direct investment is only 0.69 percent of the world's total.[18] Appendix 8B's list of technological needs illustrates the nature of the technological stagnation prevailing in India today.

The Birth of a New Policy

Realizing the critical technological need of the country, Prime Minister Rajiv Gandhi has started to liberalize the industrial and foreign investment policies. The main elements of the liberalization of these policies are:

Licence exemption for 25 industries.

A higher investment limit for small and ancillary units, with an increase from Rs. 2 million to Rs. 3.5 million and from Rs. 2.5 million to Rs. 4.5 million, respectively.

Increase in the limit of fixed assets, from Rs. 200 million to Rs. 100 million, for companies covered under the Monopolies Act.

Broad banding of licences for electronic items such as entertainment electronics, electronic toys, computer peripherals, electronic testing and measuring equipment, and discrete semiconductor devices. This facility also extends to sectors such as chemical machinery, machine tools, and two-wheelers and other vehicles.

Permission for the private sector to participate in the field of telecommunications equipment.

Withdrawal of a number of electronic items from the purview of the Monopolies Act, enabling larger houses to set up industries in these areas.

Permission to foreign companies and large houses for manufacture of electronic components.

Withdrawal of capacity constraints for the manufacture of entertainment and professional electronic equipment and computers.

Permission for the manufacture of micro- and minicomputers, such as personal computers, by any Indian company.

Classification of software development and manufacturing as "industry."

Policy relating to import-export for a period of 3 years.

Exemption from import licence requirement for actual users of 201 capital goods items.

Decanalization of a large number of items.

Increase in value limit for imports of technology, know-how, and machinery under Technical Development Fund from Rs. 0.5 million to Rs. 10 million.

Import liberalization of computer systems. No licence is required for systems costing less than Rs. 10 million.

Greater power to Regional Licencing Authority for clearing of applications.

Fiscal incentives include:

Reduction of 5 percent in the basic rate of income tax on companies as of April 1, 1985.

A further 5 percent reduction as of April 1986.

Abolition of surcharge and surtax as of April 1987.

Increase in the exemption limit for personal income tax from Rs. 15,000 to Rs. 18,000.

Extension of tax holiday concession to 5 more years for all new units.

Reduction of customs duty on project imports from 65 percent to 45 percent.

Withdrawal of customs duty on equipment for fertilizer projects.

No duty on import of pulp and wood chips.

Reduction in import duty for power projects to 25 percent.[19]

Reactions to the New Policy

Overall, the response from foreign companies has been positive. Japanese and European companies in particular have shown eagerness to cash in on India's new open door policy. Here are some results:

Japan's Suzuki Motor Company is investing $70 million to secure 25 percent equity in the nationalized automobile company.

Chevron International Oil has agreed to invest $27 million for oil exploration.

All major Japanese automobile companies (Toyota, Honda, Nissan, and Suzuki) have invested huge sums to manufacture cars, motorcycles, and trucks in India.

Major European governments have shown willingness to subsidize financing for the purchase of jet planes, industrial machinery, and other capital goods.

In a few years, the Indian consumers will be given opportunities to purchase new automobiles with sleeker bodies, powerful engines, front-wheel drive transmission, power-assisted steering, and automatic gears.[20]

To sum up, competition already seems to be yielding results. Prices are falling, product brands are multiplying, and markets are expanding. Computers, television sets, electronic typewriters, and even hotel rooms are getting cheaper. As *Business India* writes: "For the first time since Independence, the customer has begun to feel that he is wanted. As the race clearly gathers momentum, the laggards are being left behind."[21]

A Negative Reaction. On the other hand, local Indian businesspeople and industrialists have shown mixed reactions to this new open door policy.

Although welcoming liberal import and foreign investment policies, they worry about bankruptcies and the death of inefficient local companies. On the one hand, they state that industry as well as the government must accept these bankruptcies as a logical part of competition. On the other, they warn that the purpose of liberalization should not be to hand over large areas of industry to the multinationals.[22]

Too Soon to Tell. It is not clear whether the Indian industrialists and public enterprises will take this new era in the Indian economic scene in their stride and learn to live with it or whether they will fight back through political lobbying and corruption. If they choose the second route, it is not clear whether Rajiv Gandhi will be powerful enough to win and to implement his new trade and investment policies. It is too soon to tell. However, one thing is clear: India is finally preparing to move into the twenty-first Century.

Notes

1. *Foreign Economic Policy for the 20th Century*, "The Rockefeller Report" (New York: Doubleday, 1958), pp. 56–57.

2. Rostow, W. W., *Process of Economic Growth* (Oxford: Clarendon Press, 1960). See also Lewis, John P., *Quiet Crisis in India* (Washington, D.C.: Brookings Institution, December 1962).

3. Mikesell, Raymond F. "America's Economic Responsibility as a Great Power," *American Economic Review* vol. L (1960): 258–70.

4. Behrman, Jack N., "Promoting Free World Economic Development Through Direct Investment," *American Economic Review*, Supp. (1960): 271–81. See also his "Foreign Licensing, Investment and U.S. Economic Policy," *Patent, Trademark, and Copyright Journal of Research and Education*, vol. IV (summer 1960): 153–72; and "Licensing Abroad of American Held Patents, Trademarks, and Techniques," ibid., vol. I (1957): 145–58. See also various issues of the same journal since fall 1959.

5. Lewis, John P., op. cit.

6. McMillan, C., Gonzalez, R., and Erickson, L., *International Enterprise in a Developing Economy* (East Lansing, Michigan: Bureau of Business and Economic Research, Michigan State University, 1964).

7. Mehta, G. L., "Investment of Foreign Capital in India," broadcast talk over All India Radio, New Delhi, March 24, 1964.

8. *Partners in Progress, 1960–1985* (New Delhi, India: Indian Investment Center, 1986).

9. For details, see Negandhi, Anant R., *The Foreign Investment Climate in India* (East Lansing, Michigan: Division of Research, the Graduate School of Business Administration, Michigan State University, 1965).

10. *Partners in Progress, 1960–1985*, op. cit.

11. Ibid.

12. "Technology Policy Statement," *Commerce* (Bombay), January 15, 1983, 80–83.

13. *India Offers Technology* (New Delhi, India: Indian Investment Center, 1983), pp. i–v.

14. Miller, Matt, "Returning Indians, Foreign Companies Create High-Tech Haven in Bangalore," *Asian Wall Street Journal,* September 8, 1986, p. 21.

15. *India Offers Technology,* op. cit.

16. Lall, Sanjay, *The New Multinationals: The Spread of Third-World Enterprises* (New York: John Wiley & Sons, 1983), pp. 257–58.

17. Ibid., p. 258.

18. "Import of Technology: Top Indian Companies Studied," *Eastern Economist,* December 14, 1979, p. 1205.

19. *Partners in Progress, 1960–1985,* op. cit.

20. "Revolution on the Road," *India Today,* August 31, 1985, p. 100.

21. "Are They Afraid of Competition?" *Business India,* September 9–22, 1985, pp. 116–24.

22. Ibid.

Appendix 8A: Salient Features of the Current Indian Foreign Investment Policy

Foreign Ownership. The foreign equity or foreign ownership is restricted to the level of 40 percent, but this can go up to 100 percent with the choice of product, the level of exports, and the location of the unit. The government provides specific facilities for export-oriented units.

Units in Free Trade Zones. The government allows foreign majority owner-ship to units in India's six free trade zones located at Bombay, Kandla, Madras, Cochin, Falta, and Noida. Units located in these zones are com-pletely exempt from income tax for an initial period of 5 years. These units also remain exempt from all other direct and indirect taxes. These units are also allowed to sell up to 25 percent of their production to valid import licence holders in the domestic tariff area. These units are allowed to import their capital goods, raw materials, components, and so forth, free of all duties. The only requirement is that the value-added component should be not less than 30 percent.

One Hundred Percent Export-Oriented Units. These units can be set up anywhere in India. They enjoy virtually all the facilities provided to the units located in the free trade zones except that they are not allowed an initial 5-year tax holiday. In turn, they are allowed a number of other incentives available to other exporting units.

Nationalization. India does not nationalize just for the sake of nationaliza-tion. Only when it becomes imperative in the public interest is nationalization resorted to and then also on a very selective basis. For example, when leading Indian banks were nationalized, the foreign banks were not disturbed and they continue to operate even today on an increasing scale.

Remittances. The government of India freely allows the remittance of income on account of dividend and interest after payment of Indian taxes.

Repatriation. Apart from the regular periodic remittance of income on foreign investment, the government freely allows the repatriation of the initial capital in the original currency. The appreciation on capital, if any, is also allowed to be repatriated after the payment of taxes.

Royalty. Royalty of 3 to 5 percent is generally allowed on domestic sales. The royalty is worked out using the internationally accepted formula: the ex-factory value of production minus bought-out and imported components, raw material, and so forth. Higher rates of royalty are permissible on exports and products involving import of sophisticated technology.

Lump-Sum Fee. Lump-sum payment, in addition to the recurring royalty, is considered for the import of drawings, documentation, and other forms of know-how. Reasonableness of such payments is decided on the basis of the value of production, based on the technology imported.

Dividend: Dividend is paid to the equity holders out of the total profits after allowing for taxes. Dividend on shares with a value not exceeding Rs. 500,000 or 25 percent of total issued equity capital can be remitted without the prior approval of the Reserve Bank of India. It is only for the repatriation of the dividends not covered by the preceding provisions and repatriation of equity capital and appreciation on it, if any, that approval of the Reserve Bank is required.

Duration of Agreement. Collaboration agreements are approved normally for a period of 5 years from the date of agreement or 5 years from the commencement of production, provided production is not delayed for a period of 3 years from the date of signing of the agreement (i.e., a maximum of 8 years from the date of signing of the agreement).

Sublicencing. The government expects that the technical collaboration agreement should generally not prohibit sublicencing of the know-how and product design/engineering design under the agreement to other Indian parties. Such sublicencing, when it becomes necessary, is subject to terms to be mutually agreed to by all parties concerned (including foreign collaborators) and to the approval of the government.

Source: *Partners in Progress, 1960–1985* (New Delhi, India: Indian Investment Center, 1985)

Appendix 8B: Areas for Collaborations: Illustrative List

Engineering Industries

Metallurgical

Razor blade strips, high-tensile strapping strips, high-tensile steel strips, cladded steel strips   Steel castings (upgrading of technology)
Close die special steel forgings
Nickel
Titanium metals
Sponge-magnesium metals

Prime movers

Kerosene engines for outboard boats
Electric motors (special types only)
Cross-linked power cable (XLPE)
Power capacitors for power factor improvement
Power protection relays
Low-tension circuit breakers (sophisticated design)
High-tension circuit breakers (upgrading)
Tungsten filaments
Motor starters and contractors
Welding electrodes (special purpose)

Automobile ancillaries

Air brakes
Delivery valves
Flywheel magnetos
Head lamps
Pistons
Piston pins
Hydraulic brake and assembly (upgrading)
Inlet and exhaust valves

Fuel-injection equipment
Shock absorbers
Multicylinder fuel-injection pumps
Single-cylinder pumps
Nozzle holders
Nozzles
Stearing gears
Tie rod ends
Wiper motors
Flywheel ring gears

Industrial machinery
Boilers and steam-generating equipment (waste heat boiler for fertilizers)
Cement mill machinery (specialized type above 3,000 TPD)
Rayon and synthetic fiber machinery (specialized types of machinery)
Chemical and pharmaceutical machinery (specialized items such as glass equipment, storage cryogenic applications, effluent treatment plants, and specialized pharmaceutical machinery)
Dairy equipment (specialized items)
Coal and other mining machinery (specialized items)
Food-processing machinery (specialized equipment)
Gas cutting and welding equipment
Packaging machinery (specialized items)
Leather and footwear machinery (specialized items)
Paper and pulp machinery (chip washers, wood grinders, refiners, dandy rolls, MG cylinders, slitters, rewinders, etc.)
Ceramic machinery (specialized type)
Air-pollution–control equipment
Tea machinery (specialized items such as machinery for making instant tea, tea-bag–making machinery, etc.)
Printing machinery (specialized items)
Rubber machinery (specialized items)
Textile machinery (sophisticated woollen/worsted spinning machinery such as woollen combers, worsted cords, superspeed gil boxes)
Air and gas compressors (such as specialized high-pressure compressors for process industries, oil-free compact compressors for instrumentation and allied applications, diaphragm air compressors)
Power-driven pumps (for nuclear applications and handling petroleum, crude, and refined products and high-vacuum pumps)
Heat-treatment furnaces (specialized type)
Industrial sewing machines

Modern flour-milling machinery
Heavy-duty industrial valves

Commercial office and household equipment
Domestic refrigerators (certain specialized components such as compressors and glassmatic terminals)
Electronic typewriters

Miscellaneous mechanical and equipment industries
Grinding wheels (bonded abrasives)
Cutting tools (gear-cutting tools and other specialized tools)
Safety razor blades (single-track and plastic-bonded–type blades)
Tungsten-carbide–tipped tools
Precision laboratory balances
Dental X-ray equipment
Special antifriction bearings (deep-groove multirow bearings, angular-contact ball bearings, combined ball and cylindrical roller bearings, high-precision heavy-duty bearings, miniature bearings, and roller bearings for special applications)
Needle roller bearings
Wrist watches, mechanical, and components
Fishing trawler accessories
Alternative energy system

Machine tools
Turning machines
Drilling machines
Milling machines
Grinding machines
Boring machines
Threading machines
Shaping and slotting machines
Gear-cutting, generating, finishing, and testing machines
Honing and polishing machines
Wire-working machines
Hammers and forging machines
Presses and sheet-metal–working machinery

Others
Leaf spring manufacturing machines
Chain-making machines
Machines for the manufacture of zip fasteners
Machines for the manufacture of needles and pins
Impact extrusion press for manufacturing of collapsible tube

Specialized machinery required for manufacture of nuts and bolts (such as cold headers, nut tappers, trimmers, and reciprocating die types of threading and pointing machines)
Fluorescent tube-making machinery
Wood-working machinery

Nonengineering Industries

Fertilizers
Fertilizers based on natural gas

Inorganic chemicals
Hydrogen peroxide

Organic chemicals
Acetone
Phenol
Cyanuric chloride
Toluene dilsocyanate
Polyols
Xylos
Benzaldehyde
Tartaric acid (food grade)
Cellulose acetate butyrate
Acetal

Miscellaneous chemicals
Leather auxiliaries
Acetylene black
Special ion-exchange resins

Drugs and pharmaceuticals
Selected drugs and pharmaceuticals
Biotechnology relevant to food chemistry and drugs

Manmade fibers
Polynosic fiber
Polyester fiber through continuous polymerization and direct spinning process
Spandex fiber yarn

Paints
Power paints and specialty paints

Dyes
Selected dyes and dye intermediates

Paper
Specialty papers such as insulation paper (electrical), base paper for laminates, and cigarette tissue paper

Rubber products
Steel-reinforced rubber conveyor belts
Radial tires
Contraceptives
Thread (heat-resistant type)

Glass and glass products
Ophthalmic and optical glasses
Float glass
Laboratory glassware

Plastics and resins
PTFE (polytetrafluorethylene)
Polycarbonate
PTFCE (polytrifluorchlorethylene)
FEP (fluoro ethylene propylene copolymer
PFA (perfluoroalkoxy)
Fluoroelastomers
TFE (trifluorethylene)

Synthetic rubber
Nitrile
Butyl
Isoprene

Floculant
Polyacrylamide

Other
Dimethyl terephthalate (DMT)
Caprolactam
Refractories such as monolithics, electrocast, magnesite from sea water, fused grains of magnesite, and alumina
H.T. insulators and bushings and solid-core insulators for railways
Industrial catalysts.

Source: *India and Japan: A Retrospect and Prospects for Bilateral Economic Cooperation* (New Delhi: Indian Investment Center, 1985), pp. 50—57.

9

Technological Domination by the Transnational Corporation in Thailand

Suthy Prasartset

T he development process in Thailand since the early 1960s may be designated as a transnationalized model of accumulation because the Thai economy has been fully integrated into a new system of international division of labor based on import substitution and export-oriented production. This integrating process has been led by the transnational power structure and its local collaborators in the bureaucracies and the corporate sector.

The transnationalized model of accumulation is based on a set of three ideological practices: developmentalism, consumerism, and militarism (or the doctrine of national security).[1] While the three ideological practices are inextricably linked together in shaping the development process taking place in Thailand, I shall deal here with the ideology of developmentalism since this is the major determining factor leading to the process of technological domination of the transnational corporation (TNC) in Thailand. The ideology of developmentalism has become the basis of the state's development strategy, which is externally oriented and outward-looking. According to this strategy, foreign capital is unconditionally welcome; foreign aid and loans are depended upon to implement a national development plan. Such a plan is structurally urban-biased and growth-oriented rather than based on redistribution and the concern for human welfare. Aids and loans become a convenient alternative to structural reform, which tends to disrupt the status quo.

In its quest for development or modernization, the state has allocated its limited resources to provide social and economic infrastructure for foreign capital as well as local big business groups. It has actively reformed and created new institutions and legal structures to serve the need of the transnational corporations and their local affiliates. In this process, the state has become increasingly dependent on foreign aid and loans to finance its treasury deficits, and the economy is increasingly facing structural imbalances.

In summary, this pattern of development is structurally externally oriented, urban-biased, and highly inequitable, as witnessed by the increasing concentration of economic and sociopolitical power. This process has re-sulted in widening income and regional disparities as well as the increase in poverty, unemployment, malnutrition, and the marginalization of the masses. This externally oriented strategy of development produces grave conse-quences for Thailand because it has brought about a devastating erosion of its capacity and potential for self-propelling and independent development. In other words, such a strategy has brought about structural dependency that is manifested in the following phenomena: trade dependence, financial and debt dependence, technological dependence, transnational corporate control of local productive processes, and cultural dependence. In the following discus-sion, I shall confine myself to the role of the TNCs in technological domina-tion and the nature and mechanism of their control over local productive processes. This will be followed by a concluding discussion.

Terms and Conditions of Technology Contracts

It is generally argued by government and business circles in Third World countries that foreign investment confers a number of benefits on the host country, primary among these being the process of technology transfer. The term *technology transfer* is, in fact, a misleading concept. Vaitsos proposes the term *technology commercialization* instead as a correct reflection of the nature of the technology market as it is.[2] Thus, technology will be viewed as an economic unit or a merchandise whose market is highly monopolist. Tech-nology is not transferred without a high cost to a host country. More often than not, the buyer of technology is bound by various kinds of agreements that limit the fuller use of imported technology for the benefit of a host country.

In consequence, what is commonly called "technology transfer" is simply part and parcel of transnational corporations' design for relocation of their industrial sites in Third World countries in order to exploit cheap labor, natural resources, and market opportunities in those regions. Third World countries' industrialization since the second World War has mostly been a result of transnational corporations' global strategy to bring about a new international division of labor, whereby production processes with lower-level or standardized technology, often relatively more labor-intensive, are shifted to the Third World, while highly sophisticated production processes are retained in the home country.[3] This is, in fact, a crucial element in the process of transnationalization.

In such circumstances, the transnational corporations are able to keep the host country as a captive buyer of their technology, so that what was under-stood formerly as "technology transfer" is, in fact, "technology subordina-tion." Renato Constantino warns us that the peoples of the Third World must be made aware of the fact that the profit motive makes transnationals and capitalist states refuse to share technology except in their own interests.[4] He emphasizes further that, in most cases, the only type of technology transferred is that which benefits the owners of the process. The countries to which it is transferred are confined to light and medium industries that produce consumer goods for other markets. Furthermore, many restrictions are imposed, such as stipulations enabling the technology supplier to control and intervene in the management of the buyer's enterprise; restrictions on research and technological development by the buyer; requirements that the host country obtain equipment, raw materials, and so on exclusively from specified sources; prohibitions on the export of goods to certain markets; prohibitions on the use of supplementary technology by the buyer; and production limits. Constantino's argument is supported by the general findings of United Nations Conference on Trade and Development (UNCTAD)'s 1973 study on the transfer of technology. How far this pattern of technological subordination occurs in Thailand has yet to be probed systematically. This is a research area that has been sadly neglected, although it is understandable for a country such as Thailand, which has consistently followed a policy in favor of the process of transnationalization. However, we are fortunate enough to have two important pioneering studies by Mingsan Santikarn[5] and Economic and Social Commission of Asia and the Pacific– United Nations Centre on Transnational Corporations (ESCAP UN-CTC),[6] both analyzing the contractural arrangements for technology transfer in Thai manufacturing industries.

A word about the sampled firms in the two studies is in order here. The two studies examined the technology contracts filed at the Bank of Thailand. This was the only collection of technology contracts available for the studies because the bank requires that the companies remitting foreign exchange and technology fees submit the contracts or those parts of the contracts relating to the terms and conditions of payments to it. The main concern of the bank is not to control or to screen the technology imported. So far, there has been no attempt by the Thai government to look into this matter. Moreover, as the bank does not require forms with technology agreements that specify payments as a percentage of import value, raw materials, or components to submit the contracts, the sampled firms can reveal only part of the situation. However, given this limitation, the two studies still give us some insight into the nature and extent of technological domination by transnational corporations in Thailand.

Santikarn's analysis of licencing agreements of local and joint venture firms in Thailand testifies to the fact that the technology buyers in Thailand are restricted by several well-known requirements and prohibitions. This is clearly shown in table 9–1.

If we classify the restrictive conditions into two major types—export-restrictive clauses (market restrictions in the table) and tie-in clauses (other conditions)—we can see that the two types of conditions are less widespread

Table 9–1
Restrictive Conditions in 184 Technology Contracts Registered at the Bank of Thailand, 1975

Conditions	Percent of contracts
Market restrictions	47.1
Export ban (5.8)	
Restricted export area (12.5)	
Export allowed only on permit (17.4)	
Others (11.4)	
Sale agents chosen by owner of technology.	7.6
Prices of output set by the owner.	4.9
Selling of intermediate products must be permitted first by the owner.	2.2
The buyer prohibited from producing other products that compete with licenced product.	7.6
The buyer must buy the machinery from the owner.	13.6
The buyer must buy the raw materials and intermediate products from the owner.	21.7

Source: Santikarn, Mingsan, "Technology Transfer: A Case Study," Ph.D. thesis, Australian National University, 1978.
Note: Conditions are not mutually exclusive.

than in Latin American countries, based on Vaitsos's report that in Bolivia, Colombia, Ecuador, and Peru about 81 percent of the contracts prohibited exports totally and 86 percent had some restrictive clauses on exports.[7] Again, in Bolivia, Ecuador, and Peru, where information was available, 67 percent of the contracts contained tie-in clauses. The imposition of relatively strong restrictive clauses encountered by these Andean countries was, in an important respect, an attempt by the transnational corporations to obstruct their integration as a common market.

The fact that in Thailand almost half of the contracts contained varying degrees of export-restrictive clauses and about one-third had tie-in clauses indicates a high degree of dependence on the transnational corporations.

The existence of market-restrictive clauses has become a major obstacle in Third World countries' attempts to produce for the world market. It has been argued in the Thai case that such clauses have run counter to export-oriented production policy.[8] On the other hand, the existence of a tie-in clause means that the seller of technology is in an advantageous position to seek maximum benefits from the buyer of technology, especially in the over-pricing of machinery, raw materials, and intermediate products. It might be argued that the fact that such an agreement has taken place at all indicates the ability of the buyer to absorb such a high price. This, however, represents an unsatisfactory social cost. This concern was succinctly expressed by Akraseni and Iamkamala, who noted that in Thailand, there was still no law or government agency to regulate and screen the purchase of foreign technology, so that the buyer and seller of technology were free to make their contractual arrangement without government intervention. More often than not, the

Thai buyer is in a disadvantaged position either for lack of information or because the buyer is not genuinely interested in mastering the technology per se. When the buyer is only interested in profit, he has to pay a high technology fee or to accept unfavorable terms and conditions in the technology agreement. Where the seller is also a partner in the joint venture firm, this is tantamount to technological domination by the foreign partner.[9]

A United Nations regional study reveals that market-restrictive clauses are also widespread in Thailand, although tie-in clauses are present on a much smaller scale. The report on Thailand shows that in 275 contracts restrictive conditions on export markets (e.g., export bans, restricted export areas, and the need to seek approval from suppliers prior to export) were found in approximately one-fourth of the contracts. In only eight contracts were there no restrictions imposed.[10] In the 388 contracts examined, market restrictive clauses were found more frequently in the following industries: food processing, wearing apparel, chemicals and chemical products, electrical machinery and appliances, and transport equipment. The report emphasizes that 40 percent or more of contracts in these industries contained restrictions with respect to marketing arrangements. (See table 9–2.)

As is shown in table 9–3, the clauses providing for tie-in purchases of machinery and raw materials are less prevalent than those for export restriction. These conditions were found in only 29 cases or about 8 percent of the 340 contracts for which data were available. It was suggested that this seemingly drastic drop in tie-in clauses could partly result from the obligation imposed by the Thai government on the vehicle industry to increase the local content of vehicles produced in Thailand. This finding was taken to be a positive sign of the reduction of the TNCs' technological domination.

However, this drastic decline might, in my opinion, be attributed rather to a sharp increase in other conditions of the technology agreement. This can be seen from the fact that there has been a marked increase in provisions specifying the guarantees regarding certain achievements in quality or quantities by the supplier. In Santikarn's study, it was found that only 6.5 percent (12 contracts) of the total contracts stipulated such a condition. In contrast, the 1984 ESCAP UN-CTC report showed that the condition requiring guaranteed quality was present in 128 contracts or 33 percent of the contracts in the sample. In respect to this drastic change, the report considered this condition to be one that enhanced technology transfer, although experience in Latin America has shown that this condition tends to be stipulated as a substitute for the tie-in purchase clause in order to circumvent government regulations. In this regard, it is important to emphasize that TNC "assistance" to local firms in manufacturing products of stated quality has become a new binding factor for local firms. It means that the buyer is forced to buy both the machinery and the raw materials directly from the seller of technology.[11] In this situation, the enhancing condition can easily be turned into a dominating or hampering condition.

Table 9–2
Restrictive Conditions with Respect to Market Arrangements
(*number of contracts*)

International Standard Industrial Classified	Export Ban	Restricted Export Area	Prior Approval from Technology Suppliers Required	Others	Not Specified	No Restriction	No Information
311–2 Food	7	1	1	—	19	1	7
313 Beverages	1	—	1	—	2	—	—
314 Tobacco	—	—	—	—	2	—	—
321 Textiles	4	1	4	—	19	2	2
322 Wearing apparel	1	—	2	1	8	1	1
324 Footwear	—	—	—	—	—	—	—
341 Paper and paper products	1	—	—	—	6	—	—
342 Printing and publishing	—	—	—	—	4	—	—
351 Industrial chemicals	3	2	2	1	22	1	—
352 Other chemical products	12	1	8	—	45	1	15
353 Petroleum refineries and products	—	—	—	—	8	1	—
355 Rubber products	1	—	1	1	2	—	1
356 Plastic products	1	—	—	—	1	—	—
361 Pottery, china, and earthenware	—	1	1	1	—	—	—
362 Glass and glass products	—	—	—	—	6	—	1
369 Nonmetallic mineral products	1	2	—	2	1	—	—
371 Iron and steel	—	—	1	—	4	—	—
372 Nonferrous metal	—	1	—	—	2	—	—
381 Metal products	—	—	—	2	2	—	1
382 Machinery except electrical	2	1	4	—	12	1	—
383 Electrical machinery and appliances	4	5	3	1	14	—	1
384 Transport equipment	4	4	4	—	18	—	3
385 Other machinery	—	—	—	—	1	—	—
Service activities	1	1	1	1	36	—	9

Source: Economic and Social Commission for Asia and the Pacific United Nations Centre on Transnational Corporations; *costs and conditions of Technology Transfer through Transnational Corporations* (New York: United Nations, 1984), p. 218.

Table 9–3
Purchasing Arrangements
(*number of contracts*)

International Standard Industrial Classification	Tied Purchase of			Approval of Suppliers Needed for Acquiring Machinery and Input from Other Sources	No Condition Specified Regarding Purchasing Arrangements	Information Missing
	Raw Materials and Intermediates	Machinery	Both Raw Materials and Machinery			
311–2 Food	3	—	—	—	26	7
313 Beverages	—	—	1	—	3	—
314 Tobacco	1	—	—	—	2	2
321 Textiles	—	—	—	—	25	—
322 Wearing apparel	1	—	—	—	16	1
324 Footwear	—	—	—	—	—	—
341 Paper and paper products	—	—	—	—	6	—
342 Printing and publishing	—	1	—	—	5	—
351 Industrial chemicals	—	1	—	—	29	—
352 Other chemical products	9	—	1	—	56	15
353 Petroleum refineries and products	1	—	—	—	8	1
355 Rubber products	—	—	—	—	5	—
356 Plastic products	—	—	—	—	3	—
361 Pottery, china, and earthenware	—	—	—	—	2	1
362 Glass and glass products	—	—	—	—	6	—
369 Nonmetallic mineral products	—	—	—	—	6	—
371 Iron and steel	—	1	1	—	3	—
372 Nonferrous metal	—	—	—	—	3	—
381 Metal products	2	1	—	—	4	1
382 Machinery except electrical	—	1	—	—	17	—
383 Electrical machinery and appliances	1	2	1	—	24	1
384 Transport equipment	—	—	—	1	27	4
385 Other machinery	—	—	—	—	1	—

Source: See table 9–2, p. 220.

The study revealed another interesting point that, in my opinion, contributes to the process of technological dependency of Third World countries. The study concluded that a high degree of foreign ownership or TNC penetration is closely associated with *high level and rate of technology fees*. As the report stated: "Foreign affiliates sampled accounted for a major proportion of fee remittances by the firms. In 1981, firms with a foreign share of more than 50 percent remitted a total amount of 758.5 million baht compared with the total amount of 1,330.3 million baht." In addition, "approximately 30 percent of firms with foreign equity share over 75 percent paid fees exceeding 5 percent of net sales, whereas only 7.4 percent of the firms with equity share below 75 percent acquired technologies at high fees."[12] This finding is presented in table 9–4.

In addition, it has been shown that there was a high degree of concentration of technology payments in the sampled firms. The report showed that the top 7 percent of the firms, each remitting more than 10 million baht, accounted for about 60 percent of the total remittances. The top 14 percent of the firms were responsible for about 75 percent of the remittances. This means that the larger TNCs tend to contribute more than proportionately to the surplus outflows from Thailand, owing to their ability to promote intrafirm activities. This point is strongly supported by the finding that intrafirm technology transactions accounted for almost three-fourths of the total remittances from Thailand in 1981. This finding is, of course, consistent with the general nature of the process of transnational corporation integration or transnationalization.

As far as the rate of technology fees and royalty is concerned, the United Nations finding does not show a definite conclusion for all industries surveyed as the ranges of fees varied from industry to industry. Before further

Table 9–4
Technology Fees Classified by Percentage of Foreign Ownership

Technology Fees as a Percentage of Net Sales	Foreign Share				
	Total	0–24.9%	25.0–49.9%	50.0–74.9%	75–100%
Total	141(100.0)	26(100.0)	40(100.0)	28(100.0)	47(100.0)
Up to 2	34(24.1)	3(11.5)	13(32.5)	8(28.6)	10(21.3)
2–5	86(61.0)	20(76.9)	25(62.5)	18(64.3)	23(48.9)
5–10	17(12.1)	2(7.7)	2(5.0)	2(7.1)	11(23.4)
More than 10	4(2.8)	1(3.9)	0(0)	0(0)	3(6.4)

Source: See table 9–2, p. 214.

Note: Numbers in parentheses represent percentages.

$X^2 = 17.2756$.

Level of significance = 0.05.

Degrees of freedom = 9.

discussion of the result of the study, it is essential to point out that the pricing of technology is affected by a number of factors. It is important to remember that technology is one of the most important component parts of foreign direct investment. Therefore, the selling of technology has as its major objective the extraction of maximum consolidated benefits for the possessor. The pricing of technology is only one of the numerous means the transnational corporation can utilize to achieve such an objective. The pricing of technology, thus, depends on the specific nature of the technology requirement of a particular industry, the structure of the technology market, the other channels that the transnational corporation can use to extract compensation for the use of its technology, and the government's policy (e.g., the rate of tax on remitted profits and other earnings).[13]

As shown in table 9–5, the range of technology fees in basic industrial chemicals, paper and paper products, rubber products, glass and glass products, and nonmetallic minerals industries is relatively narrow and low. On the other hand, higher fees were found in industries with a high degree of product differentiation, especially those in other chemical products.

In general, the majority of contracts (73.9 percent) stipulated fees between 2 and 5 percent of gross sales. Those between 5 and less than 10 percent accounted for 13.8 percent of the contracts and about 12.3 percent of them paid fees in excess of 10 percent.

However, at the level of particular industries, it was reported that the pharmaceutical industry exhibited extreme pricing practices in respect to technology fees. For example, the fees for a local anesthetic were as high as 28 percent of net sales. The royalties and technical fees for a simple and

Table 9–5
Percentage Ranges of Running Royalties

International Standard Industrial Classification	Industry	Royalty Base	
		Net sales	Gross sales
	Total	0.25–28.00	0.00–22.50
311–2	Food	1.00–7.00	2.50–14.00
321	Textiles	0.75–5.00	1.75–2.00
322	Wearing apparel	3.00–8.00	2.00–5.00
324	Footwear	1.40–3.50	—
341	Paper and paper products	1.00–2.00	—
351	Industrial chemicals	1.10–5.00	0.00–5.00
352	Other chemical products	0.40–28.00	1.00–22.50
355	Rubber products	1.14–3.60	—
361	Pottery, china, and earthenware	1.00–3.60	—
362	Glass and glass products	0.25–5.00	—
382	Nonmetallic mineral products	2.25–5.00	2.00–7.00
383	Electrical machinery and appliances	1.00–11.00	1.50–6.00
384	Transport equipment	1.50–6.00	2.00

Source: See table 9–2, p. 210.

well-known analgesic amounted to 20 percent of gross sales. The study, therefore, concluded: "Considering that the pharmaceutical manufacturing process involves mixing of imported chemicals with neutral agents and flavoring ingredients (except for one drug), the above fees can obviously be considered exorbitant."[14]

As a further example of such exorbitant charges for technology fees, the study noted that a British agricultural tool company supplies the technology to its subsidiary for the production of a very simple agricultural hand tool for a fixed fee £25,000 per annum plus 2 percent of annual sales revenue, with the terms of the agreement covering 20 years.

In other cases, the report gave a mixed picture. It stated that in the garment industry, for instance, a fee of 8 percent of net sales was imposed for the purchase of a well-known brand for producing blue jeans. Fees for brands of high-fashion shoes were 3 to 4 percent of net sales, while the same fee for a lesser-known brand was 1.4 percent of net sales. One recipient paid 10 percent of gross sales to produce a well-known brand of perfume. It cost another recipient 14 percent of gross sales to produce a famous brand of chicken stock. When duration is taken into account, technology fees in Thailand can be considered very high. This is in sharp contrast to the situation in other Southeast Asian countries, such as Malaysia and Indonesia, whose governments impose some ceilings on fees and duration. Thai industrialists, however, are faced with a relatively wide range of fees and relatively longer duration. (Contract durations are detailed in table 9–6.)

Apart from exercising its power through restrictive contractual arrangements and the pricing of technology fees, the transnational corporation can also exert influence through joint venture operations and not necessarily through explicit contracts. As the technology is in great demand on the part of local partners, most of these enter into joint ventures with foreign firms in order to obtain existing technology from them.[15] As technology is usually embodied in intermediate products, machinery and equipment, technical and managerial skills, systems of production and distribution, and so on, it is through this complicated package of technology that the transnational corporation exerts its dominating power in order to maximize its benefits from the sale of technology to local affiliates. On the other hand, the local partners and local firms often do not know what type or degree of technology they are buying until they have bought it. Sometimes, they may know what they are buying but have no other choice, as the range of actual technological choice is limited by the technical specification of the equipment to produce such products.[16] The technological domination of the transnational corporation in Thailand, as evidenced in the preceding discussion, confirms Vaitsos's statement that technology, as an indispensable input in industrial development, "becomes through the process of its present form of commercialization a major factor limiting such development."[17]

Table 9–6
Duration of Contracts Classified by Industry
(number of contracts)

International Standard Industrial Classification	Total	Duration of contracts						
		Less than 5 Years	5 Years	More than 5 but less than 10 Years	10 Years	More than 10 Years	Open	Data Missing
Total	388 (100.0)	43 (11.08)	52 (13.40)	30 (7.73)	54 (13.92)	32 (8.25)	138 (35.57)	39 (10.05)
311–2 Food	36	4	2	2	6	3	12	7
313 Beverages	4	—	—	—	1	2	1	—
314 Tobacco	2	—	—	—	—	—	2	—
321 Textiles	28	3	2	7	6	1	7	2
322 Wearing apparel	16	2	3	1	4	1	5	—
324 Footwear	2	1	—	—	—	—	—	1
341 Paper and paper products	6	2	1	—	—	—	3	—
342 Printing and publishing	5	1	1	—	1	—	2	—
351 Industrial chemicals	30	2	1	4	4	4	14	1
352 Other chemical products	82	6	10	1	11	3	37	14
353 Petroleum refineries and products	9	2	1	1	1	—	4	—
355 Rubber products	6	—	2	—	—	1	2	1
356 Plastic products	3	1	1	—	—	—	1	—
361 Pottery, china, and earthenware	2	—	—	—	—	2	—	—
362 Glass and glass products	7	—	1	3	1	—	—	1
369 Nonmetallic mineral products	6	1	—	—	3	2	1	—
371 Iron and steel	5	1	2	—	—	—	2	—
372 Nonferrous metal	3	—	1	—	—	—	2	—
381 Metal products	6	1	2	1	—	—	1	1
382 Machinery except electrical	20	2	1	1	4	1	8	—
383 Electrical machinery and appliances	28	2	5	1	8	4	9	—
384 Transport equipment	33	2	11	5	2	—	11	1
385 Other machinery	1	—	—	—	—	—	1	2
Service activities	48	10	5	4	2	6	13	8

Source: See table 9–2, p. 216.

Note: Numbers in parentheses represent percentages of all contracts.

TNC's Domination over Local Productive Processes

Another important feature of the process of transnationalization of Thailand is that major industrial production of the country has been dominated by transnational capital. For a nation to follow a policy of independent national development, the state must be able to obtain a certain measure of control over important industrial branches of the country, so that they do not fall into the hands of transnational capital.

Since the mid-1970s, there have been marked changes in the economic structure of Thailand, especially the rising share of the industrial sector. Although this sector has registered a rapid rate of growth, we cannot be proud of its "achievement" as several important industrial branches have fallen under the control of TNCs. Instead of indicating a relatively rapid growth of the Thai industrial sector, this successful performance signifies a high level of TNC domination of the Thai economy.

In his seminal study, Krirkkiat Phipatseritham has clearly pointed out that the TNCs have a firm control over major industrial branches of Thailand, particularly in petroleum refining, tin smelting, car assembling, textiles, and electrical and electronic equipment.[18] This is set out in table 9–7.

It is clear that the TNC derives its dominating power from the control of technology (e.g., licencing and patents) and international marketing channels. In the tin smelting and textile industries, for example, the TNCs concerned have a tight control over the distribution of finished products. Some TNCs even go so far as to pressure Thai partners to accept certain local trading agents as the local distributors. In the pineapple canning, tapioca, and to-

Table 9–7
Major Industries under TNC Domination, 1982

Industry	Sale (million baht)	Domestic Use	Export	Approximate Degree of Control
Total	98,010			
Petroleum refining	35,000	All	None	Total
Tin smelting	10,720	Little	Almost all	Total
Car assembling	12,000	All	None	Most
Motor bicycles	3,300	All	None	Most
Fertilizer	1,270	All	None	Most
Tires	2,000	Almost all	Little	Most
Textiles	20,000	Most	Some	Most
Electrical goods	8,000	All	None	Most
Electronic equipment	2,000	Some	Most	Total
Condensed milk	1,320	All	None	Most
Canned pineapples	1,200	Some	Almost all	Most
Tobacco	1,200	Some	Almost all	Most

Source: Phipatseritham, Krirkkiat, *The Distribution of Ownership in Thai Big Business* (Bangkok: Thammasat University Press, 1982), p. 283.

bacco leaf processing industries, the TNCs exercise strong control over trademarks and foreign marketing channels.

Control of technology and inputs for manufacturing industries by TNCs posed major obstacles in the process of industrial development of Third World countries. In the Thai case, Akraseni and Chongthanasarnsombat put this point clearly when they reported that, owing to the lack of technology for producing local material and parts, the electrical products and equipment industries have to import a high proportion of raw materials and parts.[19] In cases where there is local production, costs are often too high for successful competition with imports. As a result, the import dependence ratios of these industries still remain at a very high level. The production for such goods as integrated circuits, electric wire, telephone wire, electric bulbs, air conditioners, color televisons, car radios, and batteries has to depend on imports for about 50 to 100 percent of the raw materials and parts used. This situation inevitably contributes to high costs of production and thereby makes the product less competitive in the foreign market. This circumstance tends to strengthen the process of dependent industrial development in Thailand.

In addition, with their ability to control inputs for manufacturing industries in Thailand, the TNCs are in an advantageous position to extract excessive surplus through transfer-pricing practices. The import-dependent nature of the Thai industrial structure tends to facilitate such practices, especially through the tie-in purchase of inputs.

Apart from the control of technology, marketing channels, and the tie-in purchases of raw materials and inputs, the TNCs also exert considerable influence on the management of their local affiliates, notably the joint venture firms. It is well known that majority equity participation by local partners does not mean a corresponding degree of majority control of the joint venture firm. The actual control of the firm can be exercised through channels or means other than majority equity participation.

Before proceeding to examine the pattern of foreign control by means other than equity control, it is necessary to outline briefly the structure of foreign-equity participation by important industrial sectors. As shown in table 9–8, it is clear that, on the average, about 60 percent of the companies surveyed are in minority foreign ownership.[20] Majority foreign-owned companies account for about 16 percent of the total, and the wholly foreign-owned firms for 22 percent. Foreign control by equity is very high in the pharmaceuticals, mining, and trading sectors.

It is interesting to note that a very high proportion of these minority-owned companies are 49 percent foreign-equity holdings. This important finding strongly supports my argument that the TNCs have a very high degree of control and domination over several important industrial branches of Thailand. While some countries still define "foreign ownership" by a criterion based on foreign majority equity participation (as in the cases of Can-

Table 9–8
Foreign Equity Control by Industrial Sector

Industry	Number of Companies	Foreign Equity Share			
		5% or Less	6– 50%	51– 99%	100%
Total	568	18	331	94	125
	(100)	(3.2)	(58.3)	(16.5)	(22.0)
Mining	17	0	2	4	11
	(100)	(0)	(11.8)	(23.5)	(64.7)
Food, beverages, and tobacco	84	4	53	13	14
	(100)	(4.8)	(63.1)	(15.5)	(16.7)
Textiles and wearing apparel	74	3	52	14	5
	(100)	(4.1)	(70.3)	(18.9)	(6.8)
Wood and wood products	15	1	9	3	2
	(100)	(6.7)	(60.0)	(20.0)	(13.3)
Paper, paper products, publishing, and printing	13	1	7	1	4
	(100)	(7.7)	(53.8)	(7.7)	(30.8)
Chemicals, oil, and rubber products	64	0	35	11	18
	(100)	(0)	(54.7)	(17.2)	(28.1)
Pharmaceuticals and toiletries	35	0	14	7	14
	(100)	(0)	(40.0)	(20.0)	(40.0)
Plastic and humanmade fibers	32	1	25	3	3
	(100)	(3.1)	(78.1)	(9.4)	(9.4)
Nonmetallic mineral products	21	2	ʹ16	2	1
	(100)	(9.5)	(76.2)	(9.5)	(4.8)
Basic metals	16	1	12	1	2
	(100)	(6.3)	(75.0)	(6.3)	(12.5)
Fabricated metal products	32	2	21	8	1
	(100)	(6.3)	(65.6)	(25.0)	(3.1)
Electrical and mechanical machinery	68	2	38	9	19
	(100)	(2.9)	(55.9)	(13.2)	(27.9)
Transport	46	1	28	12	5
	(100)	(2.2)	(60.9)	(26.1)	(10.9)
Other industries n.e.c.	21	0	14	3	4
	(100)	(0)	(66.7)	(14.3)	(19.0)
Trading	30	0	5	3	22
	(100)	(0)	(16.7)	(10.0)	(73.3)

Source: Tambunlertchai, S., and McGovern, I., "An Overview of the Role of MNCs in the Economic Development of Thailand," paper submitted to the Conference on the Role of Multinational Corporations in Thailand, 1984.

Note: Numbers in parentheses are percentages. Rows may not add to totals because of rounding.

ada, Austria, India, and Spain), there are others that define it differently, as shown in the table on page 159.[21]

In my opinion, 20 or 25 percent foreign-equity participation should be an appropriate criterion for determining whether a firm is controlled by foreign capital, given the many other advantages the TNCs possess. The 20 or 25 percent foreign-equity participation will adequately account for the existence of foreign control by other means than equity participation. I shall deal with this point shortly.

Country	Criterion of Foreign Ownership
	(percent)
Australia	25 and more
Turkey	10 and more
France	20 and more

Apart from control through technology, the TNCs can also exercise control by financial and managerial means. In the case of financial control, the foreign firms may take only a nominal shareholding in the so-called joint venture. The foreign shareholders either lend money to the company or guarantee loans extended by local banks. The loan guarantees include a straightforward legal guarantee and the issue of a letter of awareness. The latter is more common among U.S. and European subsidiaries of the TNCs. A 1984 study concluded that "the guaranteeing of loans by both these methods is a powerful means of control, since both can be withdrawn at the discretion of the parent or foreign investor."[22] The report also established a close relationship between nominal shareholding and high debt/equity ratio of the firm concerned. This obviously means that the TNCs are in good position to impose various conditions on the local firm through such financial arrangements.

Regarding managerial control, it has been reported that the pattern of control is consistent with the investment pattern followed by specific countries of origin. For example, in industries with a high degree of Japanese investment, there tends to be a greater control of finance and marketing, but less of general management. On the other hand, in those industries dominated by U.S. and European firms, greater control is often the case in general management, but less in finance and marketing.

When the pattern of managerial control was examined over time, it was reported that, regardless of the nationality of the investors or of the industries in which they operated, the degree of control did not change over time. Companies operating in Thailand for more than 30 years still had as much expatriate control over key managerial functions as companies that were only recently incorporated. Quite clearly, there was no "indigenization" of management control as these companies grew older, and this may have important implications for the future development of the economy.[23]

In another study dealing with the managerial behavior of Japanese firms in Thailand and other Asian countries, Weinstein pointed out how the Japanese TNCs maintained their control over the joint venture in spite of their minority equity participation.[24] This can be effected in three ways. First is by nominal shareholding by the local partners, who often obtain large loans from the Japanese partners. Sometimes the Thai partners may put in their land or buildings as part of the capital. More often than not, they are allocated a large number of shares regardless of the cost of land and buildings. However, they must tacitly agree to allow key management positions to go to the hands of their foreign partners. Weinstein quotes Japanese embassy sources as saying that it is not uncommon for under-the-table money to be paid to local nationals for the use of their names. Second, the two partners agree to maintain a very low level of registered capital in order to help the Thai partners to acquire a majority shareholding in order to comply with the law prohibiting foreign partners from holding a majority share in certain industries. However, the joint venture firm set up under such an arrangement will depend on loans from the Japanese partner's parent firm. Thus, it is not surprising to find that a joint venture firm tends to operate with a relatively high debt/equity ratio. Weinstein quotes U.S. embassy sources as saying that the debt/equity ratios for Japanese-controlled firms are as high as 8 to 1 or even 10 to 1.[25] This is definitely made possible by the supply of credits provided by Japanese partners, especially for the importation of machinery, equipment, and parts from Japan. Needless to say, heavy use is made of suppliers' credit.

The last method of maintaining control over local firms while complying with the law requiring majority local participation is the use of "basis agreements" that explicitly delineate division of responsibility regardless of the degree of equity participation. Through this form of agreement, the local firm has effectively allowed crucial responsibilities to be under foreign control, these being the operation of the factory, the procurement of raw materials, and the marketing of the product. On the other hand, the local partner is normally in control of such positions as labor relations, payroll, and similar noncritical functions. By controlling these dominant positions in the joint venture, the foreign firms, with their worldwide network of operations, are in a strategic position to extract substantial surplus from the Third World countries through transfer-pricing practices in intrafirm transactions. It is these transactions rather than the overall profitability of the joint venture that provide the principal earnings for the transnational corporations.[26]

Conclusion

As a result of unremitting integration into the world capitalist system, Thailand tends to suffer from a high degree of domination by transnational capital, especially from the technological point of view, as the preceding discussion has clearly shown. From the late nineteenth century on, Thailand was integrated into the system of colonial international division of labor as a producer of primary products. There was only a brief period of delinking during the Great Depression of the early 1930s and the second World War. During those few years, Thailand exhibited a satisfactory capacity for self-reliant development: dependence on external markets, resources, and technology was reduced markedly and the internal production process started to develop independently.

However, soon after the war, the process of reintegration into the world capitalist system again consolidated itself within the framework of the new international division of labor. Such long-term integration into the world capitalist system has inevitably resulted in structural dependence for the Thai social formation as a whole. This process also brings with it a disarticulated and truncated economic structure for Thailand. In such a situation, Thailand's expanded reproduction is highly dependent on imports of capital goods and technology. Thailand has never been able to develop a substantial scientific and technological base that will support a self-propelling expanded reproduction process.

Moreover, such a long-term and almost continuous process of integration into the world capitalist system has resulted in a distorted sociopolitical structure. The growth of industrial bourgeoisies has been strangled by such an incorporation process. Instead, the comprador bourgeoisies' position has been strengthened. The integration of Thailand into the new international division of labor had brought about the transformation of the mercantile compradors into industrial compradors.[27] The industrial compradors' infatuation with the most modern technology becomes a channel whereby transnational capital can control Thailand's crucial productive process through its technological power. Thus, the Thai bourgeoisies became relatively weak, so that they are unable to challenge the bureaucracies for a meaningful share of state power, not to mention their will to challenge the transnational capital. The Thai state, for its part, has followed a transnationalized model of development, so that no effective measures are taken to ensure that the operation of the transnational corporations will contribute adequately and fairly to national interests. Such is the situation for Thailand, which can be designated as a case of integration into the world capitalist system with weakening bargaining power.

China's recent open door policy can be interpreted as a process of selective relinking into the world capitalist system. This selective process has relatively greater bargaining power with transnational capital than that of most Third World countries. After a period of incorporation into the world capitalist system within the framework of the colonial international division of labor, China managed to delink completely from the system and reconstruct an autocentric socioeconomic structure by building up a meaningful scientific and technological base and an articulated economic structure. This has been achieved by following the principle of self-reliant development as laid down by the late Chairman Mao. On the other hand, China has succeeded in improving its position in the world states system. With its reinforced internal socioeconomic and political structure and international position, China is now ready to reintegrate selectively into the world capitalist system in order to exploit some of the advantages and strengthen its self-reliant development, or to pursue "socialist modernization." However, such a relinking process is also full of pitfalls, traps, and dangers. If China allows it to move beyond a certain point, it may well cause financial and technological dependency as well as cultural disruption in terms of emulation of transnationalized life-styles and tastes. Such problems have now overwhelmed most of the Third World countries, including Thailand.

Notes

1. See Prasartset, S., "The crisis of the Transnationalized Model of Accumulation: The Thai Case," paper submitted to the United Nations University Southeast Asian Perspectives Project Meeting, Penang, Malaysia, October 1985.

2. Vaitsos, C., "The Process of Commercialization of Technology in the Andean Pact," in *International Firms and Modern Imperialism* (Hugo Radice, ed.) (London: Penguin, 1975), p. 73.

3. See Fröbel, F., Heinrichs, J., and Kreye, O., *The New International Division of Labor* (NY: Cambridge University Press, 1980).

4. Constantino, Renato, "Global Enterprises and the Transfer of Technology," *Journal of Contemporary Asia,* vol. 7, no. 1 (1977).

5. Santikarn, Mingsan, "Technology Transfer: A Case Study," Ph.D. thesis, Australian National University, 1978.

6. Economic and Social Commission for Asian and the Pacific–United Nations Centre on Transnational Corporations (ESCAP–UN-CTC) *Costs and Conditions of Technology Transfer Through Transnational Corporations* (New York: United Nations, 1984).

7. Vaitsos, op. cit., pp. 192–97.

8. Akraseni, N., et al., "Industrial Development in Thailand and Industrial Development Policy for the Years 1982–1986" (Bangkok: TURA, mimeo, 1980).

9. See Akraseni, N., and Iamkamala, C., "Restructuring of Metal Products Industry" (Bangkok: TURA, mimeo, 1981) (in Thai).

10. ESCAP UN-CTC, op. cit., p. 217.

11. See Vaitsos, op. cit.

12. ESCAP UN-CTC, op. cit., p. 213.

13. See Plasschaert, S.R.F., *Transfer Pricing and Multinational Corporations: An Overview of Concepts, Mechanisms and Regulations* (Surrey: Saxon House, 1979), chapter 4.

14. ESCAP UN-CTC, op. cit., pp. 210–11.

15. See Prasartset, S., "The Impact of Transnational Corporations on the Economic Structure of Thailand," *Alternatives* (Institute for World Order), vol. VII (December 1981), pp. 431–50; Kerdpibul, U., *Thailand's Experience with Multinational Corporations* (Bangkok: Kasetsat University, 1974).

16. Pancharoen, W., *Multinational Corporations and Host Country Technology: A Case Study of Thailand,* Project No. 78–3–03 (Council for Asian Manpower Studies, 1980), p. 45.

17. Vaitsos, op. cit., p. 195.

18. Phipatseritham, Krirkkiat, *The Distribution of Ownership in Thai Business* (Bangkok: Thammasat University Press, 1982).

19. Akraseni, N., and Chongthanasarnsombat, S., *Restructuring of Electrical Products Industry* (Bangkok: TURA, 1981, mimeo) (in Thai).

20. See Tambunlertchai, S., and McGovern, I., "An Overview of the Role of MNCs in the Economic Development of Thailand," paper submitted to the Conference on the Role of Multinational Corporations in Thailand, 1984.

21. See Newfarmer, R.S., *Transnational Conglomerates and the Economics of Dependent Development: A Case Study of the International Electrical Oligopoly and Brazil's Electrical Industry* (Greenwich, Conn.: JAI Press, 1980), pp. 4–5.

22. Tambunlertchai and McGovern, op. cit., p. 28.

23. Ibid., p. 30.

24. Weinstein, F. B., "Multinational Corporations and the Third World: Case of Japan and Southeast Asia," *International Organization,* vol. 30 (summer 1976).

25. Ibid., p. 390.

26. Ibid., p. 391.

27. Prasartset, S., "The Capitalist Class in Thailand: Genesis and Consolidation," in Ernest E. Boesch, ed., *Thai Culture* (Report of the Second Thai-European Research Seminar) (Saarbrucken: University of the Saar, 1982).

10
Hungary and the Transnational Corporations

Mihály Simai

General Policy Issues

The understanding of the role, strategy, and practical work of transnational corporations has gone through several stages in Hungary in the past decades.

After the socialist transformation following the second World War, ideological and political factors dominated the attitudes of government and the academic community. This approach placed exclusive stress on the systemic role of the large international firms in terms of their place in world economics and politics plus their dominating role in the Western system, characterized as monopoly capitalism. They were not seriously studied and understood as economic actors, partners, or organizations, whose mechanism was relevant to large firms in Hungary as well as elsewhere. In the next stage, the increasing role of TNCs in the world economy and the growth of Hungary's trade with the West demanded a new approach to dealing with TNCs, since they were the dominating actors of the Western economic system in the fields of production, technology, trade, and capital flows. Experiences in Hungary's relations with them in trade were basically satisfactory. They have been strong and reliable partners. Very often they proved to be more flexible in their practices than the smaller firms in the West. Their international network facilitated the different swap techniques often necessary in East–West trade. Sometimes they were less restrictive and discriminatory than Western governments in their policies. They were, of course, realizing large profits as a result of these activities.

The third stage was characterized by the changes in the forms of cooperation. As the environment became politically more favorable to East–West relations and the growth of trade required new impetus, different forms of industrial cooperation ventures were established, many of them with TNCs within and outside Hungary. This period also brought changes in the system of planning and management in some socialist countries, which facilitated greater flexibility for the firms. The spread and smooth working of these cooperative joint ventures were hampered by the lack of a legal framework and guarantees as well as by difficulties in evaluating the local and international contributions, the pricing of products, and so on.

The fourth stage, since 1986, represents qualitatively new elements in cooperation. The changes taking place as the result of the ongoing reform of the Hungarian economy, the new legal framework facilitating the participation of foreign capital in different firms, and the free trade zones established in the country are some of the important features of the present environment.

The development of the Hungarian reform process facilitated the new stage of cooperation. The increase in the autonomy of enterprises as a result of the new Enterprise Law facilitated the establishment of different ventures. The system of appointing top managers was changed and the Enterprise Councils were authorized to select the top executives. The direct participation of Hungarian firms in international ventures was encouraged. Bureaucratic procedures for authorizing different international operations were greatly simplified. The price system became more flexible and price formation was tied in many areas to international price movements and reflected real domestic costs more closely than before. In a large segment of the economy, price formation became "free," reflecting supply and demand movements. Foreign exchange legislation became simpler and a realistic "managed float" system was introduced. A new bankruptcy law was adopted, and Hungary joined the IMF and World Bank.

Present Forms of Cooperation between Hungary and Transnational Corporations

Hungary's relations with TNCs include traditional trade, trade cooperation in third markets, and industrial cooperation.

Traditional Trade (Exports and Imports). It is very difficult, of course, to isolate trade with TNCs from overall trade relations. According to the estimates of the author, based on enquiries, about 35–40 percent of the total East–West trade of Hungary was carried on with TNCs during the first half of the 1980s.

Trade Cooperation in Third Markets. Hungarian companies have participated together with such firms as Fiat, ICI, BBC, Krupp, and CEC in several large-scale projects, mainly in power-generating supplies, the chemical industry, and railway equipment.

Industrial Cooperation. This form of relation includes several different areas. The three most important are:

technological cooperation

large and continuous supply of materials and spare parts

marketing cooperation

In 1986, there were about four hundred different valid industrial cooperation agreements, many of them with transnational corporations. About half of them represented subcontracts in Hungarian processing for export, some of them only with TNCs. There was a high concentration in light industries. Many cooperation agreements were connected with the importation of licences, know-how, and other technologies by Hungarian firms. There were cooperation agreements for product specialization and marketing as well.

These industrial cooperation agreements represent relatively small-scale ventures and their total sales volume has been rather limited. Some of these cooperation ventures failed and were discontinued. The difficult world economic environment discouraged some of the Western partners from continuing industrial cooperation because of the lack of demand in the market.

As the failures proved, the expectations of the Hungarian and Western partners did not materialize fully. Only a part of the industrial cooperation ventures were successful and survived very difficult economic storms. These were the ventures in which both partners had stronger interests.

Cooperation between Hungarian firms and such TNCs as Siemens, AEG, Bosch, Bayer, Ciba-Geigy, Ericsson, and ITT, for example, dates back to before the second World War. Since the late 1960s, cooperation with Siemens has contributed to the technological development of Hungarian medical equipment industries. ICI and Wellcome have become important partners in the production of herbicides. Cooperation with Krupp has been particularly important in the machine tool industries.

Licence purchases were also important in consumer goods industries. Products made under licence from Pepsi-Cola, Nestlé, Philip Morris, and AEG became very popular in the Hungarian market.

The main targets of Hungarian firms in their cooperation with TNCs (namely, the speedup of technological development, the increase of hard-currency exports, and the establishment of stable production and trade relations) were only partially achieved. With the exception of some important cases, technology transfer by the TNCs was limited in volume and the technology received was not the most up-to-date. The additional costs were very high and an increase of one-sided dependence because of sales of spare parts, components, and materials resulted from the new relations. A continuous flow of new technology was not achieved through the cooperation ventures.

Cooperation did, however, contribute to the technological upgrading of domestic consumption and exports (especially exports to the Council for

Mutual Economic Assistance (CMEA) countries), though, in spite of the favorable changes, the share of exports based on the cooperation ventures was under 5 percent of the total Western exports. In addition, cooperation ventures helped to strengthen relations with TNCs in many other areas, especially in third markets.

In addition to the industrial cooperation ventures, nineteen of the forty-six important TNCs in Hungary's Western economic relations also had general cooperation agreements with Hungarian partners. These agreements included provisions for scientific and technological cooperation, medium-term trade contracts, and longer-term agreements for compensation. The partners on the Hungarian side included firms, ministries, research institutes, and various other agencies.

The most important targets of the TNCs in Hungary are connected with the expansion of their markets. (In certain isolated cases, they are interested in local technology as well.) On the Hungarian side, technology imports and marketing facilities are the most often mentioned motivations.

Equity Participation and Joint Ventures

Industrial cooperation already resembles certain elements of joint venture operations. It already integrates the interests of the partners. Direct capital participation may also be involved. The more developed forms of cooperation between TNCs and Hungarian firms (namely, joint ventures) required, however, a different economic environment within the country. A new system of planning and management was facilitated to a great extent by the just-mentioned reform measures.

By the end of 1986, there were forty-four joint ventures with Western capital participation operating in Hungary. In the Hungarian legislation, they are called "economic associations." They are independent juridical persons. In other words, they are registered firms that possess their own separate assets and conduct their own accounting, and they may sell their products and services, in accordance with Hungarian legal statutes, abroad or within Hungary.

The first decree permitting the establishment of joint ventures with foreign capital was issued in 1972. Since then, the regulations have been updated several times to make participation more attractive for foreign investors. Since the early 1970s, the most important changes have taken place in the following areas:

The number of branches where foreign capital participation is encouraged has increased quite remarkably.

The limitations relating to direct foreign management activities have been removed.

The provisions for Hungarian majority interest have been changed.

Important tax concessions have been given to the foreign partners in areas regarded as priorities in the Hungarian economy.

With the establishment of custom-free zones, special conditions have been offered in the fields of foreign exchange rules, wages, prices, and foreign trade activities.

Despite these changes in the conditions for foreign capital investment, progress in joint venture operations has been relatively slow. The slow progress achieved in foreign capital participation can be explained by the following problems:

The slow growth of the Hungarian economy during the first half of the 1980s did not encourage foreign partners to enter into a rather small market. Entry to the CMEA market through these ventures was not automatically secured.

The incentives given to the foreign partners were not strong enough in comparison with those offered by some other countries competing for foreign direct investment.

The regulations affecting foreign firms were only very slowly liberalized and the bureaucratic procedures were rather complicated.

Some elements in the mechanism of the Hungarian economy were too rigid and hampered the activities of the joint ventures, especially in the fields of price formation, foreign exchange regulations, exchange rates, and imports.

The risk factors (including political risk) were still considered too high by Western partners.

Conclusion

It is too early to make an overall evaluation of the impact of cooperation between Hungarian firms and TNCs. Diverging concrete interests and the limited volume of ventures do not permit any longer-term projections concerning the changes.

What is already evident is that the mentality of the Hungarian firms has been changing as a result of the cooperation ventures. The forms of participation of Hungarian firms in international operations have been broadened. The intensity of their international operations has not increased sufficiently, however, especially not on the scale necessary to promote more efficient adjustment. The intensity of cooperation has also been adversely influenced by East–West political tensions.

11

Code of Conduct, International Investment Contracts, the Debt Crisis, and the Development Process

Carsten Thomas Ebenroth
Joachim Karl

T
he Code of Conduct on Transnational Corporations, which has been the subject of negotiations in United Nations bodies for more than 10 years, has an ambiguous impact. Some people in legal science maintain that—apart from its nonbinding character—the code is of little relevance since it has not yet been possible to achieve final confirmation of the draft. Nevertheless, the Code of Conduct has an important impact as far as the development of cross-border direct investment is concerned because it is very difficult for the negotiating parties to accept either the law of the investor or the law of the investee. The People's Republic of China is a good example of the development of foreign investment regulations. Since the opening up of Chinese foreign policy some years ago, China has been developing a legal framework for cooperation with foreign firms. The Code of Conduct can in that respect be a guide for the negotiation of an international investment contract, since it allows the negotiating parties to find an internationally acceptable frame for the drafting of such a contract. The impact of the Code of Conduct cannot be appreciated without first reviewing the historic development of foreign direct investment in less developed countries since 1945.

The Three Phases of Foreign Direct Investment in Less Developed Countries since 1945

As a result of the political transformation process whereby former colonies achieved independence, foreign direct investment predominated in the less developed countries during the first 25 years after the end of the second World War. Exceptions such as Tanzania (where the former colonial mo-

Reprinted with permission of the authors and editors from the Winter 1988 issue of *The International Lawyer*, Volume 22, No. 1 Copyright 1988, American Bar Association, Section of International Law and Practice.

nopoly of the Lonrho Group was transformed into the parastatal National Development Corporation under President Nyerere's Arusha Declaration of 1967, showed no encouraging results in the long run.

The misuse of power and the interference of some transnational corporations in national economic policy (as in Chile) was the inspiration for the development of a Code of Conduct within the United Nations family. It had a predecessor in the discussion within the OECD, where the potential misbehavior of transnational corporations because of their peculiar potential to outpace national regulations was examined. The 1974 U.N. Declarations on the Establishment of a New International Economic Order and the Charter of Economic Rights and Duties of States formed the basis for the world organization's Draft Code of Conduct on Transnational Corporations. Paralleling this development was the expanding capital transfer to the developing countries as a result of the first oil-price explosion in 1973 and the recycling of petrodollars through private banks. The excess liquidity lent by the OPEC states was transferred to the less developed countries in the form of short-term loans on a rollover basis from 3 to 6 months with a linkage to the London interbank offered rate (LIBOR) plus a spread for the risk of the credit facility. The excessive petrodollar liquidity was a supply that found relatively small demand and, until 1978, interest rates remained comparatively low. The devaluation of the U.S. dollar under the Carter administration and the tight-fisted policy adopted by the U.S. Federal Reserve Board to beat inflation induced an increase in the value of the dollar and a rise in interest rates. The impact of the 1970s policy against foreign direct investment in developing countries and the low interest rates alleviated the credit expansion and domestic investment in developing countries through the transfer of external resources via the market (imports of goods, services, and technology).

The rise in interest rates at the end of the 1970s and the subsequent rise in the value of the U.S. dollar seriously exacerbated the balance of payments problems of the developing countries. Deteriorating terms of trade due to the diminished income from the export of raw materials caused the de facto default of many developing countries. Mexico was the first large debtor country to apply for assistance from the International Monetary Fund in adjusting its economic policy in 1982. As of 1986, the International Monetary Fund was negotiating external debt problems with more than 62 countries, after having alleviated the situation in Argentina and Brazil. Mexico is at the brink for the second time because of falling oil prices and natural catastrophe in the form of a serious earthquake that further squeezed its economy.

The International Monetary Fund's old policy of restructuring and financing (import substitution and increasing exports) can only be successful if the additional fresh money for financing the necessary structural adaptation process can be channeled into the growth areas of the national economy.

Despite this fact, credits by private banks in industrialized countries can no longer be considerably enhanced because of the high risk involved in the transfer of hard currency. An increase in public development aid also seems impossible because of continuing financial constraints in the capital-exporting countries. (Moreover, a developing country is running very close to its limits in an import-substitution policy.) There is the potential danger that a less developed country may be cutting the supply lines for necessary technological goods that are the prerequisite for its own development process. Export orientation is therefore the only suitable remedy whereby less developed countries can earn foreign exchange for the repayment of their debts.

In this situation, foreign direct investment has regained importance. The LDCs have already begun to reconsider their previous negative attitude toward it. They have recognized that foreign direct investment is an appropriate way to overcome the debt crisis. Compared to commercial credits, foreign direct investment has the advantage that there are no interest rates to be paid and that profits must only be transferred when they have actually been gained and not been reinvested. Moreover, foreign direct investment creates new jobs, increases the transfer of technology, provides professional education, and fosters the development of the work force. It has spillover and growth-pole effects for the whole industry of the host country. Consequently, the plan of the U.S. Secretary of the Treasury James Baker, presented at the annual meeting of the International Monetary Fund in Seoul in October 1985, proposes that the volume of foreign direct investment in the developing countries should be increased parallel to the external transfer of resources via fresh money. The present strategy of adaptation should be enriched by growth-oriented elements. The 1986 financial package for Mexico is a first test of this new strategy.

Prerequisities for Foreign Direct Investment in LDCs

The Process of Internationalization

The world economy today is concentrated in three major regions: the United States, Japan, and Western Europe. When the so-called newly industrialized countries (NICs) in the Third World are also considered, the present status of the world economy can be characterized as a polycentric order. In the competition between these regions, it is only those enterprises that are able to strengthen their technological and managerial capacities that can survive. Shorter product life cycles and a fierce competition in research and development between all nations demands larger market potentials. This increasing importance of capital-intensive technologies and the high speed of their evolution result in high expenditures for the enterprises involved and force management to optimize the use of its entrepreneurial capacities. As a consequence, only contemporaneous worldwide market penetration is able to secure the required cost minimization. Otherwise, the high start-up and running costs involved in the modernization and restructuring of factories, research and development centers, and marketing forces will not be sustainable. The home markets are too small to amortize the investment costs at this increasing speed.

The Entrepreneurial Strategy

Each entrepreneurial strategy provides first for the development and use of exclusive capacities and the strengthening of this competing advantage over other competitors. These advantages may exist in technology, in organizational and managerial know-how, in innovatory capacities, or in product differentiation. In transnational corporations, they may be a consequence of the fact that affiliates of these corporations are able to use worldwide resources and the experience of the enterprise as a whole.

In a second step, a decision has to be made whether these core skills should be internalized by way of direct investment or externalized by way of cooperation with other independent enterprises.

The traditional forms in which cross-border transfer of resources takes place are trade and foreign direct investment. The market-economy approach to alleviating the present problems of the world economy requires new forms of international transactions, which to a large extent make possible global cooperation, with a new sharing of investment risks, control, responsibility, and profits, as well as a combination of the transfer of capital, technology, and goods. Such new forms of international investment are, for example, licencing contracts, subcontracting, consulting contracts, cooperation contracts, and joint ventures. There are also new kinds of export financing, such as barter trade, compensation contracts, contract packages, and turn-key and repurchase contracts. These new forms of internationalization are appropriate to reduce the transaction costs of cross-border resource transfer. Growing forms of protectionism support internal transfers inside a transnational corporation network instead of external transfer of resources between unrelated parties.

The question of whether internalization or externalization is more suitable for the enterprise concerned can only be answered with respect to the relevant local market. This is the third step in the entrepreneurial strategy. The enterprise has to find the best possible combination between its own entrepreneurial advantages and the local-specific advantages of the host country. In this respect, the size of the relevant market, the competition, and the degree of regulation are of prime importance.

The Host-Country Strategy

From the viewpoint of the host country, the choice between external transfers of resources (between two unrelated parties) and internal ones (within transnational corporations) depends on its own entrepreneurial capacity to use the resources. External transfers between unrelated parties are only favorable if the recipient in the host country is in a position to use the transfer object in an optimal way. If the transfer is financed through the international money markets, the products should be internationally competitive in order to receive hard currency. Most of the developing countries, therefore, need a marketing and distribution network in the global market to achieve their plans to gain financing facilities in order to repay their debts.

Many developing countries sought to protect their domestic industry against foreign competitors by high tariffs. In this artificial situation, entrepreneurs were not forced to adapt their industries to world market competition standards. Today, the LDCs are mainly successful in industrial sectors with a low technological profile—for example, the leather, shoe, steel, textile, machinery, and electrical industries. Also, capital-intensive technologies where the production technique is mainly standardized and does not sustain considerable electronic development are sectors in which these countries have advantages. On the other hand, in high technology industry, only foreign direct investment can lead to a successful position in the world market, because it is based on specific know-how in research and development as well as on important financial and managerial capacities. Moreover, the investor bears the risk in amoritizing an investment.

When considering the host-country strategy of increasing exports, one must not forget that there exists today a strong current of opinion in the industrialized countries in favor of measures of a neoprotectionist character. Technological progress leads to a painful process of economic structural adaptation. The ensuing high rate of unemployment and social unrest brings entrepreneurs and trade unions together in demands for the implementation of import quotas and other protectionist remedies to salvage the domestic industry.

Many countries prefer, in times of a constantly expanding economic adjustment process, to implement neoprotectionist measures, not realizing that they cannot protect these failing industries against international competition. The idea of free world trade and globalization is only supported if benefits can be shown for local industry. Politicians tend to have the next election in mind and are thus sometimes unable to stand against requests from trade unions and entrepreneurs for protection. For instance, the European Community regulates and subsidizes the production and marketing of agricultural products, reduces the price of export goods, and impedes imports. Other examples are the coal, steel, and textile markets.

Such a policy cannot be successful in the long run. A rise in exports and the securing of foreign markets can only be achieved if the recipient country has enough foreign exchange to finance its imports. The recipient country must therefore be in a position enabling it to sell its products on foreign markets. In this respect, what the world economy needs is not one-way–traffic national economic policies to encourage each country's own exports and to impede imports, but reciprocity for free world trade.

The Impact of the Draft Code of Conduct on Transnational Corporations for Foreign Direct Investment in LDCs

The Competition between LDCs to Attract Foreign Direct Investment

There exists today a highly competitive market for foreign direct investment. In this market, natural, economic, technological, political, and legal factors can be distinguished in the conditions for investment, although it is not possible to draw a clear borderline between these items. These investment conditions taken together form the specific host-country "offer" for a potential investor. Foreign direct investment will only take place if host country strategy and entrepreneurial intentions act in unison. The investor will use the package of production factors only if it is the best fit with its own entrepreneurial strategy when compared with the investment conditions of other competing host countries. With the exception of the legal factors, a host country cannot change its investment picture in a short period of time. The legal structure is therefore a key element in attracting or hindering foreign direct investment. It enables the host country to compensate for and balance out possible disadvantages in its natural, technological, political, or economic investment conditions. The more unattractive its factor market for foreign direct investment may be, the more it is obliged to offer legal investment incentives to foreign investors.

The Importance of the Draft Code of Conduct for the Formation of the Legal Investment Conditions

The Investment Contract as Legal Framework for the Investment. Increasingly, the main instrument for the regulation of foreign direct investment in LDCs is the investment contract between the host country and the foreign investor. In this contract, the investor and the host country can optimize the specific aims of the investment. They can minimize the investment risks and focus the contract on the economic development goals of the host country.

The investment contract therefore enables the harmonization of the host-country strategy with the entrepreneurial intentions. The traditional hierarchic model of investment regulation is replaced by a market-economy–oriented process of establishing a consensual determination of the specific investment conditions. The principal aim of the investor is to gain appropriate profits and to minimize risks. The intention of the host country is to make the investment useful for the process of developing the national economy.

One of the main problems in negotiating the terms and conditions of the investment contract is to find common legal values that are acceptable both to the host country and to the investor. Most legal systems are not adapted to international transactions. They were developed for national transactions, and the various conflicts of laws and systems do not smooth the negotiating process in the final drafting of an investment contract. In international negotiations, the choice of law is a sensitive factor because one contracting party has to renounce its own well-known legal system. There are other problems which may hamper the conclusion of an investment contract, such as the lack of relevant statutes, information problems in respect to existing legal norms, and the difficulties of inforcing the existing investment contract against a parent company abroad.

The Function of the Draft Code of Conduct

Overview. An important attempt to overcome these difficulties is the United Nations Draft Code of Conduct on Transnational Corporations. Other noteworthy codes include the Tripartite Declaration on Multinational Enterprises and Social Policy by the International Labor Office and the United Nations Conference on Trade and Development (UNCTAD) "Set of Multilaterally Agreed Principles and Rules for the Control of Restrictive Business Practices." There are also two special codes of minor importance concerning breast-milk substitutes and the utilization of pesticides. Still being negotiated is the UNCTAD Draft Code on the Transfer of Technology.

These codes establish multilaterally acceptable investment standards at the international level. They can therefore play an important role as a GATT for international investments. This is particularly true of the Draft Code of Conduct on Transnational Corporations. This code already corresponds in its structure to an investment contract as it distinguishes in its two major parts between the duties of the investor and those of the host country. It deals with almost all relevant investment topics, such as general and political questions, ownership and control, balance of payments and financing, transfer pricing, taxation, competition and restrictive business practices, transfer of technology, consumer protection, environmental protection, disclosure of information, nationalization, and compensation, as well as jurisdiction. It creates a fair balance between the partially differing interests of the investor and the host country. In the fields of labor law, transfer of technology, environmental protection, consumer protection, and antitrust law, it is supplemented by the other previously mentioned special codes and drafts.

The Draft Code and the Formation of Investment Contracts. The Draft Code of Conduct builds a basis for the negotiations between a foreign investor and the host country. Because of the differences between the legal systems of industrialized and developing countries, it is important to avoid solving such conflicts in unilateral favor of one contracting party. In this respect, the Draft Code contains guiding principles for the interpretation of international investment contracts. Moreover, the code creates an internationally accepted system for the consensual determination of investment conditions.

The guiding principles of the Draft Code show differing degrees of concretization and differentiation in their single components. According to the intensity with which each particular topic is treated, the code can either offer a concrete model for the contractual fixing of the investment conditions or, as a minimum, present the contractual scope of the final agreement. The Draft Code of Conduct thus forms a basis for the negotiation of investment contracts in accordance with internationally accepted values. These principles are the starting point for further specification of the investment conditions. Moreover, they address themselves to the transnational corporation as a whole and preclude the danger resulting from the fact that the national legal order can only be made effective within its own territory.

The Influence of the Draft Code of Conduct in Alleviating the Debt Crisis. The United Nations Draft Code of Conduct also has an influence at the macroeconomic level. By making foreign direct investment easier, it seeks to improve the investment climate in LDCs and to strengthen worldwide free trade. In this respect, it plays an important role in the necessary increase of foreign direct investment in debtor countries according to the Baker Plan. This will remain true even if final agreement on all provisions of the code cannot be achieved.

After a phase of repression in the 1970s, foreign direct investment is regaining importance in developing countries. The less developed countries have recognized that it can help them to overcome their serious financial problems and to reduce the technological gap between them and the industrialized countries. Today, competition exists among those applying for foreign direct investment. In this competition, those countries whose local investment conditions fit best with the entrepreneurial strategy have the best chance. The investment conditions of the host country can be separated into natural, technological, economic, political, and legal elements. Of special importance are the legal investment conditions because they are the only ones that can be created and modified within a short period of time. These conditions must fulfill the difficult task of harmonizing the investor's interest in minimizing the investment risks and gaining appropriate profits with the host country's aim of making the investment as useful as possible to the domestic economy. The United Nations Draft Code of Conduct is, through its structure and its content, able to support this process and can therefore serve as a guide for the creation and interpretation of the investment contract between the host country and the investor.

Part III
Chinese Policies and Experiences

12

The Economic Environment and China's Model for the Utilization of Foreign Capital

Zhang Yangui

E ver since the adoption of the open door policy at the Third Plenary Session of the Eleventh Central Committee of the Communist Party of China, the utilization of foreign capital has become one of the important forms of China's contact with foreign countries in terms of funds, materials, technological exchanges, and economic cooperation. The choice of a strategic model for China's use of foreign capital is becoming more and more significant.

A Survey of Foreign Models

As a component of a country's strategy for foreign economic relations and trade, the use of foreign capital can be classified into four types:

1. The import-substitution type whereby foreign capital is used to increase the products of the country's basic and backbone industries, which will eventually take the place of their import. These industries, thus boosted, will in turn pave the way for the successful realization of the overall strategy for developing the country's economy and trade.

2. The export-promoting type whereby, as the primary strategic objective, foreign capital is used with a view to developing export-oriented industries and increasing labor-intensive production. Success in this objective will help accumulate abundant foreign exchange and consequently give a push to the nation's economic take-off.

3. The export-substitution type, which acts as a catalyst in the transition of the export of labor-intensive products to that of technology- and capital-intensive ones.

4. The resource-exploiting type whereby foreign capital is applied to the exploitation of the country's rich natural resources, stimulating the ex-

port of agricultural and mineral products, in particular processed products. By doing so, a great amount of foreign exchange and internal funds can be raised for the introduction of a variety of relevant technology and equipment. All this will serve the purpose of diversifying the industrial structure through the export of the country's natural resources.

The determination of a type that can constitute a strategic model unique to the country, then, depends to a great extent on the external and internal economic environments, including the economic management system. Other decisive factors include the level of economic growth, industrial structure, natural-resource endowments, labor force, and size of GNP. The last variable is closely related to the size of the home market and the capacity of the international market to absorb the export of the country's commodities and labor. It follows that the larger the size of GNP, the lower the capacity. In short, all these factors must be taken into consideration when we formulate our own strategic model for using foreign capital.

External and Internal Economic Environments for China's Use of Foreign Capital during the Period of the Seventh 5-Year Plan

So important are these environments that they will exert a formative influence on the form of foreign capital utilization within a specific model, its macro-management, the structure of the sectors using foreign capital, and their geographic distribution. Some features of the international economic environment in the latter half of the 1980s related to China's use of foreign capital are as follows:

1. The growth rate of the world economy will increase faster than in the first half of the decade, which will provide China with a more relaxed external environment.

2. Most of the foreign direct investment of the developed countries (which is uneven in its geographic distribution) is made among themselves, while approximately 90 percent of the rest is concentrated in 22 developing countries and regions. It should be remembered, of course, that some developing countries, such as India and China, with a vast domestic market and a fairly good industrial foundation, are attracting ever-increasing foreign direct investment. Be that as it may, the difficulty in this respect dictates that we should formulate a reasonable strategic model for the use of foreign capital that can accommodate a large amount of indirect investment.

3. Great changes have taken place in the geographic distribution of foreign direct investment of the United States, which remains the world's biggest investor. In the 1960s and 1970s, that investment found its way mainly into Canada and Western European countries. However, the increase in investment in those areas in the 1980s, if any, is insignificant. In contrast to the declining trend in Latin American countries, direct investment in the Asian Pacific area is on the increase. Moreover, this increasing momentum will continue in the latter half of the 1980s. This investment priority of the United States is undoubtedly beneficial to China, but its disadvantages should not be overlooked. As China's current economic reform and open door policy have been in motion only since the late 1970s, a problem meriting our attention is whether China can compete with other developing countries in the same area in attracting foreign capital and whether it can do so without heavy socioeconomic cost. All this demands that China's model for using foreign capital should not simply copy any purely inward/outward-oriented framework, nor should it give priority to equity investment.

4. The direct investment of the developed countries in the different sectors of the developing countries has been restructured. Before the 1970s, the majority of investing countries invested in the main in sectors engaged in the exploitation of natural resources and the primary processing of their products. Since the 1970s, however, the proportion of investment in manufacturing industry has been increasing. This change in sector structure will continue in the latter half of the 1980s. Unlike that of the other developed countries, Japan's investment in the exploitation of the natural resources of the developing countries, though on the decrease, still constitutes the major part of its foreign direct investment. In view of different priorities of foreign investors, China should make use of foreign capital in resource-developing sectors and in the manufacturing industry (the processing industry as it is termed in China).

5. The amount of funds raised by international bonds considerably exceeds consortium loans, owing to high interest rates and the debt crisis, resulting in diversified means of international financing. Correspondingly, China should, to some extent, adapt its model for using foreign capital so as to secure more loans in diversified ways and through various channels. This is facilitated by the good credit of Chinese banks that deal in foreign exchange and preferential terms.

6. International trade is becoming "softened" and "technological" (in the sense that the percentage value of material factors such as raw materials and fuels will be reduced and trade in finished products of ordinary industries will be at a relative standstill), whereas trade in high technology products and technological trade such as licence agreements will increase. The new trend in world trade requires China's strategic model to be elastic so as to make China's export commodities also "softened" and "technological."

With regard to the internal economic environment that will act on China's model for using foreign capital in the latter half of the 1980s, three aspects should be mentioned:

1. Because of its vast territory, China's economic development varies greatly from region to region. Its population, though great in number, is of low cultural and technological quality. Its natural and agricultural resources, though second to few countries in terms of the total amount, are scarce compared to the world average in terms of per capita share. Although rich in mineral resources, its western part lacks the human and agricultural resources possessed by its eastern part, which is in turn poor in mineral resources. Although there is a good foundation for economic growth, China's energy, transportation, communications, and raw materials can hardly meet the aim of quadrupling the total output value of industry and agriculture by the end of this century. Short of infrastructure facilities and funds, its industry and technology in general remain at a low level. Nevertheless, many of its industrial products are quite competitive (potentially) on the international market. Advanced as its socialist system is, its economic management system needs improving and restructuring. All these conflicting factors exercise a strong influence on the long-range strategy of China's economic development, its model for using foreign capital, and the relations of the components of the strategic model.

2. A number of breakthroughs in China's economic restructuring have been made in the past few years. For example, the forms of ownership and business operations have been varied, the vitality of enterprises strengthened, and enterprise policy-making power expanded. Market regulation in the pricing of industrial products and means of production is bringing about their reasonable circulation, while horizontal economic cooperation between the different sectors is beginning to take shape. The practice of state allocation and purchase of agricultural products has primarily been replaced by the market mechanism under the guidance of the state plan, which is conducive to the adjustment of the agricultural setup and the development of a commodity economy in the country. These ever-increasing elements of a new system brought about by the breakthroughs have created an internal environment favorable to our use of foreign capital, the introduction of technology, joint sponsorship of enterprises, and overall cooperation with foreign countries. They also stand China in good stead in holding and tapping its international market, particularly the market for agricultural and side-occupations produce, their processed products, and light and textile goods. These breakthroughs, coupled with China's general condition, suggest that the strategic model for using foreign capital should contribute to its opening to the outside world in multilayers, through multichannels, and in varying forms. The fourth, on the other hand, indicates that foreign investment in the

agricultural resources and related light and textile industries sectors can bring much greater economic results than the others, earning enough foreign exchange to pay off the principal and interest of foreign investment incurred in the light of the import-substitution type.

3. As envisaged by the Seventh 5-Year Plan, China will undergo further changes in its strategy of economic development in the latter half of the 1980s. Five of these concern the use of foreign capital: (a) the change from the stress on quantitative increase to emphasis on improved efficiency; (b) the change from the extensive type of expanded reproduction to the intensive type; (c) the change from the adjustment of the structure of agriculture and light and heavy industries to that of primary, secondary, and tertiary industries; (d) the further implementation of the open door policy; and (e) the bringing into full play of the distinctive advantages of the eastern, middle, and western parts of China on the basis of the adjusted relationship between the coastal and interior regions. The first two changes require that the makeup of the strategic model should be beneficial to the introduction into China of advanced technology and critical equipment. The third makes it necessary to give investment priority to infrastructure facilities and material industry. The fifth makes it clear that China's use of foreign investment should be differentiated in terms of geographic distribution. The fourth shows that China's model should help to expand the extent of its opening to the rest of the world in the decades to come.

Suggestions for China's Strategic Model for Using Foreign Capital during the Seventh 5-Year Plan

The analysis of the four types of utilization of foreign capital in connection with the internal and external environments leads us to the conclusion that, in determining China's strategic model, no single type can be adopted as it stands, despite the fact that different regions and sectors in China may have the necessary conditions for any particular one to be functional. Inevitably, there must in practice be some overlapping and coordination among them. China's eclectic strategic model, after all, should distinguish itself in its composition. In this connection, the import-substitution type will function as the dominant component of the strategy, the export-stimulating and resource-exploiting types will serve as the basis, and export-substitution will be a supplement. This model is in keeping with the implementation of China's open policy by multilayers, through multichannels, and in varying forms during the period of the Seventh 5-Year Plan. The rationale of the strategy is spelled out as follows.

Why is the import-substitution type in basic and mainstay industries regarded as the dominant framework? There are three reasons.

First, China, as a country with a vast territory and very large population, enjoys a big home market, particularly a potential one, the capacity of which can be matched by no other national market in the world. If China's export volume per capita corresponded to Japan's, it would equal the total world volume. What is more, China's proportion of import or export trade, which accounts for 12 percent of Japan's GNP, is not high compared to that of other countries. At any rate, China's export volume would be such that it would obviously be beyond the capacity of the world market. Therefore, China's foreign trade and its strategic objective in using foreign capital will have to be geared to its domestic needs from a long-term point of view, particularly so through the end of the twentieth century.

Second, an outward-oriented type of use of foreign capital is usually based on a high level of economic development and a sound market mechanism. China's economic growth, though on the increase, will remain at a low level for several years. By the same token, although more breakthroughs in economic reform (such as an improved market system) can be expected, it takes time to have a perfect market mechanism.

Third, as expounded earlier, China's economic strategy will be reoriented through the adjustment of the structure of agriculture and light and heavy industries to that of primary, secondary, and tertiary industries so as to ensure that infrastructure facilities such as energy, transportation, and post and telecommunications are commensurate with direct production sectors. For this purpose, a number of key projects will be launched. To complete these projects with good quality and high efficiency, China will in the main rely on its own efforts, but a considerable amount of foreign investment and technology also needs to be assured as a necessary supplement. Foreign investment should be used to the advantage of various measures aimed at modernizing the structure of China's industries. Given the circumstances, the import-substitution–led strategy for using foreign capital can best be applied in these projects.

In the final analysis, China can make use both of foreign funds and of nonequity investment in the import-substitution type. It can exploit to the greatest extent possible the characteristics of the international economic environment (that is, the uneven geographic distribution of foreign direct investment, easier inflow of foreign funds and nonequity investment rather than equity investment, and the increasing accumulation of funds through international bonds). The strategy dominated by the import-substitution type will help attract and accommodate a greater amount of indirect investment.

The export-promoting type for the light and textile industries and the resource-exploiting type for the agricultural and mineral sectors constitute the basis of China's strategic model for the following reasons.

China, with its enormous labor force and relatively low wage level, enjoys an international comparative advantage in developing these labor-intensive products and in promoting the export of light and textile products. But in terms of machinery, electrical products, and instruments, China does not, and will not by the early 1990s, have this edge. Consequently, the expansion of the export labor-intensive products and of labor will become one of the most profitable means of increasing exchange earnings. In addition, the advantage in labor force—in combination with the sizable number of technological personnel, the processing capacity of the coastal areas and industrial centers, and transportation facilities—will give an impetus to the processing and assembling industries. The increased foreign exchange will, of course, add to the introduction of foreign advanced technology and equipment.

Needless to say, increasing the export of the labor-intensive products of light and textile industries cannot provide a support for the import-substitution framework for the simple reason that agricultural and mineral products account for a great share of China's exports. (Oil, for example, brings in a quarter of the total export revenue.) The introduction of foreign capital and technology with a view to developing China's natural resources and exports will necessarily form the basis of its strategic model. Will the increased export of resource products, then, come into conflict with one of China's general conditions (that is, that its natural resources are rich in terms of total amount but poor in terms of per capita share)? The answer is no, for China's level of economic growth will remain low and the demand of its population for natural resources will be limited for several years. This also accounts for the continuous increase in the absolute amount of exported agricultural and mineral products since the founding of the People's Republic. Although the proportion of primary and labor-intensive products in international transactions will decrease through around 1990, their absolute amount is on the increase. And we can be optimistic about the prospect that even a slow pace will not affect the increase of the export value of China's light and textile goods and its resource products.

In the strategic model, the processing sectors (such as machinery, electricity, and instruments) play a complementary role in the use of foreign capital because of the reorientation from the adjustment of the structure of agriculture and light and heavy industries to that of primary, secondary, and tertiary industries. In secondary industry, China's material and processing industries are out of proportion, with the latter greatly exceeding that of countries with the same per capita income. Its products are, at present, mainly home-market–oriented and of poor quality, but of high production cost. Something must be done to redress this imbalance. Under the circumstances, if the major thrust in using foreign capital is aimed at the processing sectors, their products cannot be expected to accomplish the export-substitution objective. Moreover, the introduction of foreign investment into the processing sectors will bring pressure to bear on the home market beyond its capacity, while the imbalance between the basic and raw-material industries on the one hand and processing industries on the other will increase.

As our eclectic strategic model is, in principle, made up of a combination of the four individual types, there crops up the problem of their coordination and, related to this, the coordination of the different forms of using foreign capital, its geographic distribution, invested sectors, and macromanagement. Different forms are easy to coordinate in that each type is characterized by its own special form. As a result, the eclectic strategic model will diversify ways of using foreign capital and the channels for attracting it. In terms of geographic distribution, the internal economic environment makes the eastern part of China the major area for investment. It is also in the vicinity of the major capital-exporting countries such as the United States and Japan, and it has formed close ties with the economically emerging countries in the Asian Pacific area.

The coordination of the sectors using foreign capital, on the other hand, depends on their input/output types, the amount of internal and external capital needed, and their ability to pay.

The complexity of the macromanagement of foreign capital utilization lies in the coordination of its administrative management and market regulation. The solving of this problem has a direct bearing on the successful implementation of China's strategy. Since the coexistence of the old and new structures is unavoidable, China should put all projects involving foreign capital under the state plan. Depending on their priority, some key projects should be subsumed under the state mandatory plan (subject to administrative management) and others under the guidance plan, giving play to the market mechanism. All things considered, the successful coordination of all the factors within the strategic model relies on the active and steadfast reform of the economic structure, including that of the management of foreign economic relations and trade, during the period of the Seventh 5-Year Plan.

In conclusion, China's strategy for using foreign capital is one of multiple objectives. This import-substitution–led strategy is different in nature from the strategy based soley on import substitution. This is because the other three objectives can minimize and overcome the defects caused by import substitution, thus making China's eclectic strategy beneficial to its opening to the outside world, introducing foreign investment and technology in different ways and through different channels, and modernizing its commodity composition and technological and industrial structures, as well as turning the inward-oriented circulation of the national economy into an inward- and outward-oriented pattern.

13

Transnational Corporations and China's Economic Development

Wang Zheng Xian

That the multinational enterprise (MNE) has become a positive and livening element in the modern world economy is no longer of any doubt.[1] Since China adopted the policy of opening to the outside world, it has constantly paid attention to the development of foreign inward direct investment, especially in the form of joint ventures. But some issues of substance have yet to be made clear, both for the good of China and for the benefit of foreign investors.

China as a Host Country

Since 1979, there has been much discussion of the policy and environment of foreign direct investment in China. Writers usually classify host countries into developed countries and developing or less developed countries (LDCs). Among the latter, China has been correctly grouped with the socialist or communist countries. Though this is perfectly logical, it could easily ignore China's uniqueness in other respects that are no less important. For example, though Vernon pointed out the heterogeneity of developing countries, he only touched on the policy side of the Chinese situation before 1978, as though policy was dominated wholly or mainly by political considerations.[2] However, as has already happened in China and elsewhere, policies can be changed almost overnight, but the other nonephemeral characteristics cannot. Four salient features of vital importance must be firmly borne in mind by economists, policy formulators, and foreign investors: (1) China is not only a socialist state but also a much underdeveloped one economically; (2) it has over 1 billion people; (3) it has a huge expanse of territory with regions at extremely different levels of economic growth;[3] and (4) for thousands of years, China has had feudal traditions. People usually recognize the first, but are apt to ignore to varying degrees the other situations, which are even more important from the point of view of successful take-off.

A huge population means a huge potential domestic market. According to Hochmuth in his 1985 review of John Dunning's *International Production and the Multinational Enterprise,* Dunning had already noticed this point when he emphasized the difference between Taiwan, Hong Kong, and Singapore and those newly industrialized countries (NICs) with large and growing internal markets, such as Mexico and Brazil.[4] Compared with other large internal markets, the case of China is indeed unique, an important fact that can never be overemphasized. Likewise, the fact that it is a large country with regions so different in levels of economic growth has considerable development policy implications. Since it is a socialist country urgently in need of take-off, its leaders must always think of the nation as a single entity. As to China's feudal ideology and traditions, these have unfortunately become, almost without being noticed, the greatest stumbling blocks in the way of its modernization drive,[5] and they have already displayed themselves in the field of foreign inward direct investment (FIDI).

It must be added that for a long time China suffered from leftist tendencies and wrong economic policies that gathered such momentum that their remnants have yet to be cleared away.

Problems of Strategy

To welcome or not to welcome FIDI, that is the question. Economists have long tried to use (social) cost–benefit analysis to solve this probem, either for the country as a whole or for a single project. But Robock and Simmonds have noticed that "the quantification of costs and benefits remains a highly ambiguous subject."[6] Dunning also admitted the difficulty of making generalizations about costs and benefits of foreign direct investment, and he identified other considerations worthy of notice.[7] Dymsza (quoting Wells) in 1984 and Stoever in 1982 also noted the shortcomings of this kind of analysis.[8] In my opinion, cost–benefit analysis should not be resorted to in the study of FIDI in China for two reasons. First, for reasons of structure and the lack of a market mechanism, the concepts of opportunity cost and shadow prices can be very vague indeed.[9] Furthermore, for the country as a whole, some very important and beneficial but unquantifiable indirect effects have arisen from FIDI since China opened to the outside world.[10]

Foreign observers have correctly noted that China's motivation for setting up joint ventures is better access to technology and foreign markets.[11] This is fully verified by the provisions promulgated by its State Council on October 11, 1986. The need for technology and exports has been the motivation for the drive for FIDI of all developing countries since the 1960s. Yugoslavia is a good example,[12] leaving aside those Asian developing countries and districts.[13] In the case of China, however, the point in regard to export has caused much confusion, which has to be sorted out.

Many economists in China have advocated export-orientation as a route for Chinese economic development, a strategy with which the author cannot agree. Instead, on the basis of the specific and unique conditions just set out, it is import-substitution in a broad sense that should be advocated.[14] In my view, the development of the domestic market should be given top priority in China's economic development. From this stance, three points follow. First, if the report by the United Nations Centre on Transnational Corporations gives a true picture of the three basic phases of industrial policy within which MNE subsidiaries have operated for the world as a whole, China presents an exception or a special case in which the third phase of export-oriented industrialization will never appear or should not be allowed to appear.[15]

Second, the expansion of the domestic market would suit most or even all foreign investors, especially those U.S. companies entering into joint ventures in China for the purpose of serving foreign markets.[16] But it must be remembered that China's immense market is only a potential one at present; China's propensity to consume can only increase as a function of its economic growth. Furthermore, as a less developed country, it is short of capital and does not wish to suffer from a permanent balance of payments deficit although it is striving to develop foreign economic relations. Those who are farsighted enough to see this point will gain from long-term cooperation with the nation. As to those urgent market-seeking investors who cannot wait, they can still benefit by entering into joint ventures even if they are asked to export a lion's share of the product. Joint ventures can easily dispose of their products in China if they can find the market, provided they can swap the exports through countertrade arrangements. Stewart rightly raised the central issue of finding "an organization which can cross the barriers between Chinese organizations so that a linkage can be offered for import and export of totally unalike products."[17] Perhaps joint ventures might be established to cope with this situation, and we can take it as a necessary evil if this is regarded as a step backward from the viewpoint of the classical theory of trade.

Third, it does not seem reasonable to welcome MNEs with high import propensities. Since China is an underdeveloped country rich in resources, backward linkage of joint ventures should always be encouraged.

Considering its characteristics, China cannot make use of FIDI to solve its employment problem. China cannot achieve this objective by establishing Special Economic Zones. This conclusion will remain the same even if it can establish joint ventures in the coastal cities, because there will be a limit set for FIDI (as will be discussed further). It must be borne in mind that China's employment problem is different in nature from unemployment problems in the West. Writers touching on this point usually relate it to the expansion of export as a means of increasing employment, apparently making use of the export multiplier.[18] But, as a planned socialist economy, China must not resort to "beggar-thy-neighbor" policies in order to solve its balance of payments problem. Furthermore, owing to the reasons just set forth, the export multiplier would not be able to operate fully in China at present.

What should a heterogeneity of regions mean to the FIDI policy of such a large country as China? Evidently, it will negate the hypothesis put forth by non-Chinese writers whereby the FIDI activities of a developing country are divided into several stages, because such a hypothesis assumes a country to be a homogeneous territory from the point of view of economic growth. For example, Stoever suggests five stages in this respect.[19] As a matter of fact, all five, with the possible exception of the fifth (outward investment) may suit different regions of China. As will be discussed shortly, the ability of a country to absorb FIDI is closely related to its level of economic growth. The same is true of the different regions of a country such as China. That is why the Chinese government has divided the country into different zones, from along the coast to inland, for FIDI arrangements. The remaining question is how to lessen the gap between the economically advanced and the backward regions.

How much FIDI should China have every year? It does not seem difficult to answer this question. Dunning has tried to demonstrate with statistical data that there is a strong relation between a country's per capita FIDI and per capita GNP.[20] Reuber et al., also noticed a correlation between the two, as did Caves.[21] This is quite logical in theory. According to Healey's study of the ratio between debt service and exports, based upon the data of 60 countries in 1968, 55 countries had debt service smaller than 20 percent of exports, and only 5 countries greater than 20 percent.[22] This conclusion could be taken to mean that this ratio should best be kept between 15 and 20 percent. It might be suggested that China could increase FIDI heavily as soon as it succeeds in expanding exports. For example, Taiwan Province had a record of an annual export rate of 22.8 percent during 1960–69.[23] Why not China? some economists asked. This is, of course, by no means feasible. It has been shown elsewhere (1) that there is a certain ratio between the rates of increase in annual export and annual GNP; (2) that, taking the world as a whole, the two rates are roughly equal; (3) that the larger the country, the smaller the ratio between exports and GNP; and (4) that when the economic growth of an underdeveloped country reaches a certain level, its per capita export will decrease. Thus, it is impossible for China to follow the example of Taiwan Province or any other small, export-oriented economy in the increase of exports, and, consequently, it is not possible for China to increase FIDI beyond a certain limit.

From what countries should China expect its FIDI to come? This may not be a problem at all. As soon as any investor can accept China's conditions, the nation should welcome it, no matter what the country of origin. However, Wells long ago noted the peculiar strengths of Third World MNEs: knowing how to reduce imported inputs, how to adapt products to environments, how to keep operating costs low, and how to deal with governments in a feasible way. Some of them have even set up foreign operations to supply export markets in the industrialized countries.[24] Jenkins in his review also remarked that, apart from the preceding ideas, Wells (in a later work) and Lecraw noticed that Third World MNEs are engaged in more labor-intensive production. Since NICs still have in their memories their lessons and experiences during the period of take-off, investors from those countries definitely understand the needs of less developed countries better than those from other countries. Experience in China shows that investors from Hong Kong, Macao, and Singapore—and ethnic-Chinese investors from other areas—usually have a better chance of success. This is understandable since they are more familiar with the cultural background, have no language problem, and can make use of their kinsfolk or friends to improve access. On the other hand, investors from advanced industrial countries have also received much attention from China owing to their possession of high technology, the strength of their companies, and their ability to take risks. On the whole, however, it seems that China should pay more attention to Third World MNEs. If possible, it might also welcome investors from Taiwan Province.

The Investment Environment

For the past few years, China has been hauled over the coals by foreign investors because of its investment environment. Ruggles, based on the experience of U.S. investors in China, has noted three sets of factors—institutional, structural, and regulatory—that constitute hurdles in the way of foreign direct investment in China.[25] He also listed quite a number of unpleasant phenomena and malpractices that do not seem to be his own fabrications. Dunning long ago pointed out that a powerful industrial nation investing in a socialist less developed country may bring forth more tensions than otherwise. Could this be taken to mean that all the unpleasant hurdles did not come unexpectedly? A popular complaint raised by investors abroad is the freakishness of China's investment policy and of the "numerous other bodies whose unseen power of veto is raised as the discussions progress."[26]

Evidently, to welcome FIDI, China must create a good investment environment. Hence, it must have a good diagnosis of the problems encountered. In my opinion, apart from the socialist system, the main causes of problems are the following: (1) Affected by leftist tendencies and dogmatism, for a long time after liberation China paid attention to social and political policies at the expense of economic policies. This, coupled with the experience of the turbulent years, caused a downturn in the management of its economy, so that it has almost no common language with foreign business people. (2) Since liberation, it has ignored the development of human resources. (3) Malpractices have been rampant. (4) China has an utter lack of legal and law-abiding traditions. (5) Feudal ideologies have remained firm in Chinese minds. The following can be at least partly ascribed to this: the concept of natural economy, the division of China's economy into almost watertight compartments and regions, the "special-privilege" mentality, nepotism, the dominance of seniority, and the concepts of the "iron rice bowl" and "big communal pot." Among these five interrelated causes, the first three could be comparatively easily done away with within a short period of time through restructuring, economic reforms, and the strengthening of party discipline. The last two can only be eradicated through a long-term educational process, a fact that should never be overlooked.

In conclusion, I believe that because of China's long-term closed economy, a sudden open-to-the-outside policy will certainly bring forth problems in the investment environment. But there is no reason to believe that these circumstances will last forever, and China should be allowed to reform and to carry out experiments. For example, I am sure that foreign investors will soon discover that corruption, low efficiency, malpractice, and bureaucracy are neither a product of its socialist system nor something inherent in the Chinese race. I quite agree with Barry Richman when he remarked in 1976 that MNEs could serve as a catalyst for achieving greater understanding between the East and the West, and that the mutual benefits derived could outweigh the negative effects and problems involved.[27]

Notes

1. In this chapter, I adopt a broad definition of transnational corporations or MNEs and avoid the sophisticated Harvard Business School definition. However, Gupta's division into two categories—classical multinationals and joint ventures (JVs)—seems helpful in the discussion of MNEs in China.

2. See Vernon, Raymond, *Storm over the Multinationals* (Cambridge, Mass.: Harvard University Press, 1977), pp. 164 et seq.

3. The first three points have been fully discussed in another paper by the author (Wang, Z., 1985).

4. See Dunning, John H., *International Production and the Multinational Enterprise* (London: Allen & Unwin, 1981).

5. This topic is discussed in another paper.

6. See Robock, Stefan H., and Simmonds, Kenneth, *International Business and Multinational Enterprise* (Homewood, Ill.: Irwin, 1983), p. 237.

7. Dunning, John H., op. cit., pp. 380–82.

8. See Dymsza, William A., "Trends in Multinational Business and Global Environments: A Perspective," *Journal of International Business Studies* (winter 1984);

Stoever, William A., "Endowments, Priorities and Policies: An Analytical Scheme for the Formulation of Developing Country Policy toward Foreign Investment," *Columbia Journal of World Business* (fall 1982).

9. For example, in 1983, a pupil of mine, Wu Neng Quan, tried to use the formula presented in a textbook (Root, 1978, p. 570) in a study of joint ventures in China for his M.A. thesis, but I found that there could be a net gain in almost every case, no matter what opportunity cost and shadow price values we chose.

10. This point is to be further discussed in a separate paper by the author.

11. Daniels, John D., Krug, Jeffrey, and Nigh, Douglas, "U.S. Joint Ventures in China: Motivation and Management of Political Risk," *California Management Review* (summer 1985): 51.

12. See Holt, John B., "Joint Ventures in Yugoslavia: West German and American Experience," *Michigan State University Business Topics,* vol. 21 (spring 1973), reprinted in *MSU International Business and Economic Studies, International Business* (1975).

13. See Healey, Derek T., "Foreign Capital and Exports in Economic Development: The Experience of Eight Asian Countries," *Economic Record* (September 1973). Note that in Western publications, Taiwan and Hong Kong have often been grouped as developing countries. This can be tolerated only on a de facto basis or for convenience in discussion.

14. This point was discussed in detail in Wang (1985).

15. United Nations Centre on Transnational Corporations, *Transnational Corporations in World Development: Third Survey,* Chinese ed. (New York: United Nations, 1983), p. 195.

16. Daniels, John D., et al., op. cit., p. 48.

17. Stewart, Sally, "Countertrade in China," *Euro-Asia Business Review* (January 1986): 27.

18. See Chen, Edward K.Y., *Multinational Corporations, Technology and Employment* (London: Macmillan, 1983), chapter 6.

19. Stoever, William A., "The Stages of Developing Country Policy toward Foreign Investment," *Columbia Journal of World Business* (fall 1985): p. 5.

20. Dunning, John H., op. cit., chapter 5.

21. Reuber, G.L., Crookell, H., Emerson, M., and Gullais-Hamonna, G., *Private Foreign Investment in Development* (Oxford: Clarendon Press, 1973); Caves, Richard E., *Multinational Enterprise and Economic Analysis* (N.Y.: Cambridge University Press, 1982).

22. See Healey, op. cit., p. 400.

23. Healey, op. cit., p. 402.

24. Wells, Jr., Louis, "Third World Multinationals," Econimic Intelligence Unit, *Multinational Business,* no. 1 (1980): 12 et seq.

25. Ruggles, Rudy L., "The Environment for American Business Ventures in the People's Republic of China," *Columbia Journal of World Business* (winter 1983).

26. Ruggles, op. cit., p. 69.

27. Richman, Barry M., "International Corporations and the Communist Nations," *Management International Review,* vol. 16, no. 3. (1970). Reprinted in *MSU International Business and Economic Studies, International Business* (1977).

14

Transnational Corporation Investment in China: A View from the Outside

S. J. Nournoff

C hina is now in a period of "consolidation and study" aimed at summing up the experiences since the historic 1978 decision of the Third Plenum of the Eleventh Central Committee. What has led to this decision for consolidation and study?

In part, the balance of payments situation reveals a need for adjustment:[1]

Balance of Payments (U.S. $)
1981 − 0.07 billion
1982 + 30.55 billion
1983 + 8.36 billion
1984 − 1.09 billion
1985 − 13.70 billion
1986 − 6.85 billion (projected from first 6 months)
    − 12 billion (projected from first 9 months)
1990 − 7.00 billion (Prime Minister Zhao's trade estimate)

Foreign exchange reserves also display some deterioration:[2]

Foreign Exchange Reserves (U.S. $)
1984 + 16.50 billion
1985 + 12.00 billion
1986 + 10.34 billion (as of March)

It is abundantly clear that China, as part of the Third World, shares the common experience of the level of productive forces being below that required for self-sustained growth. The historic legacy of feudalism, semifeudalism, and mutant capitalism combined with imperialism has contributed to this phenomenon, which is present regardless of the social system in control of the Third World state. While the socialist states of the Third World are in a better position than the rest in the group to overcome the historic limitations of small-scale production, the objective existence of corresponding productive forces must be recognized. Socialism is not the sharing of poverty, but rather the systematic establishment of the concrete material conditions necessary for prosperity with equality. The failure to fully recognize this has resulted in errors at both levels, of both theory and practice. Xu Dixin accurately portrays immature socialism as a period of two coexisting forms of (1) public ownership—and (2) collective and social—*with principles specific to each stage*. It is also necessary to point out, as Xu does, that the imperfect correspondence of productive relations with productive forces further inhibits the development of those productive forces.[3] From this, one can distill the following principle: in the historic tradition from one mode of production to another, the productive forces are dominant; within a given mode of production, however, the relations of product may, under certain circumstances, need to be revolutionized in order to free the forces of production for further development.

General Economic and Social Conditions

For the role of TNCs to be properly evaluated, it is first essential to briefly survey the current situation. The gap in per capita GNP between China and the advanced countries is estimated to be growing by between 2 and 3 percent per year.[4] In order to catch up by 2050, per capita income would have to rise annually on the average between 5.5 and 6.5 percent.

With 70 percent of China's population still engaging in agriculture, it is clear that for the foreseeable future, this sector will remain the linchpin of development. If one accepts the assumption that one-third of the present agricultural labor force is superfluous, this is no mean task. To set this agricultural sector in context, it must be recalled that China has 20 percent of the per capita cultivable land of Japan and less than one-half the per capita cropland of India.

Rural income varies significantly throughout the country. Notwithstanding this, real per capita income increased by 80 percent between 1981 and 1985, with production growing by 10 percent per annum. Self-sufficiency replaced reliance on the outside for grain and cotton.[5] Simultaneously, the proportion of rural poverty decreased from 31 percent of the rural population in 1979 to 13 percent in 1982 (poverty being measured as 2,185 cal per person per day).

These beneficial changes, however, have not been cost-free. With cash market value increasingly dictating crop choice, a 60-million–ton feedgrain shortfall is projected for 2000, representing 12 percent of total grain production and one-third of feed grain requirements. Grain production in 1985 was 380 million tons, 7 percent below the 1984 level.[6] Although the average gross output per agricultural worker will almost double between 1981 and 2000, the gap between rural and urban incomes is expected to grow. The proportion of brigades covered by health insurance decreased from 81 percent in 1975 to 58 percent in 1985. Fertilizer imports doubled between 1979 and 1983, contributing to very rich crop yields. However, though nitrogen-rich, these fertilizers were poor in potassium and phosphorous, resulting in a long-term problem of soil depletion. Chinese-produced nitrogenous fertilizers are both low in quality and unstable, thereby compounding the problem.

While a fourfold increase in agricultural production has been targeted for 2000, it must be understood that if the urban–rural income differential is to be stabilized at a ratio of 2:1, the relative price of crops must increase by 17 percent between 1981 and 2000. Diet composition is also projected to change by the end of the century, with animal-product consumption increasing from 6 to 15 percent of the diet. Two facts are significant here: (1) an increase of 10 percent in animal products is equivalent to the disappearance of 35 to 40 percent of cultivated land and (2) one kg of meat contains 25 percent fewer calories than one kg of grain directly consumed.

China's industrial growth compares most favorably with that of other Third World countries. Notwithstanding fluctuations, the per annum rate of growth between 1957 and 1982 was 8.5 percent, and, even during the 1965–74 decade, manufacturing as a percentage of annual fixed investment rose to 40 percent. In the 1981–85 period, light industry grew by 10 percent per annum, state revenues doubled, workers' income increased by 20 percent per annum, and 6 million new jobs were created each year.[7] As impressive as this last figure is, it pales in comparison with the need to absorb 140 million people into the job market between 1985 and 1990 (30 million new job entrants, 10 million workers from the reconsolidation of collective enterprises, and 100 million workers released from the agricultural sector). This would require 26 million new jobs per annum.

China is the world's fourth-largest energy producer and third-largest energy consumer. It employs 2.5 times more energy per gross domestic product dollar than the world average.

With 20 percent of its total population being students, China is far ahead of most Third World countries when primary school enrollment is calculated. There is a drastic drop, however, in the postprimary school sector, where China lags behind other Third World countries. This characteristic is accentuated when we note that the gross enrollment ratio in secondary school dropped from 40 percent in 1980 to 30 percent in 1982.[8] It is also of significance that, in the rural areas, the lower the income level, the smaller is the percentage of postprimary enrollment, especially for girls. In addition, there is a noticeable decline in students attending schools designed to train skilled workers. This is of particular significance if we recall that the percentage contribution of education to national income in the United States between 1927 and 1957 was 33 percent, while for Japan between 1930 and 1955, it was 25 percent.

It is clear that each new initiative generates its own contradictions that must be squarely faced. 1985 saw the rate of inflation climb to 12 percent, the highest it has been since 1949.[9] The economy has become overheated. In 1985, the rate of growth was 22.8 percent while a rate of only 7 percent was called for in the Seventh 5-Year Plan.[10] If the goals targeted for the year 2000 are all to be met, serious attention will have to be given to the side effects.

Role of Foreign Trade

Two clear principles emerge when we examine the role of foreign trade and the role of foreign inputs: (1) domestic resources are and will continue to remain central to China's development, with foreign inputs in a bolstering role, and (2) expanded foreign-exchange–earning exports are the key to expanding direct purchase and indirect acquisition of foreign inputs.[11] As Professor Teng Weizao has said, "you cannot buy modernization."[12]

The composition of China's exports has demonstrated a marked shift.[13] The share of agricultural products in total exports declined from over a half in 1955 to one-fifth in 1979. By the 1980s, manufactures constituted the bulk of exports.[14] While China's foreign trade doubled between 1978 and 1983 to $40.7 billion, technology and equipment made up 37 percent of the $18.5 billion import component, and machinery exports comprised only 4 percent of the $22.4 billion total on that side of the ledger.[15] It was observed in 1983 that China's export of mechanical and electrical products, instruments, and meters totalled only 0.14 percent of world exports of these items.[16] The 1985–90 target of a further expansion of 40–50 percent can only be achieved if the three-point strategy (improving the mix of exports from primary to finished product, expanding the international market, and arranging for the production of export commodities) is realized.[17]

Objectives of Foreign Investment and TNC Involvement

The involvement of foreign capital is seen within the context of a two-pronged general strategy:

> To supplement self-reliance (although this term itself is under some dispute owing to its previous use as a euphemism for autarky) in line with absorptive and repayment capacity

To balance two types of investment: (1) big project, long-term, low- or no-interest investment with long-term payoff probability and (2) small-scale projects of a short-term, immediate-payoff nature.[18]

The specific goals of the process have been articulated as (1) to absorb advanced technology and management with a view to improving quality, quantity and both energy and material efficiency, (2) to technically upgrade existing enterprises with the aim of reducing investment while increasing the rate of return, (3) to increase exports and foreign exchange earnings, and (4) to train local personnel, both technical and managerial.[19]

A number of areas have been targeted as key elements in the economic renewal process. The weak links have been identified as energy, communications, and transportation, while farming, forestry, animal husbandry, and fishing have been characterized as inadequately developed. Technical renovation priority has been set in five industries (iron, steel, nonferrous metals, machine building, and chemicals), while areas where supply is short are consumer goods, materials for construction and packaging, urban infrastructure, and public utilities.[20]

In response to these needs, technology acquisition through state allocation of foreign currency was $600 million in 1983, $1.56 billion in 1984, and approximately $5–6 billion in 1985, not including energy and transportation.[21] To this must be added the $16 billion of joint venture capital invested as of 1986. In total, China absorbed between $23 and 24 billion between 1983 and 1986. This is significantly above the $12 billion figure cited by Prime Minister Zhao in 1984.[22] The total must be set against the fact that in 1978 China went beyond its absorptive capacity when $7.8 billion was invested in 22 plants.[23] The penalties to Germany and Japan alone for cancelling the next phase of the Baoshan steel complex came to well over $120 million. The full magnitude of the problem during this period can best be understood if we recall that more than one-half of the plant and technology imported between the early 1970s and the end of 1980 was shipped in during 1980.[24]

During the final three years of the Sixth 5-Year Plan, a three-year rolling plan for technology import was adopted, aimed at integrating 3,000 items of foreign technology. (The rolling plan will bridge the two 5-Year Plans—1985–1987—and is aimed at national and sectoral priorities with input from local authorities and end users.) In 1983, the first year of this plan, 80 percent of the $600 million worth of equipment was of advanced design.[25] For the period of the Seventh 5-Year Plan (1986–90), some new priorities have emerged. Computer software, advanced technology and key equipment have been emphasized, combined with a commitment to progressively reduce the employment of foreign components, to avoid the long-term use of foreign exchange to import raw materials, and to institute an import licencing system to avoid the duplication of imports.[26] These last three points must be seen as an expression of the existence of significant problems in these areas.

Transnational Capital and China

Given the background just described, it is clear that in the current phase of socialist development, the key factor requiring remedy was the underdevelopment of productive forces. Once the semiautarky of the earlier approach had been rejected, it was necessary to craft a new stage in the period of transition of immature socialism plus a new mechanism for acquiring and integrating appropriate technology. This stage is a new form of state capitalism differing in character from both the New Economic Policy in the Soviet Union and the New Democratic period in China.[27] This new stage might conveniently be called the *stage of socializing capital*. This occurs simultaneously with the entry of the capitalist mode of production into a new phase of globalization, concentration, and integration. This is not meant to remotely imply systemic convergence, but rather to explain the conjuncture of opportunity that lies behind the policy.

This stage of socializing capital is predicated on a number of assumptions, the most prominent of which are:

1. The need to integrate within the shortest possible time the cutting edge of the most advanced technology and technique.
2. The provision of inducement to those possessing these properties through the opportunity to benefit from unequal exchange (read; make profit) while eliminating the conditions perpetuating that unequal exchange—in other words, the recognition that China will be exploited for a limited time, but during that time constructing the conditions to eliminate that exploitation. Poverty left unaddressed is also exploitation. The choice is consequently seen, not as one between exploitation and nonexploitation, but rather between exploitation with a plan to overcome it versus the exploitation of permanent poverty.
3. Uneven development between regions of the country, with some areas inevitably leading the way, to be followed by those areas in the second tier.
4. The functioning of the leading regions, in the words of Prime Minister Zhao Ziyang, as a double window—one looking to advanced foreign experiences and the other looking to the other parts of China.

While a comprehensive assessment of China's experience may be premature, I should like to address the following three areas, on the basis of research conducted in 1981 and 1985: (1) uneven development, (2) negative experiences with transnational capital, and (3) positive experiences in integrating transnational capital. Even in these areas, there is no pretense of anything more than an indication of the general direction.

Uneven Development

The problems of uneven development, unbalanced growth, and the emergence of a dual economy are well-known features in the literature on the Third World. As a matter of policy, China is committed to uneven but shared development. Recently, the policy was expressed in the following fashion. The push will be from the eastern economic region to the center and, last, to the West. The East is to concentrate on new methods and techniques for both old and new industry that are knowledge- and technology-intensive and that will produce high-quality consumer goods. The central economic region is to undergo a two-stage process. In the first stage, energy, iron, nonferrous metals, phosphorous, and building materials are to be emphasized, to be followed by a knowledge- and technology-intensive second stage. The western economic region is to pursue farming, forestry, animal husbandry, transport, local resources, processing, and the manufacture of products for the national minorities.[28]

The thrust of policy initiatives, however, must be seen in the context of the historic background of the unevenness itself. In 1980, 62 percent of industrial production, 57 percent of gross agricultural output, and 75 percent of exports were concentrated in the municipalities of Beijing, Shanghai, and Tianjin and in Liaoning, Hebei, Shandong, Jiangsu, Zhejiang, Fujian, Guangdong, and Guangxi provinces. By 1982, 45 percent of the national industrial plant facilities were also concentrated in these localities.[29] Of the 3,000 units designated as priority units for modernization, one-third were in the Beijing, Shanghai, and Tianjin municipal areas.[30] This geographic distribution was further compounded by the initial policy of allocating foreign exchange. The foreign exchange quotas were linked to the amount provided prior to the institution of the reforms themselves. It was clear that on this basis those who had high allocations before were to continue to receive those allocations and consequently were in a better position to improve their future foreign exchange earnings, which in turn became the basis for determining the new allocation.[31] The fourteen open coastal cities also became the prime beneficiaries of the state capitalist sector, including foreign-investment and technology-transfer projects numbering 1,400, valued at $1.85 billion in 1985 alone.[32] Decentralization of decisionmaking certainly has its positive aspects, but concomitantly it has given further priority to the open cities. Tianjin and Shanghai can independently authorize projects up to a $30 million limit,

Dalian and Guangzhou up to $10 million, and the other ten up to $5 million, qualified only by the fact that if foreign currency is involved, the Planning Commission, the Economic Commission, and the Ministry of Foreign Economic Relations and Trade have a role. Other cities are left with the policy of no limit if a project is totally foreign-financed, with a product not covered by the state plan, marketed by the state, or having a fixed quota.[33]

The test of overall policy must be seen in its implementation. The proposal of the Central Committee for the Seventh 5-Year Plan called for correcting the relations between different regions.[34] Within two weeks of the publication of the proposal, a foreign investors' conference was convened in Lanzhou, resulting in $1.27 billion in agreements for the western region. Xue Muqiao, in commenting on the importance of the conference, stated: "The gap between east and west is growing because the state gives investment priority to the east."[35] In the final analysis, how can the degree of success of the policy be measured? In broad terms, I suggest in two ways: (1) the extent to which technology is transferred from the initial recipient to the interior and (2) the degree to which the gap in both per capita productivity and income is being narrowed between the more advanced and less advanced parts of the country. While my sample is limited, it may nonetheless be indicative. The extent to which technology transfer has occurred is reflected in table 14–1.

In addition, Shanghai appears to have the most developed plan, being responsible for the Shanghai Economic Zone comprising the four neighboring provinces of Jiangsu, Anhui, Zhejiang, and Jiangxi, as well as being designated as the national pivot for technology dissemination. In 1984, Shanghai had 779 projects under the Technology Cooperation between Mu-

Table 14–1
Technology Transfers in China

Advanced Area	Less Developed Area	Technology Transferred
Jiangsu	Inner Mongolian A.R.	Woolen textiles
Beijing	Tibet	Machine tools
Wuxi-Tianjin-Beijing	Inner Mongolian A.R.	Cake, candy, beer, food processing, chemical fertilizer, textiles, paper
Tianjin	Qinghai	medicine
	Taiyuan	steel
	Xinjiang	aluminum
	Qinhai	carpets
	Shanxi	bicycles, plus training of 200 students in exchange for long-term low-cost coal
Guangzhou	Interior provinces	textiles
Shanghai	Hainan Dao	Design, installation and supervision of rubber tire factory
	Sichuan	upgrading of textiles
	Hubei	clocks
	Inner Mongolian A.R.	wool

nicipalities, and between Municipalities and Provinces program. In addition, contacts have been directly established between enterprises in backward areas and Shanghai for the purpose of improving equipment and product quality. Unfortunately, requests have been relatively few from the three high-priority areas of Yunnan, Ningxia, and Xinjiang, and those that have been forthcoming are mostly in the food and clothing sectors.

The various methods for arranging technology transfer may be summarized as follows:

1. Natural-resource development:
    (a) Exchanging raw material for technology transfer and the training of a specified number of students
    (b) Investment of an agreed amount in exchange for raw material.
    (c) Coproduction agreement, whereby the developed area pays for financing a project in an underdeveloped area in exchange for preferential treatment on price and supply.

2. Profit sharing in exchange for technical and personnel assistance:
    (a) The developed area will receive one-third of enterprise profit over 10 years.
    (b) The developed area will receive at least 10 percent of enterprise profit.
    (c) The developed area will receive 5 percent of enterprise profit for a period of 4 years.
    (d) An internal joint venture agreement is signed in which the developed area provides resources, technicians, and expertise, while the underdeveloped area provides buildings and labor.

3. Salary inducements:
    (a) Workers from advanced areas receive three times their normal salary to work in an underdeveloped area.
    (b) High salaries plus the defraying of local expenses.
    (c) Payment of 450 Yuan per month.

4. Short-term development program management consulting arrangement between more advanced and less advanced units.

5. Experimental trial production organized and paid for by an advanced unit in an underdeveloped area.

6. The acquisition by an advanced area of foreign patent rights that are in turn resold to an underdeveloped area.

7. Advanced areas engage in compensation transfer with underdeveloped

areas by providing technical assistance in exchange for the end product after the production line has been fully installed.

8. Advanced areas train middle school, college, and university students as well as workers and specialized engineers from underdeveloped areas for a consideration.

The general trend revealed by these examples is quite positive, but the scale is far too small. The major deficiency from an operation standpoint is of a somewhat broader nature. The signals from the center need to be more precise in establishing priorities. When localities are instructed simultaneously both to learn-adapt and transfer advanced foreign experience, and to earn foreign exchange as rapidly as possible, cadres will inevitably overemphasize the latter. In earning foreign exchange, there is an immediate and tangible payoff—but in transferring technology to less developed parts of the country, the payoff is less visible. Export earnings are employed to develop new export earnings. Balanced growth is given rhetorical expression, but the newly acquired technology is never quite shared with the interior. Once markets are secured for a new product, they are seen as permanent sources of revenue, not to be shared with other parts of the country. The desire to dominate a market becomes explicit. The fact that only 1 percent of foreign exchange was allocated for technology transfer to the Inner Mongolian Autonomous Region (A.R.) is ample evidence of the problem. This problem is further exacerbated when we note that official policy indicates that, when a conflict emerges between domestic and foreign sales, it should be resolved in favor of foreign sales.[36]

There must obviously be a balance between technology acquisition and the sharing of benefit. One of the lines that emerged at the June 1985 Chengdu Academic Conference on the theme of balanced growth is questionable. Development cannot take place simultaneously in all parts of the country. Unevenness is a general feature of the current period. This having been said, it is equally incorrect to continuously postpone significant technology transfer on the grounds that it is premature. If the pace of transfer is inadequate, administrative intervention from the Center may be required. Passively relying on requests from underdeveloped areas should give way to active promotion through the more formal process of twinning both industries and regions.

The most promising sector in the underdeveloped regions is clearly mining. It is important to recall that China ranks first in tungsten, tin, antimony, zinc, titanium, tantalum, and rare earths, and it has some of the largest reserves of lead, nickel, mercury, molybdenum, niobium, copper, and bauxite.[37] While the infrastructural investment would indeed be substantial, it would surely be offset by the benefits of a forward processing and manufacturing sector.

Negative Experiences with Transnational Capital

China's 1978 decision to open to the outside world directly exposed it to the century-long cumulative experience of multinational capital.[38] To paraphrase an old Chinese saying: "This was like sending a goat and a dog to fight a tiger." China was at a substantial disadvantage, with little experience except for direct-purchase or turn-key acquisitions. China was, and is, a Third World country, and was dealt with by multinational capital in full recognition of that fact.

In 1981, still very much in the shakedown period, there were ten major negative features of the China–multinational-capital relationship.

1. China was the recipient of outdated and backward technology.
2. The value of foreign technology was greatly overestimated.
3. China was the recipient of some of its own exported components as part of full production lines.
4. Contracts were vaguely worded, especially concerning fee-payment schedules and raw-material supply.
5. The inexperience of the Chinese negotiators, whose skills were more in the area of foreign language than in economics, was fully exploited by the multinational-capital side.
6. The Chinese side was undervaluing its contribution to joint ventures, as foreign capital was employing a "commodity price" and the Chinese side a "socialist price."
7. Compensation trade agreements were signed that denied the Chinese side any share of profit until full payback had taken place.
8. Inadequate specifications provided on foreign-supplied equipment required the fast assembly of inspection teams travelling abroad at substantial cost and project delay.
9. Chinese nonparticipation (sometimes at China's own request) in foreign marketing resulted in profit loss and the failure to gain marketing experience.
10. Joint ventures were proposed whereby foreign equity contribution would be limited to patent rights transfer, while the Chinese side was to be responsible for cash contribution plus operating capital guaranteed by the Bank of China.

A Few Examples

A few detailed specific examples should suffice to illustrate the issues during that period.

The Remi-Martin (HK)/Tianjin Wine Joint Venture. The Remi-Martin (HK)/Tianjin wine joint venture reflected multiple problems.

Pricing. The Chinese side undervalued their capital construction and infrastructural contributions, calculating value on the basis of a noncommodity price.

Profit Distribution and Marketing. As a consequence of the Chinese side's noninterest in foreign marketing, the final distribution of profit was not proportionate to each side's equity contribution. With 38 percent of equity, Remi-Martin (HK) earned 2.37 times the profit of the Chinese side, which held 62 percent of the enterprise equity. (See appendix 14A for detailed calculations.)

The Chinese side subsequently requested a reopening of negotiations on the distribution clause of the contract, which was rejected by Remi-Martin (HK). The only agreed-to modification in terms permits the Chinese side to increase its share for the internal market from 10 to 30 percent. This, however, is only a verbal agreement.

Transfer Price. A multi-year agreement was concluded to supply bottles from an Australian company linked to Remi-Martin. While it is not clear what a competitive bid price would have been, the matter should have been investigated, but was not. It is of course perfectly proper to raise the question of how Remi-Martin, or any other company for that matter, is to be compensated for its technology transfer. In the first instance, technology transfer is folded into the "price" set on equipment and related technical support, expressed through the value of equity contribution. In addition, ancillary support, supply, and anticipated profit provides further compensation. Market penetration, opening up further prospects of gaining profit, adds to the value. In sum, technology transfer is compensated for by the opportunity of making profit.

Two Steel Projects. The Wuhan Iron and Steel Works contracted with the Japanese for the acquisition of equipment without addressing the issue of compensation to the Chinese side if major innovations in the equipment were introduced. Chinese engineers had, in fact, made major improvements in the Japanese equipment, requiring a new round of negotiations to determine the extent, if any, of compensation. This was subject to a determination in Japan of whether the Japanese were prepared to integrate Chinese innovation into their entire production process.

While a great deal has been written on the appropriateness of the Baoshan steel complex, there are some features of that experience that are germane to our current consideration.

Equipment supplied was not up to specifications.

Untested and experimental equipment was provided.

Deliveries were short by as much as 10 percent.

Many components were shipped in as part of a package that could have been supplied at a cheaper price from within China.

Watches and Shirts Ventures. Outmoded and overpriced technology was further apparent in Chengzhou and Wuxi. An export-oriented electronic watch factory was acquired by Chengzhou in 1978 at a cost of U.S. $290,000. By 1981, the factory had virtually closed with the total investment at risk as there were no orders. In some senses, the equipment was outmoded at the time of installation. Product style and production techniques were simply unadaptable to a rapidly changing international market.

The Guang Ming Shirt Factory project in Wuxi illustrated similar problems in the area of packaged technology. The foreign partner was responsible for providing equipment for an entire workshop as well as for marketing control. Three difficulties emerged:

The equipment included some components originally manufactured in China and carrying a markup of 19 percent above the original sales price.

Some of the components were locally available at a cheaper price.

Some of the equipment was second-hand, resulting in delayed production pending arrival of new replacements.

The municipal level plays no significant role in project planning. The responsibilities of the municipalities are limited to fulfilling the quota and the repayment of loans. In addition, while Beijing states that local municipalities can sign contracts on their own initiative, this right is exercised only at the provincial level and not the municipal level.

Repayment agreements for foreign-financed projects also revealed problems. The same Guang Ming shirt project was for foreign finance to be repaid in 3 years. While the factory met its obligation 9 months ahead of schedule, the modality for arriving at the per unit value was questionable. A "floating formula" was agreed to by both sides. The price of the commodity was to be readjusted semiannually at the Guangzhou Fair, while the interest rate on the capital borrowed from abroad (70 percent of the capital outlay) was to be readjusted monthly by the Bank of China. The original price was $20 per dozen, rising to $30 by the conclusion of repayment. Interest, on the other hand, rose in the same period from 7 percent to between 17 and 20 percent. The asymmetry of adjustment periods is self-evident. Among the more bizarre repayment proposals is one that emerged during discussions over installing a major nuclear power facility in Guangdong. The Hong Kong side claimed that, as the main generator would continue to be productive after the expiration date of the joint venture, a share of profit should be reserved for them until the plant ceased to be productive. This was most fortunately not accepted.

Export of Labor. Since 1979, five hundred workers from the Tianjin region have been sent abroad in two general groups: (1) foremen and seamen and (2) technical cooperation workers. Their average stay has been 2 years, although this has recently been shortened to one year. An experimental program has been instituted for sending individuals (cooks) abroad for one-year terms with an optional extension of one year. In addition, dozens of individuals have been sent to Japan for experience. The wage scale for this group is extremely low, 50–80 Yuan per month plus overtime and bonus.

Two significant problems have arisen from the export of labor.

1. Individuals going abroad and then reintegrating into their old units obviously bring back skills that can be selectively applied to improving the work of the unit. Teams of workers assembled to work on technical cooperation projects, however, present a somewhat different problem. After completion of their assignment and the return home, this team is disbanded and workers go back to their previous units. The organizational skills gained as a consequence of working in a larger team are nullified if the workers are dispersed back to their old units.

2. Large-scale contracts that were signed (as in the case of the United States) or under negotiation (as in the case of western Canadian farmers) carry with them potentially very damaging effects. In light of the high level of unemployment in the recipient countries, the use of Chinese workers would be seen as a method for driving wages down and breaking the trade unions, the ultimate effect being to increase unemployment among local workers. In addition, it would fan the racism latent within these countries. The use of these labor teams in other Third World countries with a low ratio of skill to population deprives these countries of the opportunity to increase their own economic independence by acquiring those skills. Chinese promotional material circulated in East Africa in the mid-1980s, offering low wages and guaranteed labor peace, is also very damaging.

The Special Economic Zone in Xiamen. The newest operative Special Economic Zone, in Xiamen, exhibited an interesting innovation in dealing with foreign investment as well as some unresolved problems. The arrangement with the R. J. Reynolds Tobacco Company permitting the Chinese side to use their new line of cigarette-producing machines without charge is a potentially significant precedent. China gains the processing fee for the production of Camel cigarettes ($1 million) as well as skill acquisition through the production and marketing of its own independent brand.

Another positive aspect of the Xiamen experience can be found in the Xiamen garment factory. Fifty percent of production is consumed locally, and 50 percent exported. This balance reflects a coordinated approach that may be applicable in other sectors; the nation gains foreign exchange and the Chinese consumer gains the direct benefit of improved production techniques.

Still, serious problems in Xiamen can be detected:

While China receives a processing fee of $1 million for the production of Camel cigarettes, there is an absence of information on the profit made by R. J. Reynolds. A study on cigarette price structure proposed by a member of the economics department of Xiamen University was rejected by local administrative authorities.

The conscious policy of competing with Shenzhen in drawing away companies already established in that zone may be counterproductive.

The construction of apartment house complexes in Xiamen, with the right of overseas Chinese to have their relatives in any part of China transferred to Xiamen in exchange for such construction, can result in speculative activity.

The joint venture for TV and video equipment displayed two weaknesses: (1) Permitting the Japanese to be in charge of the technical side without insisting on the training of Chinese personnel placed the process outside both Chinese control and the ability to master these techniques in the shortest period of time. (2) Selling the products only within China until the Japanese agree to sell to the outside market prevented China from gaining any foreign exchange earnings.

An Overview of the Negative Experiences

Two final observations are warranted for this 1981 period.

1. Some cadres dealing with foreign businesspeople have used the opportunity for personal gain:
   (a) by "borrowing" vehicles such as motorbikes from foreign residents,
   (b) by having hard currency deposits made in a Hong Kong bank or other foreign bank in the name of the official or a relative,
   (c) by financing education abroad for a relative,
   (d) by receiving personal gifts.

2. Some representatives of Chinese export corporations are depositing money in the foreign accounts of local businesspeople or government

officials in exchange for placing orders for the purchase of Chinese goods.

While many of the problems were adequately addressed between 1981 and 1985, some remain unaddressed and new ones have surfaced.

Cost of Equipment. The Quing Hai County granite quarry on Hainan Dao accepted the foreign partner's unsubstantiated claim that the value of its equipment contribution was $1.42 million (U.S.), only to find within a year that the value on the open international market was no higher than $700,000 (U.S.).

Marketing. The Quing Hai County granite quarry agreed to a unit price of $19 (U.S.) per square foot of finished granite, while the international price was $50 (U.S.) per square foot.

The Hainan Dao nylon zipper factory signed a cooperative coproduction agreement with the provision that 70 percent of the product should be exported. The foreign partner violated this provision and, in the absence of a penalty clause, the factory was required to turn to the internal market. While product demand is high, anticipated export earnings are not forthcoming. Foreign marketing brokerage fees were found to be prohibitively costly.

Taking over direct marketing after the foreign side has violated its agreement has also proved costly for the Hainan Dao granite factory. They anticipated a profit, but are now confronted with anticipated losses of 600,000 Yuan per year between 1985 and 1990.

Outmoded Technology. The Hua Nan Computer Company in Guangzhou acquired a solar computer line from France at a cost of $12 million (U.S.) in addition to 30 million Yuan. Sales have been 10 percent of capacity owing to the microchip revolution, which was foreseeable at the time of acquisition. The blending of technology and documentation by the French side as 40 percent of value did not permit an adequate evaluation of the package.

Consulting Agreements. Consulting contracts signed with the Stanford Research Institute (U.S.), Albert of Germany (F.R.), and Nomura (Japan) did not include a Chinese training component.

Contract Terms. Because the Hainan Dao granite factory failed to include a penalty provision, it was confronted with the expenditure of foreign exchange for spare parts when the foreign partner failed to accept responsibility for repairs.

Compensation trade agreements should specify production. Hainan Dao granite found itself locked in another controversy, claiming its maximum annual production was 50,000 square meters, while the foreign partner made a counterclaim of 80,000 square meters.

Pressure. The palm oil industry on Hainan Dao was subjected to the threat of investment withdrawal unless the proposed site of the venture was changed, despite adverse local experience. The site was altered and the results were poor.

Flooding the Market. Ningbo's plan in late 1985 to open a color TV joint venture would have brought the national total to more than 75 such factories—notwithstanding the fact that 3 years earlier, the Center limited the Fujian-Hitachi facility to 230,000 sets (despite its 300,000 set capacity) and prohibited Fujian from shipping to other provinces.[39]

These seven points are essentially linked to foreign exploitation of China's inexperience. There are, in addition, a variety of internally generated conditions that compound the issue.

Cost of Export Earnings. In mid-1985, the average expenditure to earn one U.S. dollar was between 3.8 and 4.5 Yuan, while the official exchange rate was 2.88 Yuan per U.S. dollar. Each dollar earned might be said to have incurred a loss of between 1 and 1.7 Yuan.

Local Financing. In the absence of adequate coordination between the Bank of China and local investment and trust corporations, foreign corporations simply seek local guarantees after having been turned down by the Center (such as the Bank of China).

Internal as Opposed to External Purchasing. For example, Hainan Dao purchased a satellite relay station from Italy rather than from a factory in Chengdu, where technically equivalent equipment was both available and competitive in price.

Chinese purchasing agents of the Shanghai-Foxboro joint venture insisted on the purchase of Hong Kong components until the American general manager pointed out that the "foreign" product about which they were so enthusiastic was in fact made in China.

Sale to the Interior of Acquired Technology. Enterprises in coastal cities have sold technology they have acquired to less developed areas of the country at substantial profit. Guangzhou reproduced a fast noodle factory at an initial cost of 900,000 Yuan and, after selling 80 of them, reaped a profit of between 14,000,000 and 23,000,000 Yuan.

Expanding Productivity prior to Market Survey. The Inner Mongolian A.R. expanded local carpet manufacturing and, in the absence of a foreign market, was forced to close twenty factories.

Sharing Technology. The unwillingness of one Guangzhou textile factory to share its technology with another resulted in the expenditure of foreign exchange for both, the first from Germany (F.R.) and the second from Italy.

Infrastructural Planning. The expenditure of 400 million Yuan for an up-graded port facility in the expectation of heavy usage was not borne out by the 20 percent employment of its 26.7 million ton capacity.

Inadequate Supply. The Guang Mei Food Company in Guangzhou was confronted with both an absence of a reliable supply of bottles for its soft drink line and a less than reliable source of electric power.

Center-Local Consultation. Significant inflation resulted from the failure on the part of the Palm Oil Plantation and Processing Corporation to consult with the Hainan Dao authorities before committing 120,000 mu of land to foreign development. There was an excessive drain on resources as land prices rose in relation to the new demand.

Cooperative Coproduction Agreements. In the absence of legislative protection, there is an unwillingness on the part of foreign investors to take advantage of this investment form.

Acceptance of Penalty. Failure to pay compensation in light of cancelling the contracts for the Sharp IC calculator, reverse cycle heater fans, and telephones on Hainan Dao resulted in some uncertainty abroad.

Commitments. Unwillingness to honor sight drafts owing to Hainan Dao's difficulty in 1985 further complicated the ability of the District Administration to encourage appropriate foreign acquisitions.

Positive Experiences with Transnational Capital

It is clear that the Chinese record in coping with transnational capital has not been one-sided. Some of the most prominent features on the positive side have been loans from the state; retention of foreign exchange; phased production; import cost/export earnings balance; mixed form of payment and investment; systematic decrease of foreign dependency; local development mix; step-by-step expansion of development zones; environmental protection; and technical assistance fees.

Loans from the State. In upgrading existing productive capacity, the state has provided loans for new technology acquisition at interest rates as low as 5 percent to be repaid within a five-year period. This has proved particularly effective with intermediate-level technology where a relatively brief training period of approximately 6 months is required.

Retention of Foreign Exchange. Units without a historic foreign exchange earnings record may retain 25 percent of foreign exchange gained from foreign sales. The No. 3 Textile Mill in Hohhot has been the beneficiary of both this retention and loans from the state.

Phased Production. In a high tech production line, a multiphase approach has proved extremely effective in the step-by-step process of acquiring worker and management skills. The Polaroid Shanghai 20-year project is organized in three stages: production of parts, sale of parts to the United States, and introduction of a full-production assembly line.

Import Cost/Export Earnings Balance. Neutralizing high tech import cost through a buyback provision has been successfully realized in Shanghai's contract with General Electric for engine production.

Mixed Form of Payment and Investment. The development of mixed forms of payment and investment has been most effectively achieved in two ways:

Shanghai and Volkswagen have adopted a three-part payment formula where part of the cost is paid in Yuan, part in foreign exchange, and part in a percentage of production and/or earnings from export. Initial production will be 30,000 vehicles, rising ultimately to 300,000, supplemented by an additional 100,000 engines of which 70 percent will be exported.

Ningbo and Shanghai have begun to coordinate investment policy, sharing cost, risk, and benefit. In addition, several unit within the same jurisdiction (Guangzhou Trust and Investment Corporation, Guangzhou First Industrial Corporation, and Guang Mei Food Company), have joined with a single foreign partner to expand the Guang Mei facility.

Systematic Decrease of Foreign Dependency. The necessity of acquiring technology from abroad and the need to develop local capacity in order to reduce this dependency are reciprocally linked. Shantou has developed a plan to produce locally 80 percent of superwave probe components by 1988.

Local Development Mix. In determining local acquisition priorities, it is essential to have a complementary mixture that:

emphasizes needed technology consistent with the local skill level,

links with more advanced experience from another part of China,

introduces nonproductive activity only to the degree that is required to initiate productive activity.

The Seven-Point Development Mix of Ningbo, concentrating on intermediate to heavy production, is far better than the mix in Hainan Dao (where 47 percent of foreign investment is in the nonproductive sector, with that percentage continuing to grow) and Tianjin (where five major projects in 1984 were in the tertiary sector). On the other hand, Hainan Dao's use of Shanghai engineers for its tire factory is excellent.

Step-by-Step Expansion of Development Zones. The Ningbo Technical and Development Zone is scheduled to cost 2.5 billion Yuan for its 3.9 square kilometers, and its Guangzhou equivalent, 28.8 billion Yuan for its 9.6 square kilometers. Each of these zone programs has been divided into stages whereby one stage must achieve a self-sustaining level before initiation of the subsequent stage.

Environmental Protection. There is no ambiguity at the policy level on the issue of protecting the environment.[40] On the operational level, however, there are mixed signals going to foreign investors. Ningbo has begun construction of a water-purification facility for the entire Development Zone, while Guangzhou has privately let it be known that it will not require pollution control as part of submissions made for project development.

Technical Assistance Fees. IBM Japan has proposed to waive its fee to the Hua Nan Computer Company in Guangzhou if the Chinese side fails to develop its independent capacity within a designated period of time.

Conclusion

When the decision of the Third Plenum of the Eleventh Central Committee was announced in 1979, it was clearly anticipated that the record would be a mixed one. No one expected the road to be easy, yet the problems confronting China were enormous and had to be addressed. Each historic stage has its own particular features, mediated by the unique historic experience of each society. An ever-narrowing orthodoxy was becoming too ossified to adequately analyze and respond to the actual state of affairs. Theoretical abstractions, increasingly divorced from that reality, were no longer capable of guiding policy. Subjective will had come to replace objective analysis. On balance, the decision to strike out in a new and innovative way, concentrating during the current stage on dramatically altering the forces of production, was appropriate.

If Chinese socialism is to have meaning, it must be measured against increasing levels of relative and absolute prosperity and a commensurate system of distribution. The policy of opening to the outside world has been defined as a central feature of this period, when capital must be both created and socialized. Transnational capital, displaying increasing characteristics of globalization and concentration, is still capable of deflecting crises with creativity.

Some of the results of this innovation are directly transferable, some require digestion and adaptation, and others are systematically specific and irrelevant. It was nonsensical in the past to adopt a posture of contempt for all things foreign. It is equally nonsensical to worship all things foreign.

So what are some of the major questions emerging from the preceding analysis?

1. Has the policy of linking China to the international division of labor resulted in the overexpenditure of foreign exchange without the desired results in terms of either trade volume or composition?

2. Has the policy of acquiring only key foreign inputs been adhered to, given the Center's reluctance to become involved beyond macrointervention?

3. Has the policy of one region leading but all regions benefiting been realized, or have we seen unwarranted delay in the internal transfer of skill and technology and the underpricing of raw materials to the disadvantage of the producing regions?

4. How is one to deal with the fact that, by strengthening the commodity sector in the realm of productive forces, one is at the same time strengthening commodity relations of production?

However these questions are answered, it is clear from the previous decades of struggle of the Chinese Communist Party that objective analysis will ultimately dictate the direction and nature of policy.

Notes

1. *Statistical Yearbook of China: 1984* (Hong Kong: State Statistical Bureau, Economic Information & Agency, 1985), p. 381; Zhu, Rongji, Speech at the forty-

eighth World Trade Conference, Chicago undated, p. 3; Yeung, Loretta Au, *New York Times,* October 1, 1986, pp. 9–10; *China Daily,* October 20, 1986.

2. Yeung, ibid.

3. Xu, Dixin "Transformation of China's Economy," in (Xu, Dixin et al., eds.) *China's Search for Economic Growth* Beijing: New World Press, 1982), p. 15.

4. Except where specified, statistics in this section are drawn from World Bank, *China: Long Term Development Issues & Options* (Baltimore: Johns Hopkins University Press, 1985).

5. Proposal of the Central Committee of the Chinese Communist Party for the Seventh 5-Year Plan for National Economic and Social Development (Adopted September 23, 1985), in "Uphold Reform and Strive for the Realization of Socialist Modernization." *Documents of the CPC National Conference* (September 1985) (Beijing: Foreign Language Press, 1985), pp. 14–15.

6. Yeung, op. cit.

7. Proposal, op. cit.

8. Proposal, op. cit.

9. Yeung, op. cit.

10. Proposal, op. cit., p. 19; Chen, Yun, Speech at the National Conference of the Communist Party of China, September 23, 1985, in "Uphold Reform," op. cit., p. 93.

11. Zhao, Ziyang, Report on the Work of the Government, fourth Session of Fifth National People's Congress, in *The Open Policy at Work* (Su, Wenming, ed.) Beijing Review Publications, *China Today* (10), Beijing, 1985, p. 8.

12. Teng, Weizao, "Socialist Modernization and the Pattern of Foreign Trade," in Xu, Dixin et al., op. cit., p. 173.

13. Ibid, p. 171.

14. *Statistical Yearbook: 1984,* op. cit., p. 381: "Communiqué of State Statistical Bureau of the People's Republic of China on National Economic & Social Development," Beijing, March 9, 1985, p. vi.

15. Chen, Muhua, "China's Foreign Trade in the Past Five Years," in *Open Policy,* op. cit., pp. 17, 18, 20.

16. Ibid, p. 17.

17. Proposal, op. cit., pp. 40–41.

18. Ji, Chongwei, "China's Utilization of Foreign Funds and Relevant Policies," *Chinese Economic Studies,* Winter 1983–84 (Armonk, N.Y.: M. E., Sharpe) pp. 42, 47.

19. Wei, Yuming, "Absorption of Direct Investment From Foreign Countries," *Open Policy,* op. cit., p. 33; United Nations Centre on Transnational Corporations, *National Legislation & Regulations Relating to Transnational Corporations* (New York: United Nations 1986), p. 84.

20. Ji, Chongwei, op. cit., p. 48.

21. Zhu, Rongji, Speech at forty-eighth World Trade Conference, op. cit., p. 3.

22. Zhao, Ziyang, "Expanding Economic & Technical Exchanges, in *Open Policy,* op. cit., p. 13.

23. Wang, Linsheng, and Chen, Yujie, "Economic Relations with Foreign Countries," in *China's Socialist Modernization* (Yu, Guangyuon, ed.) (Beijing: Foreign Language Press, 1984), p. 690.

24. Chen, Huiqin, "Jishu yinjin de fangziang bixu zhuanbian," *Jingji Guanli*, no. 4 (1981), pp. 22ff; in Klenner, Wolfgang, and Wiesegart, Kurt, *The Chinese Economy* (Hamburg: Verlag Weltarchiv GmbH, 1983), p. 54.

25. Zhu, Rongji, "Technical Transformation of China's Existing Enterprises and Import of Technology," Speech at Symposium on Chinese Economic Cooperation with Foreign Countries, Beijing, October 4, 1984, pp. 1, 4.

26. Proposal, Point 43, op. cit., p. 43.

27. Wei, Yuming, op. cit., p. 36.

28. Proposal, op. cit., pp. 30–32

29. Fahui yanhai diqu youshi-jiaqiang duiwai jingji maoyi, *Renmin Ribao*, January 1, 1982; Zhang Peiji, "Stick to Open Door Policy and Expand Foreign Trade," *Economic Reporter*, no. 5 (1982), pp. 2ff, in Klenner, op. cit. p. 120.

30. Ibid, p. 81.

31. Ibid, p. 122.

32. Zhu, Rongji, Speech to forty-eighth World Trade Conference, op. cit., p. 4.

33. Gu, Mu, "Policies for Coastal Cities," in *Open Policy*, op. cit., p. 26

34. Proposal, Third Objective, Point 17, op. cit., p. 20.

35. Hsinhua, *New York Times*, August 11, 1985.

36. Proposal, Point 42, op. cit., p. 42.

37. *Beijing Rundschau*, No. 10, 1982, p. 7, in Klenner, op. cit., p. 84.

38. The following sections are based on interviews conducted by the author in 1981 in Beijing, Tianjin, Wuhan, Shanghai, Nanjing, Chengzhou, Wuxi, Xiamen, and Guangzhou, and in 1985 in Beijing, Tianjin, Hohhot, Dalian, Shanghai, Ningbo, Haikou, and Guangzhou.

39. *Japan Economic Journal*, June 22, 1982, quoted in Klenner, op. cit., p. 95.

40. Proposal, Point 60, op. cit., p. 56.

Appendix 14A: The Remi-Martin Joint Venture

During the initial negotiations, Remi-Martin (HK) offered to share both internal and external wine distribution rights with the Chinese side. The Chinese side, concerned about its inexperience, rejected this proposal and an agreement was arrived at which provided for the Chinese side to purchase 10 percent of production, to be marketed within China, while Remi-Martin would purchase 90 percent of production for the external market. Each side was to be exclusively responsible for its designated market. Each side agreed to purchase its quota at 10 percent above production cost and to market the wine with an additional 15 percent profit. The following analysis displays the consequences of this decision.

Equity: Remi-Martin has 38 percent; the Chinese, 62 percent.

Capacity: 150,000 bottles annually

Cost: Original estimate: 2.5 Yuan per bottle

Actual cost: 2.9 Yuan per bottle

Distribution: Remi-Martin: 90 percent, all for international market; Chinese: 10 percent, all for internal market (can be increased to 30 percent if requested).

Terms: Each side will purchase market share for cost plus 10 percent. Each side will retail at cost plus 10 percent plus markup.

Calculation: 150,000 × 2.9 Yuan = 435,000 Yuan

plus 10 percent profit (43,500 Yuan)

Remi-Martin's share (38 percent) = 16,530 Yuan

Chinese Share (62 percent) = 26,970 Yuan

Remi-Martin markets 135,000 bottles at 3.668 Yuan per bottle (2.9 + 0.290 + 0.478) cost + 10% + 15%

Remi-Martin profit = 135,000 × 0.478 = 64,530 Yuan

Chinese market = 15,000 bottles at 3.668 Yuan per bottle

Chinese profit = 15,000 × 0.478 = 7,170 Yuan

Total Remi-Martin Profit (gross): 16,530 + 64,530 = 81,060 Yuan

Total Chinese Profit (gross): 26,970 + 7,170 = 34,140 Yuan

With 38 percent equity, Remi-Martin earned 2.37 times the amount of profit earned by the Chinese with 68 percent equity.

Remi-Martin fixed capital totals 264,199.27 Yuan (including freight).

Remi-Martin earns back its entire investment in 3 years, 100 days.

15
Selected U.S. Law Aspects of Technology-Transfer Contracts between U.S. and Chinese Parties

Preston M. Torbert

L aw influences the terms of technology transfer contracts and their negotiation between Chinese and U.S. parties in three ways. First, the contracts are affected by the governing law of the contract as provided in a choice of law clause in the contract or as determined by arbitrators in the event of arbitration when the contract has no choice of law clause. Second, the contracts are affected by certain public-policy provisions of the law of either country even if that law is not the governing law of the contract. The Foreign Economic Contracts Law of the People's Republic of China, for example, provides in Article 9 that contracts that are against the laws and public interest of the People's Republic of China are null and void. As a result, a contract between a Chinese party and a U.S. party that was against the public interest of the People's Republic, even if it provided for U.S. law as the governing law of the contract, would not be inforceable in China. Third, the contracts are also affected by certain aspects of the contract, corporation, and administrative laws of each of the parties' countries. For example, even if a contract is governed by U.S. law, many aspects of the execution and implementation of the contract by the Chinese party are governed by Chinese law. The same applies for the U.S. party if the contract is governed by Chinese law.

In order for each party to understand fully the legal basis for the contract, it must understand how the laws of the other party's country, even if the law of that country is not the governing law, may affect the contract. It is not sufficient for a U.S. or Chinese party simply to know its own law and general international practice. It is also necessary to understand certain aspects of the

This is the text of a paper presented at both the Symposium on New Opportunities for International Technology Transfer (sponsored by the Chinese Academy of Sciences and Northwestern University and held in Beijing, October 27–29, 1986) and the International Symposium on Transnational Corporations in World Development and China's Open Policy (sponsored by Nankai University and UNESCO and held in Tianjin, October 27–30, 1986). The author gratefully acknowledges the assistance of Messrs. Yuk Tong Cheung, Frederick E. Henry, and John E. Morrow, Baker & McKenzie, Chicago, in the preparation of this chapter.

contract law, corporation law, administrative law, and tax law of the country of the other party.

From my Chinese friends I have learned much about these laws in China and how they affect technology transfers with U.S. parties. In the spirit of reciprocal exchange, I would like to mention a few aspects of U.S. law that influence the execution and implementation of technology-transfer contracts by U.S. parties but that, in my experience, seem to be little understood in China. I hope that an explanation of these aspects of U.S. law may promote more efficient and successful contract negotiations between entities of the two countries.

There are four aspects of U.S. law affecting technology-transfer contracts that I would like to address, if only in a preliminary and incomplete manner. The first is the U.S. law regarding bank guarantees and standby letters of credit; the second is U.S. income tax law; the third is U.S. export-control regulation; and the fourth is U.S. law relating to corporate takeovers. I shall try to answer the following questions:

1. Why do U.S. parties refuse to give bank guarantees?
2. Why would a U.S. party insist on a breakdown of payments under a technology-transfer contract?
3. Why would a U.S. party insist on prohibiting sales by the Chinese party to certain countries of products made with the technology?
4. If the U.S. party to a technology-transfer contract that has become effective is the object of a corporate takeover, what legal effect will this have on the contract?

U.S. Laws Affecting Bank Guarantees and Standby Letters of Credit

In most technology-transfer contracts between Chinese and U.S. parties, the Chinese party agrees to make payment in several installments. Generally, the first payment is a down payment made within a certain number of days after the contract becomes effective and before the Chinese side has received any technology documents, training, or technical assistance. In this situation, the Chinese side naturally wants to protect itself against the danger that the U.S. party will take the down payment and not perform the contract. The Chinese party, therefore, insists that the contract contain a provision stating that the other party will submit a bank guarantee under which the Chinese party can receive the down payment back from the bank if the U.S. party does not perform the contract. This is surely a reasonable request by the Chinese party, but it often leads to much frustration and delay in the negotiation or implementation of the contract.

The problem is not one of good faith. The U.S. side understands the Chinese party's desire for protection and is generally willing to agree to give the Chinese party such protection. The problem is in the form of the protection given to the Chinese party. Historically, and at present under U.S. law, U.S. banks have no, or very restricted, authority to issue bank guarantees (i.e., to guarantee the indebtedness of other parties).

The doctrine that a bank may not serve in the capacity of guarantor dates back to the early history of the banking industry in the United States. The New York Banking Act of 1838 and the National Bank Act of 1864 were generally interpreted to mean that a bank could not act as a guarantor. The main reason for this rule was that guarantees by a bank could pose a great threat to the solvency of the bank.

This general rule is incorporated in the regulations governing the activities of national banks in the United States today. The controller of the currency's Interpretive Ruling No. 7.7010 states that a national bank may not lend its credit, bind itself as surety to indemnify another, or otherwise become a guarantor.[1] There are, however, two exceptions: (1) when a bank has a "substantial interest in the performance of the transaction involved" or (2) has a segregated deposit sufficient in amount to cover the bank's total potential liability. It is difficult to say when a U.S. bank might have a "substantial interest" in the transaction and, in most cases, a customer of the bank will not want to put on deposit with the bank an amount equal to the guarantee. U.S. banks, therefore, generally do not issue bank guarantees.

The ruling allows foreign branches of U.S. banks to provide bank guarantees in order to allow them to compete with foreign banks that offer guarantees, but it subjects guarantees by foreign branches of U.S. banks to certain credit limitations. It may be impossible or inconvenient for the U.S. bank to open a bank guarantee through a foreign branch. In some cases, the U.S. bank has no foreign branch. In other cases, where the U.S. bank does have a foreign branch, it is inconvenient to have the bank guarantee issued by the foreign branch while the U.S. head office is handling all of the other payment procedures. Further, practical difficulties may occur where the foreign branch is used. For example, the signature agreement between the U.S. bank and the Bank of China may not include the signatures of the personnel in the foreign branch. In such a case, the Bank of China will not accept the bank guarantee issued by the foreign branch.

For these reasons, U.S. banks tell their customers (the U.S. parties to technology-transfer agreements) that they cannot or will not issue a bank guarantee. Instead, U.S. banks suggest standby letters of credit.

A standby letter of credit is similar to a commercial letter of credit widely used in the purchase of goods in international trade. However, the function of the standby letter of credit is similar to that of a bank guarantee. The U.S. party requests its bank to open the standby letter of credit in favor of the

Chinese party with payment to be made upon delivery to the bank by the Chinese party of a document indicating that the U.S. party has not performed its obligation to transfer the technology documents or other obligation under the contract.

The standby letter of credit is generally cheaper and more efficient than a bank guarantee because it is a "documentary transaction," while a letter of guarantee is not. Under a standby letter of credit, the issuing bank (the U.S. bank in this case) inspects only the document presented and, if it conforms with the terms of the letter of credit, the issuing bank pays the beneficiary (the Chinese party in this case). In contrast, under a bank guarantee, the guarantor (the bank) must examine the facts described in the documents presented in order to determine if the obligor (the seller) actually has defaulted. A bank issuing a guarantee, therefore, bears a higher risk than a bank issuing a standby letter of credit because determining if documents comply with specified standards is not as difficult and as risky as determining if the obligor actually has defaulted.

Although much depends on the particular circumstances, it can be said that in the event that the bank disputes the beneficiary's claim, it is generally easier for the beneficiary to prevail in case of litigation under a standby letter of credit than under a bank guarantee. With a standby letter of credit, all the beneficiary need show is that the documents comport with the terms of the credit—a single issue of fact. Under a bank guarantee, the beneficiary must show that the customer actually defaulted.

If Chinese parties to technology-transfer contracts can understand the use of the standby letter of credit and accept it in their contracts with U.S. parties, they could make a great contribution to successful contract negotiations between Chinese and U.S. parties concerning technology transfer.

U.S. Income Tax Law

The tax laws of a country affect all types of transactions performed by companies of that country. In particular, U.S. income tax law affects certain aspects of technology-transfer contracts with China. The new income tax law of the United States is being studied to determine its impact on U.S. trade and investment abroad.

One important effect of the new law will be the reduction of corporate income tax in the United States to a maximum rate of 34 percent. The new income tax law, like the prior law, allows a credit against U.S. income taxes for foreign taxes paid by U.S. corporations on foreign-source income, but subject to certain limitations. Since in many cases Chinese income tax rates will be higher than U.S. income tax rates under the new law, U.S. corporations that pay taxes in China will try to arrange their activities to reduce in a lawful manner the taxes they pay in China. This may affect certain technology-transfer agreements.

Generally, technology-transfer agreements provide for the U.S. party to perform three obligations: provide technical documentation, provide personnel training in the United States, and provide technical services in China. In most cases, the compensation paid by the Chinese party is not allocated to each of these three obligations separately, but is divided simply into initial payments and a running royalty. Under the Foreign Enterprise Income Tax Law of the People's Republic of China, assuming that the U.S. party does not have an establishment in China, the Chinese transferee will withhold tax at the rate of 20 percent on all payments made by it. (The withholding tax is 10 percent under the income tax treaty between the United States and China that became effective January 1, 1987.) The U.S. party, however, under U.S. tax law, will not be allowed a credit for the Chinese taxes withheld on the portion of the payments attributable to the training performed in the United States. The reason is that under U.S. income tax law, the compensation the U.S. party receives for the training is considered to be U.S.–source income because the training was provided in the United States. Since the income is U.S.–source income and not foreign-source income, no foreign tax credit will be allowed.

If the U.S. tax authorities were to audit the tax returns of the U.S. party to a technology-transfer contract with a Chinese party, they would disallow any tax credit taken by the U.S. party for the income derived from the training services performed in the United States. If the contract did not state what amount of income derived from these services, the U.S. tax authorities might conclude that an unreasonably large portion of the compensation under the contract was attributable to the training performed in the United States. To avoid such a result, the U.S. party may well insist during contract negotiations that the compensation for the technical training be expressly stated in the contract.

From the Chinese point of view, this request may seem unreasonable and even self-defeating. In some cases, it appears that the Chinese party to the contract or its superior authority wants to believe that it is obtaining the training free of charge.[2] If a value is put on the training in the contract, the Chinese party cannot believe that the training is free of charge. Further, pursuant to the Provisional Regulations of the Ministry of Finance of the People's Republic of China Regarding the Reduction and Exemption of Income Tax on Fees for the Use of Proprietary Technology of December 13, 1982, an exemption from withholding tax on payments under a technology-transfer contract is available where certain conditions are met. One of these conditions is that the contract terms are "preferential." It appears that one criterion that the Chinese tax authorities employ to determine whether the terms of the contract are "preferential" is whether the contract provides for free training.

The U.S. party, then, in insisting that the value of the training be stipulated in the contract, may be reducing the chances that it will receive an exemption from income tax on the compensation it receives for the technology transfer as a whole.[3]

Of course, if the value of the training is a relatively small part of the compensation the U.S. party receives under the contract, then it may not be so concerned about the lack of a tax credit and it may want to improve its chances of a tax exemption by including the value of the training in the technology price and providing for "free" transport. However, where the value of the training is a significant portion of the contract and the chances of otherwise qualifying for the exemption are not great, then it is understandable that the U.S. party may wish to clearly stipulate the value of the training in the contract. It is hoped that the Chinese parties will understand the reasons for this.

U.S. Export-Control Regulations

The difficulties that U.S. export-control regulations pose for technology transfers between U.S. and Chinese entities are well known. However, most of the attention has been focused on the problem of the U.S. party's obtaining a validated export licence that, in many cases, is necessary for the technology to be transferred without a violation of U.S. export-control regulations. There is another aspect, however, to the U.S. export-control regulations that is not widely known in China. These are the restrictions that the U.S. export-control regulations place on the transfer of the technology or products made with the technology to third countries.

Currently, it is a violation of the U.S. Export Administration Act for the Chinese transferee to reexport technology or to export any direct products of the technology transferred by a U.S. party under a validated export licence to any one of five countries: North Korea, Kampuchea, Cuba, Vietnam, and Libya. If the U.S. party had "reason to know" (either at the time of concluding the technology-transfer contract or subsequently) that the Chinese party was intending to or actually did reexport the technology or ship the products of the technology to any of those countries, the U.S. transferor would be subject to fines and imprisonment for a violation of the law.

In order to protect itself against any possible violation of the law, the U.S. licensor may request in the contract negotiations that a specific clause be inserted in the technology-transfer contract stating that no reexport of the technology or any export of the products of the technology will be made without the prior written consent of the transferor or that no reexport would be made to the five prohibited countries. In addition, the U.S. transferor might also request that the Chinese transferee acknowledge the effect of the

U.S. export-control regulations on the transferor and agree to abide by them.

It is easy to understand that the Chinese transferee would feel offended by the demand for insertion of such a clause in the contract. In many cases, the U.S. party also would prefer not to insist upon such a clause. However, the U.S. party cannot choose whether it is subject to the restrictions of the Export Administration Act. It is its duty to obey U.S. law. The requirements of U.S. law may compel the U.S. party to insist on receiving assurances that the law will not be violated. If both sides show goodwill and flexibility, often a result satisfactory to both sides can be reached.

U.S. Law Relating to Corporate Takeovers

During the past several years, the United States has been the scene of many corporate acquisition or takeover battles. In the typical case, one corporation purchases a large portion of the stock of another corporation in order to elect new management and control the target corporation. Once control is obtained, the target corporation may be merged or consolidated or some or all of the assets of the corporation may be sold to other parties.

In a number of cases, after a technology-transfer contract has been signed, but before full implementation of the contract, the Chinese party has received a telex from the U.S. party indicating that the U.S. company has become the target of a corporate takeover and has been acquired. In such cases, the Chinese party may wonder whether the original U.S. party to the contract is still legally bound to perform the obligations under the contract.

The mere acquisition by one U.S. company of the stock of another U.S. company does not have any effect on the acquired company's corporate identity. Thus, existing contracts of the acquired company, including a technology-transfer contract with a Chinese party, would not be affected. After the acquistion, the U.S. party that signed the technology-transfer contract is still the same party and its respective rights and obligations remain the same.

The issue is more complex when a corporate takeover results in a merger, consolidation, or sale of assets. The first question is what law should determine the legal effects of a merger, consolidation, or sale of assets of the U.S. party to a technology-transfer contract. U.S. contract and corporate law will surely govern the general legal effects of any merger, consolidation, or sale of assets between U.S. corporations. It may also govern the effects on contracts with foreign parties of the U.S. party that is merged or consolidated or whose assets are sold. This is particularly true as a practical matter where the contract between the U.S. party and the foreign party does not have a governing law clause or a clause regarding the assignment of rights under the contract. This is very often the case in technology-transfer contracts between Chinese and U.S. parties.[4]

Under U.S. law, a merger, consolidation, and purchase of assets and their legal effects can be described in the following manner: A merger refers to a situation in which one company becomes a part of or merges with another company; the former company ceases to exist, but the latter company continues. In a merger, the company that continues to exist acquires the assets and rights as well as liabilities and obligations of the company that ceases to exist. It may also retain its name and identity, but in many cases the name is changed. In a consolidation, two or more companies unite to form a new company and the original companies cease to exist. Thus, in a merger of company A and company B, one will survive; but in a consolidation of company A and company B, a new company (C) will be formed. A merger and a consolidation are similar in that the surviving or consolidating company issues its shares or pays fair compensation for the shares of the former company, acquires the assets and rights of the former company, and assumes its liabilities and obligations.

For a Chinese party that has entered into a technology-transfer contract with a U.S. party, the effects of a merger or a consolidation of the U.S. company are basically the same. The Chinese party can treat the surviving or consolidating company the same as if it were the original U.S. party. The surviving or new company is entitled to all rights and must abide by all obligations under the existing contract.

A purchase of assets refers to the situation in which one company acquires in exchange for compensation all or part of the assets of another company. Under U.S. contract law principles, rights under a contract are generally assignable without the consent of the other party to the contract, but obligations are not. This principle could put the Chinese party to a technology-transfer contract in a difficult position because the U.S. company that has purchased the assets of the original U.S. party is entitled to the rights of the contract with the Chinese party, but is not bound to perform the obligations under the contract. However, in most cases where assets are purchased, the purchaser assumes the obligations of the business to which the assets are related. Consequently, although the seller cannot transfer its contractual obligations without the consent of the other original contracting party (i.e., the Chinese party), the purchaser will customarily assume the obligations of the contract that it has acquired by assignment. Thus, both the seller and the purchaser would be bound to perform the obligations of the original contract to the Chinese party.

In summary, it can be said that generally under U.S. law, after a corporate takeover involving the sale of assets, the original U.S. party to the technology-transfer contract will remain bound to perform its obligations under the contract unless the Chinese party has consented to the transfer of the obligations to the other U.S. party acquiring the assets. In practice, the purchaser of assets also generally agrees to perform such obligations. Where a merger or consolidation occurs, the surviving or new company that has the assets of the original U.S. party will be bound to the same degree as the original party.

These principles of U.S. corporate and contract law and practice are not detrimental to the interests of the Chinese party. In fact, they protect the Chinese party's interests. However, two points should be noted. First, although the obligations of the original U.S. party to the contract will continue in one form or another in any case, they may not be performed by the same legal entity or by the same personnel as contemplated in the original contract. In such case, the Chinese party may feel that the corporate takeover has damaged the very important relationship of mutual trust between the parties and has made implementation of the contract difficult. The Chinese party may even desire to terminate the contract. The U.S. party may have a similar reaction. Often when there is a corporate takeover, management is changed and thus the corporate policies may change as well. A technology-transfer contract that appeared to be very beneficial to prior management may not appear so to new management. New management may be less enthusiastic about performing its obligations and, in some cases, may even try to find in the contract a valid reason for termination.

Second, the Chinese party may further strengthen its rights by including in the technology-transfer contract a clause granting it a right to terminate the contract in the event of a sale of shares or other transaction that would result in a change of control from the original U.S. contracting party.

Conclusion

Technology transfer between Chinese and U.S. parties has played a very important role in economic relations between the two countries. Since President Nixon's trip to China in 1972, and particularly since the establishment of diplomatic relations between China and the United States in 1979, technology-transfer contracts between Chinese and U.S. parties have increased in number and importance quite rapidly.

While great progress has been made, certain difficulties remain in successfully negotiating such contracts. One difficulty is the lack of greater mutual understanding. In particular, each side needs a greater understanding of the laws and regulations of the other party's country that will affect the other party to a technology-transfer contract. Such an understanding will allow each side to realize that in negotiations, certain demands made by the other side regarding the terms of the contract may not be the result of any intention by the other side to complicate or make impossible successful negotiations, but instead may be a reasonable good-faith request based on the law of the other party's country. In some cases, changes in the terms of the contract due to such demands may benefit both parties. Any party, whether Chinese or U.S., should listen carefully to the demands of the other side in contract negotiations. They should also consult their legal advisors to determine whether to accept such demands and, if so, on what terms and whether to make demands themselves.

I believe that a better understanding by each party of certain laws and practices of the other party's country will over the long term redound to the mutual benefit of both parties to contract negotiations. This chapter is a modest first step in an effort to promote such an understanding.

Notes

1. I understand that one U.S. bank, Morgan Guaranty Trust, is exempt from the restrictions on issuing guarantees because of a provision in its charter.

2. Of course, from the economic point of view, the training is rarely "free." If the compensation for the training is not separately stated in the contract, it will generally be included in the price of the technology.

3. It is true that, if the U.S. party receives an exemption from tax, it will not be concerned about a tax credit. I understand, however, that in most cases, the contract must be negotiated and signed before the tax authorities will review it to determine whether it qualifies for an exemption. Therefore, the U.S. party will not know at the time the contract is negotiated and signed whether an exemption will be granted.

4. China's Foreign Economic Contracts Law does provide in Article 26 that prior approval of the other party is required for the assignment of rights and obligations under a contract, but this provision does not appear to reflect a strong public policy that would be applied to a contract despite a governing law clause that resulted in the application of a different rule of law. Assuming for the moment that Article 26 did apply in such case, the following points would require clarification: (1) what constitutes an assignment and (2) whether transfers or rights and obligations by force of law are covered.

16
Human-Resources Policies for Transnational Corporations in China

Murray E. Bovarnick

T his chapter is based on a research project conducted by Organization Resources Counselors, Inc. (ORC), a New York–based international management consulting firm, during the second half of 1985. The purposes of the study were to learn how employees of Western multinational firms live and work in the People's Republic of China, and to examine the consequent human-resources issues. Several research methodologies were followed:

1. Sixty-six companies, primarily U.S.–based multinationals, responded to an ORC questionnaire about their China expatriate personnel policies and practices. At the time, these companies employed 755 expatriates in China, including 450 from their respective home countries, 189 third-country nationals, and 116 Hong Kong Chinese.

2. A second survey questionnaire was sent to expatriates then living in China to enquire about their personal living circumstances and expenditure patterns. Seventy-six responses were received, primarily from U.S. citizens. Among other things, the expatriates reported what kinds of goods and services they purchased in China. An ORC pricing agent then visited Beijing, Shanghai, and Guangzhou to price out those goods and services at the establishments typically patronized by Western expatriates.

3. An ORC study team in New York reviewed the relevant academic and professional literature. It also interviewed U.S. and Chinese officials, former expatriates, and others with current knowledge about China.

4. Two special studies were commissioned. Arthur Young International, Hong Kong, prepared a study of individual income taxes in China. The international law firm of Paul, Weiss, Rifkind, Wharton and Garrison wrote a paper on labor relations in foreign–Chinese joint ventures.

5. Finally, a field study team that included representatives of ORC and Arthur Young, Hong Kong, visited Hong Kong, Beijing, Shanghai, Guangzhou, Shenzhen, and Zhanjiang in May and June 1985. Team

members conducted over sixty interviews, each lasting two to three hours, with Western expatriate employees and their spouses, Chinese officials, and U.S. consular officials in Beijing, Shanghai, and Guangzhou. The team also visited expatriates' homes, offices, and factories as well as numerous stores, restaurants, hospitals, and Chinese- and English-language schools.

A complete report of this study, entitled *Multinationals in China: Human Resources Practices and Issues in the PRC,* is available from ORC, and a brief descriptive article appears in the *Columbia Journal of World Business,* spring 1986.

This chapter focuses on one aspect of the total research, namely, the human-resources policies and practices that appear to have been followed by the Western—primarily U.S.—multinational corporations with respect to their expatriate staffs in China.

Two sets of terms must be defined. First, who are the expatriates and what do they do in China? They are almost all men. Of the five female expatriates that ORC interviewed, two were in the consular service and three were ethnic Chinese. Occupationally, the expatriates are either managers or professionals. If managers, they manage organizations ranging in size from four- or five-person representative office up to a manufacturing or minerals-extraction enterprise of several hundred employees. Beijing Jeep, the largest venture visited by ORC, employs several thousand people. Professionals (such as geologists, engineers, and accountants) usually work with the larger ventures and are responsible not only for their own professional work, but also for training (without necessarily supervising) their Chinese counterparts. There are no Western factory workers in China and very few Western office workers. Finally, with the possible exception of the petroleum companies, Western representation within any given venture is likely to be limited. Beijing Jeep, at the time of our visit, employed only five or six Westerners, and several other manufacturing ventures employed only two or three.

Multinational Human-Resources Policies

Background

What do we mean by *human-resources policies and practices?* As a general rule, the term encompasses all of the activities that companies undertake to attract, retain, develop, motivate, and reward their employees. Because the leading multinational corporations are characterized by a notably high regard for the indispensability of human talent, their human-resources activities, designed to husband and nurture this talent, are numerous, comprehensive, and intricately interrelated. Needless to say, human-resources policies are not identical from company to company, nor is the objective of such policies necessarily identical for different categories of employees within a company. It is safe to say that, in the United States today, increased productivity is the principal purpose of personnel policies for manufacturing employees. But, for managers and professionals, who make up the larger part of the expatriate ranks, career development has traditionally been the central theme. Thus, human-resources policies and practices have customarily been designed to recruit into the organization people with high potential for managerial and professional achievement, to socialize them rapidly into the organization, and to provide progressive measures of hierarchical and financial advancement that will induce them to remain with the company until retirement. One giant corporation summed up its entire human-resources philosophy with a single word: *sustainability*. This meant assured, steady, and, above all, predictable growth.

This course of conduct is most feasible in a corporation that has developed the culture and acquired the resources that permit its top management to view the company's organization chart as a giant chessboard with an unlimited number of squares on which it can deploy the necessary number of pawns, which can be maneuvered until (through the Darwinian process known as career planning) there emerge the desired number of knights, bishops, castles, queens, and kings. Selection, training, placement, and compensation systems are all designed to support this process.

When Western organizations venture abroad, however, especially into the less developed areas of the Third World, they tend to lose control of the rules of the game. As a prime example, Aramco once held near-colonial power and status in Saudi Arabia; today it is an entity of the Kingdom. In country after country, the Western industrialists have been required to adapt their business practices to the laws, customs, and standards of their host nations. Thus, in China, as elsewhere, the multinationals cannot transport either their employees or their human-resources policies with quite the degree of uniformity and sustainability they might prefer.

To begin with, they cannot now place on the chessboard as many employees as they could 20 or 30 years ago. Although China itself does not restrict the employment of expatriates, there is a substantial cost obstacle. If the total pay and benefits expense of a U.S.–based manager amounts to, say, $80,000, the total support cost in China may be as much as three to four times that amount, depending primarily on the employer's policies regarding overseas and hardship premiums and the assumption of increased living expenses. Furthermore, there are some Chinese joint venture partners who will not allow the joint venture to bear the full cost of what they regard as excessive premiums and allowances.

Second, there are not as many squares to be filled on the chessboard as one might imagine. The Chinese expect each member of a Western joint venture cadre to train his or her own replacement. Thus, in a typical startup joint venture, for each Western manager, there is a Chinese deputy manager; in many firms, the relationship between the two is that of mentor to protégé. "Each one teach one" is not merely a pedagogical slogan in China. It is an important vehicle for the creation of an indigenous management and professional work force.

Third, human-resources policies based on an objective of sustainability can be themselves sustained in an environment that meets minimum standards of predictability. A U.S. multinational with operations in, say, Belgium or Italy, can make reasonable assumptions about the respective political and economic environments and can plan its business strategy, including its labor needs, accordingly. Western enterprises in China can make no such predictions. They and their Chinese hosts are engaged in a political and economic experiment that has only just begun and whose outcome is still highly uncertain. It is hardly possible to plan quarterly operating budgets, let alone careers.

Finally, portions of the underdeveloped world are so new, so strange, and so altogether alien that we may not even be able to frame human-resources policies that will produce effective adjustment to the day-to-day work and the environment, let alone sustainability and career development. Many of China's unique conditions cannot be envisaged by human-resources policymakers who have not themselves lived and worked in China. Consider the implications of the reaction of a recently married young engineer, whose first overseas posting was in an interior Chinese city:

> When we arrived at the hotel, it had, in two rooms, one desk, one hatrack, twin beds, and that was all the furniture. There was an inch of water in the bathroom. There was a sort of shower, but it didn't work. The toilet was flooded. The walls were filthy. The carpet was filthy. And this was where we were going to live for the next year. I don't think I'll ever forget that feeling.

Selection

ORC interviewed more than forty expatriates, along with several of their spouses. By and large, they seem to have been drawn from four distinct employee pools. One pool included the "career expatriates," those peripatetic wanderers who spend most of their working lives outside their home countries. Many of these career expatriates were in the petroleum industry and had lived in other Asian locations as well as in Africa and the Middle East. They move from Lagos to Guangzhou as routinely as their domestic counterparts might move from Denver to Houston.

A second group included what we shall call the "natural selections." One subset within this group consisted of ethnic Chinese, foreign nationals of Chinese descent. Some had been born in China and some in their present home country; all were bilingual. One large multinational was reported to have been stockpiling ethnic Chinese for several years in anticipation of its Chinese venture. The second subset included western Sinophiles, primarily younger people, who had studied Chinese history, culture, or language, and who had thus been attracted to employers who had or were interested in Chinese operations. As a matter of collateral interest, many ethnic Chinese expatriates had strong negative reactions to living and working conditions in China, whereas the Sinophiles were often quite satisfied.

The third employment pool, the largest of all, simply consisted of people with the necessary professional qualifications who were willing to accept, and in many cases volunteered for, assignment to China.

Regardless of the pool from which they were drawn, most of the interviewees had some characteristics in common. In general, they had had several years of prior experience with their current employers, either domestically or abroad. Several of them had also represented their employers during earlier negotiations with the Chinese. They were believed to be the best qualified for the jobs at hand on the basis of their employment records. The expatriates believed that their qualifications are rated against two scales. The first of these is technical and professional competence; knowledge of Chinese language or of China is the second. Finally, all of them were willing to accept assignment in China, although in several cases they had no real choice.

Sixty to 70 percent of the companies require medical examinations before a China posting. However, very few of them report having systematic programs to evaluate prospective expatriates for emotional stability, cultural adaptability, social self-sufficiency, tolerance of ambiguity, or, above all, patience to endure the snail's pace at which business events proceed in China. Rather, it seemed to us that:

1. The candidates who eventually became expatriates resident in China were known quantities, so that further in-depth assessment would have been superfluous.

2. China itself was an unknown quantity. Thus, no validated assessment methods were available in any case.

If our interpretation is correct, the selection processes are not much different from those used in most cases of reassignment, whether domestic or foreign. Typically, there is an early search to identify, first, the "natural selections" and, then, others with the required professional competence. A first screening may eliminate prospects with known physical disabilities, school-age children, or other evident barriers to relocation. The executives with selection authority then make preliminary selections on the basis of the requirements of the job and the qualifications of the candidate, meaning qualifications both to do the work and to function effectively in the foreign environment. In time, a final selection is made and an offer extended. (If the selection group truly knows its candidates, the offer will not be rejected.) In the case of China, there is likely to be only one deviation from this norm: the selecting executives simply may not know as much about China as they know about Minneapolis, London, Riyadh, or Caracas.

Orientation

The foregoing observations reflect primarily our interviews with expatriates; the employers themselves were not extensively queried about their selection processes. Both groups, however, were questioned about preassignment orientation and training. About one-quarter of the companies have formal orientation programs conducted either by outside consultants or by internal staff. Somewhat less than one-third of the companies expect employees with prior China experience to orient those about to leave for China, while the remaining companies in the survey reported no orientation at all. About 40 percent of the employers provide mandatory language training when the nature or duration of the assignment seems to require it, and almost 70 percent apparently bear some or all of the expense for language training voluntarily undertaken by the expatriate and, in most cases, the expatriate's dependents as well.

Several of the expatriate interviewees had gone to China without any pretense of orientation; this was notably true of the career expatriates, some of whom had relocated from another foreign country without even touching home base. Another group had never had the benefits of formal orientation, but had been in China before as members of a feasibility study or negotiating team; this group was clearly the best prepared. The third group had been through some sort of orientation, ranging from a few casual conversations with "old hands" to formal courses conducted over a 6- to 8-week period.

By and large, the expatriates were critical of their orientation experiences. Several of the internally conducted programs were described as anecdotal, impromptu, and improvisational. If the program was conducted by outside consultants, the focus was likely to be culture rather than commerce, and the training methodology academic rather than pragmatic. The expatriates were also skeptical about the value of language training, unless it was of the immersion variety and conducted over a much longer period than most of the employers were willing to tolerate.

Many of the expatriates, and certainly all of the spouses, favored preassignment visits, at least in principle. However, there was a contingent that held a negative view not only about preassignment visits but about orientation as well. Life and work in China are so far beyond the realm of our conventional experience and expectations, they said, that there is no way in which one can prepare or be prepared for it. Anyway, if it were possible to accurately describe life and work in China, and that can *only* be accomplished through a careful visit, most assignments would be turned down. The most emphatic advocate of this viewpoint was the young engineer quoted earlier.

Career Development

Employees are typically assigned to China for a period of one to three years, but this may be extended by mutual consent. Many of the expatriates volunteered that this is too short a time, by two or three years, for a Western expatriate to reach full effectiveness in China. Yet they, and we, have no doubt that candidates for assignment to China would strongly resist a longer initial assignment.

Be that as it may, what impact does a China tour have on one's career progress? Our collective experience with China is both too short and too limited to permit more than speculation. Our first speculation is that, for the most part, experience in China is more likely to advance than to retard one's long-term career prospects.

If the foreign enterprises in China in general, and one's own enterprise in particular, are successful, then we can expect that both the number and the size of such ventures will increase. The managers and professionals now in China will be among the very few with legitimate claims to successful hands-on China experience. They will be scarce commodities and will surely be able to market, either inside or outside their own companies, their new-found and hard-earned value.

If we instead postulate that the Chinese experiment is not successful and that the first wave of Western investors turns out to be the last, then I would argue that the successful completion of one's own tour of duty in China would still have positive career consequences. Expatriates who manage to meet their own performance expectations, even in the course of fighting a losing battle, will have:

- Acquired and demonstrated substantial reserves of patience and perseverance;
- Expanded through continuous challenge their own personal and professional resources;
- Developed their negotiating skills to a hitherto untested level;
- Had the opportunity to enjoy a culturally enriching experience;
- In all probability held a position of higher professional and commercial responsibility than might have been possible in their home country.

However valued these attributes might be, there may be, for some, a price to be paid for their acquisitions. There is always the risk of failure on the job, and the risk in China is intensified by the physical, social, and cultural constraints under which Westerners must labor. In particular, the Chinese environment will be threatening to employees who function best in a supportive network of family, friends, and colleagues.

In addition, home-office or otherwise domestically oriented employees who accept a first assignment abroad clearly take themselves out of the mainstream flow of action. Their visibility is diminished, their network of connections is weakened, and their professional and political currency may be threatened. The hazard of being "out of sight, out of mind" is not unique to China, but China is doubly hazardous because of the concurrent risks of business and personal failure. Of fifty companies answering questions about premature expatriate recalls, nine reported at least one repatriation at the expatriate's own request, and six reported at least one recall because of unsatisfactory performance.

By way of contrast, China may be simply another port of call for the career expatriates. Professional expatriates move from station to station like the airplanes on which they fly, and personal success or failure in China is neither more nor less significant than the same outcome in, say, Nigeria. For some of them, however, the Chinese experience may have unique personal and professional significance. One oil industry manager, who was not at all appreciative of life in China, nevertheless described his overall feelings in these almost poetic words: "There was a time to be on the North Slope and a time to be in the North Sea. If now is the time to be in China, this is where I want to be."

Compensation

Most U.S. multinationals compensate their expatriates on the basis of what is known as the "balance-sheet" methodology. The balancing act starts with the assumption that an employee transferred from the United States to, say, France, will have to dedicate more or less income for housing, for other essential goods and services, and for income taxes, than in the United States. The exact differentials in each case vary with the employee's income level and family status, the relative rates of inflation in the two countries, foreign exchange rates, and the prices and availability of goods and services in the host country. These differentials are periodically calculated through comparative expenditure and pricing studies, similar to the study completed by ORC as part of its China project. On the basis of these studies, which are conducted worldwide several times a year, the multinationals undertake to maintain the purchasing power that expatriates would have in their home country, despite differences in living costs at the foreign post. This is accomplished through a combination of positive and negative living allowances.

In addition to balance-sheet adjustments, most multinationals offer an overseas premium to compensate the expatriate for the personal and family dislocations and inconveniences occasioned by an overseas posting, and most pay additional premiums for assignments to areas characterized by hardship or hazard.

At the time of the ORC study (summer 1985), the expatriates assigned to China were well compensated compared with those assigned elsewhere. Virtually all of them were paid overseas premiums of 10 to 25 percent of base salary, with 15 percent as a common figure. Over 60 percent also received separate hardship allowances, generally ranging from 15 to as high as 40 percent of base pay in Beijing, and even higher in some of the less hospitable areas. A typical allowance was 20 percent of base pay. In some cases, however, hardship allowances were at the same high levels as those reported for Beirut and San Salvador.

In addition, we would judge that at least 60 percent of the Western expatriates in Beijing, Shanghai, and Guangzhou were reimbursed for out-of-pocket housing, subsistence, transportation, and miscellaneous other expenses at levels consistently more liberal than would be the case in other parts of the world. The nature of housing accommodations in China explains this apparent generosity. Most Westerners in China live either in joint venture hotels or in apartment complexes located on hotel property and managed by the hotel itself. In the major coastal cities, and increasingly in the interior as well, these hotels are large tourist complexes. Their facilities include two to six restaurants; laundry, dry-cleaning, and maid services; English-language newsstands; gift and sundry shops; bars; and, in many instances, recreational facilities such as swimming pools, tennis courts, and even bowling alleys. Most of the hotels also have assigned to them their own fleets of taxicabs, which are the principal means of urban transportation for expatriates. Thus, Westerners, even those who do not have kitchens, can purchase all they need to purchase in China without ever leaving the hotel premises.

When transient business visitors stay at these hotels, their expenses are charged to expense accounts. At the time of the ORC study, many of the expatriates enjoyed the same privilege. Their room bills were paid by their employers, sometimes but not always after a deduction of a housing contribution from their base salary. Meals, transportation, and personal service expenses were often reimbursed on presentation of hotel bills or receipts. Even for those with kitchens, whose food expenses could be expected to be lower than in the home country, very few companies implemented a negative goods and services differential. In addition, the expatriates in China, as elsewhere in the world, were protected from double income taxation through either tax-equalization or tax-protection programs. As the result of these pay and reimbursement practices, many expatriates were able to save a considerable portion of their total compensation. This privilege was not necessarily shared by expatriates maintaining separate households in their home countries.

Leave Policies

Expatriates in China were rewarded with substantial time off. The typical practice was to allow four weeks of home leave or local vacation, with the employer often paying the family's transportation costs between China and the employee's home country. In addition, most companies granted their expatriates rest and recuperation leave amounting to three weeks per year, with transportation and per diem expenses usually paid by the employer.

Thus, the expatriates interviewed by ORC generally received the equivalent of seven weeks paid vacation, as well as reimbursement for a substantial portion of their vacation expenses. While an uninformed observer might question the rationale for what appears to be recreational largesse, the expatriates claimed, and ORC agrees, that time off and away from China is virtually a therapeutic necessity. Swimming pools and tennis courts notwithstanding, life and work in China were seen not only as challenging, but also as frustrating and demanding. Although Westerners live in tourist hotels (some approaching a state of luxury), they are, for the most part, tourist hotels from which there is no escape. For cultural reasons beyond the scope of this chapter, the Westerners have virtually no interpersonal relations with the Chinese, and their recreational and social opportunities are severely restricted. They flee to Hong Kong primarily and to Singapore and Tokyo to a lesser extent; they claim they would not or could not remain in China without these periodic respites.

Hong Kong is also regarded as a medical haven. The expatriates generally had a low regard for, and in some cases a genuine fear of, the Chinese health-care system, including its facilities, medicines, practitioners, and techniques. They were also concerned about what they perceived to be health hazards imposed by the Chinese environment. The conditions most often cited as threatening were air pollution, undrinkable water, unrefrigerated food, primitive sanitary facilities, frequent dust storms, and obsolete systems of protection against fire and industrial hazards. Some of the diplomatic offices have Western-trained health-care personnel on staff, and there are also Western-staffed clinics in Guangzhou and Zhanjiang maintained by multinational oil companies. These few outposts of Western medicine are not sufficient to relieve the almost universal fear of becoming ill or injured in China.

Education

One other condition bears mention because it has implications for expatriate selection and retention. There are at the moment only four English-language schools in China, and they are associated with the diplomatic offices in Beijing, Shanghai, Guangzhou, and Shenyan. Children of the respective diplomatic staffs are given first preference for admission; only after their needs have been met are other children considered. Expatriate families with school-age children must therefore be prepared to have them educated elsewhere; half of the multinationals underwrite some or all of the resulting expenses, including transportation. From a selection standpoint, the educational facilities in China tend to discourage the posting of expatriates with school-age children.

Conclusion

In essence, multinational human-resources policies applicable to China are about the same as some covering employment in other areas of the world. The principal exception is probably the reimbursement of housing and subsistence expenses through the employee's expense account, rather than through the more customary approach of positive and negative living allowances. That there is little variation in such policies from country to country is not surprising; in order to move home-country nationals throughout the world, as dictated by the employer's business needs and the employee's career development, the multinationals must of necessity maintain consistent worldwide policies. However, one can make the argument that China is not simply another less developed country and that there is good reason to consider China-specific practices, applications, and interpretations.

Evolving Directions in Human-Resources Policies

Necessity for a Supportive Environment

As long as there are only a handful of Westerners in China, and as long as these few expatriates live and work in the artificial environments of the tourist hotels, debarred from social relationships with their Chinese hosts and from participation in Chinese cultural and recreational life, there is a strong presumption that a married couple, unaccompanied by dependent children, is a more stable and "complete" working unit than a single, unaccompanied employee.

All of us have a need for professional, intellectual, social, and emotional support, none of which are available from the local population. Typically, the expatriates work with only a few other Westerners on whom they can rely for the first three kinds of support. For many Westerners, single life in China is solitary, cold, and incomplete.

Staffing of Ventures in Inland Cities

Rigors of all kinds are reported to be most acute in the inland cities. One expatriate found he was the only Western businessman in a city with a population of well over one million. Had he not been accompanied by his wife, he quite possibly would not have stayed there; indeed, neither of the two would have accepted the posting if they had first visited the city.

Inland assignments will become increasingly common as China seeks to expand and modernize its industrial infrastructure. Multinationals should accordingly consider staffing their interior positions with pairs of expatriates, possibly a home-country Westerner and a bilingual offshore Chinese ethnic. Failing that, unaccompanied Westerners may find that they are totally dependent not only for support, but even for conversation, on the English-speaking Chinese liaison officer.

Desirable Qualifications

What qualifications should be sought in candidates for China postings? These have been implied earlier in this chapter and are briefly summarized here.

First, competence and self-assurance in the performance of one's own job, whether it be administrative or technical, is of overriding importance. While this requirement is standard in a domestic posting and is critical in any overseas posting, it is doubly urgent in China. The expatriates normally work with only two or three colleagues. There may be back-up staff support as close as Hong Kong, but the regional office may instead be as far away as Tokyo, Manila, or even San Francisco. Furthermore, communications may be erratic and unreliable. Interviewees told us of interior cities where there were no external communications facilities of *any* kind for as long as two weeks at a time. In these circumstances, anything less than unwavering professional competence is likely to border on inadequacy.

Second in importance are self-sufficiency, resourcefulness, patience, and perseverance. China is not only a less developed nation, it is also a communist state, a planned economy, and a nation whose mores and traditions arise out of a culture and a history unfathomable to most Westerners. It is also the site of a unique social-political-economic experiment—the controlled introduction of Western capitalist business management processes and market-driven incentives into a largely agrarian, state-dominated, communist society. All of these circumstances conspire to produce a pace of business activity that, according to the expatriates, is infinitely slow. Getting *anything* done is likely to require more time, effort, negotiation, and imagination than might be required anywhere else on earth. Some executives have been known to fail in their home countries because they "can't stand the pace." There will be similar personal failures in China, and for the same reason, but not for the same kind of pace.

Third, knowledge of the Chinese language would be an asset for many expatriates, but, on the whole, it is less important than the two sets of qualifications mentioned previously. Interpreters may be employed through various Chinese sources, or they may be hired in Hong Kong or elsewhere in the Far East. Most of our interviewees, excluding the offshore Chinese, did not speak Chinese, and did not feel overly handicapped in their assignments because of it.

Finally, several of the persons interviewed offered the opinion that expatriates in China will find their life more satisfying and their work (especially with the Chinese) more effective if they have personal empathy, professional interest, or both in the welfare of the Chinese people and the future of the massive experiment in which they are taking part. The establishment of U.S.–owned instrument assembly plant in, say, France or Italy is a commercial event of no great significance. In China, however, and to the Chinese, such a venture represents a meaningful milestone in the modernization of the Middle Kingdom. China is still a frontier, both professionally and socially, and expatriates who are able to appreciate the excitement of frontier life will adjust to its hardships better than those who do not or cannot.

More Intensive Orientation

As previously noted, the interviewees had mixed feelings about the value of preassignment orientation and visits. The ORC study team, including both its Chinese and U.S. members, fully supported orientation. It is clearly desirable, from an employee-relations viewpoint, for expatriate employees and their dependents to be given a description of how they can expect to live so that they may make the necessary preparations. From a business standpoint, it is essential that expatriates be briefed on how they are going to work. Westerners in China are subject to Chinese laws, Chinese regulations, and Chinese business protocol. Most of their customers and suppliers—as well as everyone else with whom they will work—are likely to be employees of either a government agency or a state-owned enterprise. Even their own staff members will be employees of a government labor service or the joint venture partner. This business environment is thus different from any other environment the expatriates will ever have encountered. Coping is difficult even for "old hands," and to enter into this milieu without the benefit of accumulated experience, wisdom, and insight is to ensure a slow and frustrating start and a serious waste of time and effort.

By and large, however, those expatriates who did receive some sort of formal orientation were unenthusiastic about the results. Rather than list their complaints, we can identify some of the characteristics of an optimum program.

The program should be intensive, and family members should be included. Instructional media should include readings, lectures, open discussions, and, if possible, videotapes of the Chinese environment, including homes, hotels, offices, hospitals, Friendship Stores, free markets, parks, and all of the street scenes necessary to depict the environment. The orientation should be given by knowledgeable persons with recent experience in China. Some of these instructors may be associated with academic or training institutions, but, wherever feasible, company employees with Chinese experience should also be involved.

Three segments of course content are suggested; language training could be a fourth. One segment would focus on living in China: accommodations, food, recreation, transportation, medical and health care, social and cultural opportunities, clothing, shopping, and the like.

A second segment would cover twentieth-century Chinese history, leading to an examination of current Chinese political, social, and cultural institutions and behaviors. While many Chinese behavioral patterns may appear odd to Westerners, they are by no means irrational or threatening, provided that one understands their origin and significance.

The third segment would be an introduction to Chinese business practices. This would include a discussion of the several state agencies the expatriate will deal with, a review of the applicable Chinese laws and regulations (of which there are relatively few), and an examination of commercial practices and customs (of which there are many). The need, purpose, and protocol of negotiations in China would also be included in this segment.

The fact that the Western visitors and their Chinese hosts do not always share the same set of goals and objectives, even though they may be engaged in 50-50 joint ventures, should be emphasized as well. For the most part, the Western firms have gone into China solely for private economic purposes. But the Chinese have invited them for purposes that are entirely public and not wholly economic. China's principal interest in the transaction is the development of an indigenous industrial economy so that it can better house, feed, and clothe its citizens; improve its international status; and, surprisingly enough, demonstrate the superiority (or at least the viability) of its communist heritage. In pursuit of these goals, the Chinese authorities will not hesitate to manage their internal business affairs in a fashion that may be displeasing to their Western partners. Thus, many Western ventures are required by contract to provide training and development to the employees assigned by the Chinese partner to the joint venture. The Chinese partner, either a state agency or a state enterprise, may thereafter at its option relocate the trained employee or employees to other enterprises, which may well be directly competitive with the original joint venture. In short, the Chinese authorities are also using the same chessboard to play the game of career development. After all, it's their chessboard.

Longer Assignments

The typical Chinese tour of duty lasts one to three years, and seven weeks of each year are usually spent out of the country. Most of the interviewees were still in their first tour. They tended to agree that two years are about right, that three years are bearable, and that four years are the absolute maximum. On the other hand, a number of them who were approaching the end of their tour suggested that they might be willing to extend it for another two years or so.

There are several reasons to believe that the typical assignment is so short as to impede the effectiveness of a business startup. One reason is that an inordinate amount of time will be consumed by negotiations with one's own partners and with the many government agencies with which the venture must work. A second reason is that doing business in China is so different from doing business elsewhere that it takes considerably more time to learn to function effectively than it would take elsewhere. A third reason is that the Chinese themselves find disconcerting the seemingly rapid rotation of their foreign partnership representatives. This concern may be aggravated if the foreign representative's superior is removed from an assignment during the representative's tour in China. When this happens, there is likely to be some change in the Western partner's policy and direction, resulting in a further round of negotiations and additional delay.

Some expatriates commented that the Chinese are not beyond taking advantage of such a situation by using the arrival of a new Western replacement as an opportunity to reinterpret, in their own favor, prior understandings and working agreements whose written terms are flexible or even ambiguous.

There are ways to compensate for these problems. Preassignment orientation and training is one. Overlapping assignments, by as much as six months, is another. Slowly increasing the standard assignment length is a third. And there is always the possibility of financial awards, such as a bonus at the end of the second tour. But perhaps the most effective inducement to expatriates to accept longer assignments would be a critical mass of other Westerners, living in Western-type communities, with homes, shops, foreign-language schools, and recreational and medical facilities. This will happen only when and if business prospects in China are sufficiently favorable to justify the additional Western investment in staff and community facilities.

In the absence of such amenities, there remain only the existing inducements: a sense of adventure, the opportunity to be a pioneer, the chance to hold a more responsible position than one might find in the home country, and the relatively liberal compensation arrangements for expatriates in China. A cynical observer might claim that the ranks of the expatriates are heavily populated with romantics, opportunists, and mercenaries; a seasoned expatriate might counter that that mix may well be the right combination in the right place at the right time. The introduction of Western business methods and institutions into China simply will not be accomplished by bureaucrats and organization people.

Human Resources and the Chinese Work Force

One final human-resources issue remains to be discussed. The Westerners in China do not now really "manage" their Chinese staffs. All Chinese workers, from laborers to managers and professionals, are supplied to the foreign ventures either by the state labor service or by the Chinese joint venture partner, and the Chinese in each case control the selection, placement, compensation, and disciplinary processes. In some of the larger joint ventures, the Western general managers were not sure how many Chinese were on the payroll, and very few managers, regardless of how small or large their organizations, knew how much their Chinese employees were paid.

At the moment, the Westerners are not rushing to impose their own human-resources programs and policies on the Chinese. But they may not wish to remain silent partners indefinitely. When asked whether his company planned to install conventional American pay systems, including performance appraisal and job evaluation, one American manager answered: "Yes, very gradually. We believe that in all these areas we have a responsibility to conduct our business the way we normally do it elsewhere, and the Chinese expect us to do that."

But which set of personnel practices did this manager have in mind, and which set do the Chinese expect to see installed? There are two sets of stereotypical human-resources practices in the United States today. The older and probably more common model is designed to support and reflect classical management practices: hierarchical organization, authoritarian decisionmaking, specialization of labor, and what amounts to an internal caste system of officers, managers, professionals, office employees, and factory workers. The newer model is designed to be congruent with a flat organization structure, participative decisionmaking, team efforts, and an egalitarian internal culture. The two models not only generate different policies and programs, but they also arise from radically different viewpoints about the nature of work, productivity, and commitment.

My research does not permit me to conclude at this time which model, if either, would be more appropriate for the Western multinationals in China. But I do suggest that it might be premature for them to export intact their own current programs from the United States or even from Taiwan or Hong Kong. We would hope that they would first evaluate what is now taking place in their offices and factories in China. Additional information about how the Chinese manage their work forces in the state-owned enterprises would be equally useful. For many years, the Chinese have had their own native systems for performance appraisal and job evaluation as well as for recruitment, selection, and training. To the extent that these systems support the culture of the "iron rice bowl," the Westerners may not wish to replicate them. But neither should they be ignored.

After all, it was a Westerner who first said, "If you want to change a man's point of view, you must first understand it."

17

China's Learning Curve in Its Relations with Transnational Corporations

N. T. Wang

The significant role of transnational corporations in China's modernization has been discussed elsewhere.[1] Frequently, the entire modernization program, and certainly the open door policy, are linked to the country's relations with the transnationals. Those in support of the current policy generally emphasize the positive achievements up to now. Critics, on the other hand, stress the numerous disappointments and horror stories.

This chapter's contention is that China is travelling along a learning curve in its relations with transnational corporations. It should not be assumed, however, that time is necessarily on China's side and that its ability to deal with these corporations will automatically improve over time. The shape of the learning curve depends on whether the lessons of the past have indeed been well learned. It is therefore essential to "seek truth from facts" by evaluating the experiences.

In this connection, it should be pointed out that the first requisite for finding truth or benefiting from experience is knowledge of what has actually occurred. The relevant facts, however, are generally not disclosed to the analyst for two main reasons. First, official information is frequently treated as confidential. Aside from the mind-set inherited from the revolutionary years that information may be used by the adversary, there is a strong incentive for bureaucrats to keep information up their sleeve. Unless disclosure is explicitly required, bureaucrats who are custodians of information are reluctant to share it with others lest they lose the monopolist power. Indeed, the ancient story of the filing clerk who deliberately scrambles the files in order to make himself indispensable because nobody else will be able to find the relevant material may be reenacted today. Even in universities, access to materials follows hierarchy. The lowly students are often not even aware of the existence of crucial books and articles being hoarded by more important people. Instruction manuals are not made generally available for perusal by the operatives using the equipment, but are kept locked up, with only a few supervisors having the key. Second, information concerning transnational corporations is particularly difficult to assemble and process. Considerations of official confidentiality are compounded by those of business secrecy. In addition, the information is so complex and detailed that it is usually outside the frame of reference of traditional statistical compilations. For instance, a single joint venture contract specifying terms and conditions may run into a hundred pages. Texts of contracts thus escape serious analysis even where confidentiality is not an issue. Those who are familiar with their content are generally too busy to share their knowledge with others. Even at conferences and seminars as well as in published reports specifically designed for the dissemination and exchange of information, the details are hardly touched upon.

Another requisite for finding "truth from facts" is proper analysis or interpretation. There are many reasons why facts may be improperly interpreted. First, since the facts themselves are so numerous, their selection may be biased. This may be done deliberately in order to serve a particular purpose. The tendency to report only good news and not bad news in government propaganda presumably extends to scholarly analyses that serve the purpose of justifying official policy and, thus, are based on preconceived conclusions. There are also, of course, unconscious differences in the perceptions of analysts. The optimist sees the bottle half-full and concentrates on the positive aspects, while the pessimist is impressed by the half-emptiness of the bottle and laments the negative features. Even if the analysis is performed objectively, erroneous conclusions may still be reached because the analytical tools may not be appropriate or sufficiently powerful. For example, the structure of the universe or that of genes can hardly be observed without sophisticated mathematical techniques or powerful optical instruments. For many years, Western medicine has dismissed Chinese herbal practices and acupuncture as superstition. Similarly, the existing tools of economic analysis may be too rudimentary and blunt to reveal the hidden truth about relations with transnational corporations.[2]

The purpose of this chapter is to assess China's experience with transnational corporations in the framework of the learning curve. First, it attempts to dispel some important popular misunderstandings about the nature of the learning curve. Second, it goes on to demonstrate why certain perceptions of some old China hands, based on their personal experiences or on dated literature, may no longer apply in the present circumstances, since China has already passed through the early stages of the learning curve. At the same time, a full assessment of the stage reached requires an understanding of what is yet to be learned as well as what has already been learned.

The Conceptual Framework

The Context

The learning curve framework is especially useful for the present purpose because the whole concept of modernization implies a desired shift from traditional to modern ways of doing things. In the economic sphere especially, China's lag behind the advanced economies is readily admitted. In aggregative terms, its per capita output and the various components of levels of living rank relatively low among the nations of the world.[3] In specific sectors, the technologies and equipment of the 1950s and earlier continue to dominate, with only a few attaining the level of technologies of the 1970s and 1980s.[4]

In order to improve the situation, two alternative and contrasting strategies have been advanced: self-reliance, and learning from and cooperating with others. The Chinese have now realized that these strategies are by no means mutually exclusive, but should be complementary to each other. Evidently, for a large and populous country such as China, no external force or resource will be enough to make a fundamental difference without reliance on the country's own efforts. At the same time, the history of innovations demonstrates that major breakthroughs must await companion advances before they become practically and economically significant.[5] China's own efforts to reinvent the wheel and in reverse engineering further show that despite some shining successes in specific instances, the pace of overall progress is slowed by the important gaps that exist. What is most damaging in a go-it-alone policy is the isolationist and xenophobic impact on the entire society. Domestic conditions are not seen in the context of the rapidly changing world outside, and attitudes and mechanisms are not developed to adjust to external circumstances. The Qing Dynasty or a Stone Age tribe could rightfully congratulate themselves on their achievements with eyes shut to the outside world. But, on this ever-shrinking globe, such a posture threatens the very survival of the whole nation.

Once the international flow of resources and knowledge is permitted, the question of what source to choose or, more specifically, "Why transnationals?" arises. Transnational corporations do have certain unique features not shared by other sources. In contrast to book knowledge, they possess practical knowledge. Experience shows that efforts to transform the former into the latter may fail for two reasons. First, book knowledge is often too abstract or general to be put into practice. For example, an international franchiser will not rely simply on accounting courses for its franchisees, but will help them to set up a whole accounting system. Second, the book knowledge often misses out details. Without hands-on experience, the essential details are frequently elusive. That is why learning-by-doing is often needed. Third, some of the practical knowledge is proprietary. The owner is unwilling to part with it without a consideration. In some cases, the consideration involves not merely a fee, but a complex package.[6] Fourth, the success of a particular task or project frequently depends on a combination of ingredients. Thus, a franchisee not only needs a good accounting system, but also many other good management practices as well as access to finance, materials, and markets. A franchiser may be able to assemble all the necessary ingredients, some of which may otherwise be beyond reach, or escape the attention, of the inexperienced entrepreneur. Fifth, the flow of knowledge may not be a one-time occurrence, but may involve a continuous process, so that new developments will be taken into account and needed adjustments made. This is possible and often implicit in transnational direct investments, especially with rapidly changing technologies. Without the assurance of a continuous flow, what has been acquired or learned may rapidly become obsolete. Sixth, in contrast to official sources, continuity of resource flow may also be promoted through transnationals. While unilateral transfers, whether official or private, may appeal to the donor for humanitarian, political, or economic reasons, the convergence of the interests of transnationals with Chinese interests for mutual benefit can be a more powerful and durable force. Certainly, it should be less subject to the vicissitudes of political sentiment. Even on the Chinese side, apart from national interest, bureaucratic interest will tend to favor continued relations with transnationals since the bureaucracy's programs will be directly affected. For example, those in charge of energy, port, or telecommunications development will realize that their own achievements are linked with transnational corporation involvement.[7] Although conflicts of interest also exist, much like those that can arise between the transnationals and local capitalists in developing countries (as in Latin America), such conflicts may be easier to manage in a socialist country if appropriate incentives for innovation and efficiency are introduced for the bureaucracy.[8]

The next question is "Through what channel or in what form?" In a sense, the choice of transnationals can be regarded as a particular channel or form in itself. The Chinese have learned, however, that in dealings with transnationals, different channels and forms serve different purposes and should therefore coexist. In contrast to earlier decades, when Chinese relations with transnationals were limited to commodity trade and complete plant imports, more and more channels and forms have been permitted. These range from manufacturing to services, from compensation trade to licencing, from joint ventures to wholly owned foreign enterprises.[9] Virtually no channel or form is excluded per se. This is in sharp contrast not only to other socialist countries but also to many other developing countries.[10]

Another question is "Who are to learn from the transnationals?" The Chinese have also become very open here. At the policy level, they have not shied away from seeking advice from the transnationals. At the operartional level, enterprise personnel from top to bottom are also encouraged to learn from the practices of transnationals. Indeed, a ubiquitous feature of Chinese contracts and agreements with transnationals is the provision for technical assistance and training.

A parallel question is "From whom are they to learn?" The Chinese have shown eagerness to learn not only from top management, but also from financial and marketing personnel, production engineers, and research and development departments.

Yet another question relates to geographic scope. Although the establishment of the Special Economic Zones and the Open Cities has been compared with the earlier designation of treaty ports to which international commercial transactions were confined, a significant difference lies in the nonexclusivity of the current arrangement. There is no rigid demarcation of zones off-limit to transnationals. Even in remote and sensitive areas such as Inner Mongolia, Xinjiang, and Tibet, transnational corporations are permitted. This reflects Chinese self-confidence as well as the abandonment of the Maoist view of the inevitability of a third World War.

The Underlying Assumptions

In spite of the usefulness of the learning curve framework in assessing China's evolving relationship with transnationals, some of the underlying assumptions need to be carefully examined in order to avoid misinterpretation. (Appendix 17A explains the learning curve.) As in most two-dimensional presentations, the decline in unit cost with time or the experience gained in such operations as the manufacture of airframes generally applies to standardized methods or products only. When applied to more complicated cases, such as the manufacture of automobiles, the changes in product design, management, and investment cannot be assumed away.[11] Indeed, the decline in production costs may well be attributed to improvement in the form of better management or new investment that is introduced deliberately and not automatically and effortlessly. There are ample cases where the curve does not slope downward.

Consideration of nonstandardized methods or products raises the question of adaptation and innovation. There is usually a trade-off between sliding along a learning curve with cost advantages but without product redesign on the one hand and forgoing the advantages of the learning curve and adopting a new model on the other, as in the case of the shift from the Model T to the Model A when Ford was confronted with stiff competition from General Motors.

These considerations have many parallels. The historic downward slide of unit cost in a number of industries as scale increases is also not a simple reflection of the engineering properties. Rather, it reflects numerous improvements as the scale increases. Even when economy of scale is evident, sharp differences among firms with similar scales of operations or even identical plants and equipment are observable. In many cases, the precise reasons for the difference are not readily identifiable and hence are referred to as x-efficiency.[12]

The S-shaped diffusion curve is another parallel. The cumulative percentage of people who adopt an innovation increases gradually at first as resistance remains strong; when the advantages of the new method become more apparent, followers multiply until in the later stages they taper off. In some cases, the adoption is universal so that the curve reaches the asymptotic limit of 100 percent; in other cases, the diffusion is more limited. The S-shaped curve does not therefore guarantee that innovation will always be successfully diffused. The conditions for wide adoption may not exist.[13]

Another parallel may be found in the familiar infant-industry argument. Many developing countries have invoked this argument to protect inefficient industries. The result is equally mixed here, as some nascent industries have matured while others have merely become old infants. In the case of the latter, the maturing process has not operated. This is often due to indiscriminate protection that offers little incentive for cutting costs or for growing up.

The preceding points to the importance not only of a host of accompanying measures, which must constantly be introduced if the downward slope of the learning curve is to operate, but also of the environment within which an enterprise operates, such as a protective or competitive framework. In the Chinese case, the determination of the top policymakers to achieve systemic reform of the entire economy is unmistakable. At the same time, the need for innovation is also apparent, as neither the classical Marxist teachings nor the models of the capitalist economies can provide a firm guide for Chinese-style socialism, which blends planning with the market mechanism and reinterprets ideology to suit practical requirements. The strategy of gradualism as well as experimentation entails an element of uncertainty. Obviously, as reforms are being progressively introduced, the rules of the game are also changing. In such circumstances, what is learned from transnationals is often inseparable from the impact of the reforms themselves.

The Chinese Experience

In assessing the Chinese experience in the learning process, ten major areas are highlighted. Although few quantitative estimates will be offered, suggestions for further analysis will be made.

The Environment

The dramatic shift from a hostile to an intentionally hospitable environment for transnationals in itself reflects progress in the Chinese learning process. Even in the late 1970s, when the open door policy had already been formulated, the Chinese still treated transnationals that sought business relations as though the foreigners were asking a favor. Only gradually have the Chinese realized that transnationals have other options and are not all longing to come to China.

One major deterrent for transnationals is that the Chinese system is both unfamiliar and difficult to adjust to. The Chinese are, of course, not about to change their system merely to suit the transnationals. Happily, the systemic reforms being introduced point in a direction more palatable to the transnationals. The establishment of a legal framework that will ensure a degree of predictability and stability serves both domestic purposes and relations with transnationals.[14] Laws and regulations relating to foreign enterprises have been drafted with important inputs from transnationals. Not only have the views of the executives and specialists of the transnationals been consulted in legislative provisions, but the lessons learned in contract negotiations have also been incorporated, especially in the detailed regulations. This in turn is reflected in a more favorable environment for the transnationals.

There are, of course, still complaints of commissions and omissions as well as uncertainties in implementation. What is perhaps not generally appreciated is that the operations of transnationals are affected not merely by rules that explicitly concern them, but also by how things are done in China in all aspects. For joint ventures in China, for example, the joint venture laws and regulations are only the top of the iceberg with which foreign partners should be concerned. Many domestic rules dealing with labor, credit, and prices are all relevant. Because of the gradual approach to systemic reforms, many inconsistencies and anachronistic provisions remain on the books. Many transnationals do not know, for example, whether they will be able to obtain the necessary inputs and to market their products, even less what the price may be or whether their profits can be remitted. The blunt measures adopted in response to macroimbalances after the "foreign leap forward" in 1980 and again in 1985 give rise to the suspicion that in this regard the learning curve has not been very steep.[15] In terms of implementation, the age-old cultural traits can hardly be legislated away. For example, the Chinese emphasis on friendly relations and aversion to litigation may render a third-party–arbitration clause useless, since resort to such action may mean the end of a business relationship. Similarly, litigation concerning compensation for damages may also be regarded as unfriendly and thus be frowned upon. Transnationals complain that, after lengthy negotiations and the approval of contracts, the Chinese sometimes request a renegotiation immediately.

On the more mundane aspects of the environment, the shape of the Chinese learning curve has been steeper. Progress is evident from such indicators as the decline in the average number of days for processing business visas,[16] the rise in the number of starred hotels in China and those accepting advanced bookings, the increase in the proportion of business cables and letters answered, and the shortening of waiting periods for local phone calls and taxis. What the Chinese do not realize is that, despite all the improvements in amenities, foreign expatriates continue to regard China as one of the worst hardship countries for assignment, as discussed in the previous chapter by Murray Bovarnick.

The Incentives

To some extent, the less than entirely hospitable general conditions are remedied by specific incentives accorded to transnationals. These include enterprise autonomy and reduced taxes. For example, the right to hire and fire workers, provided in the Joint Venture Law or in negotiated contracts, is reassuring to the transnationals at a time when overall enterprise and labor reform is still in the early stages. Reduced taxes are useful in their announcement effect; they serve notice to the world that the transnationals are welcome. On the other hand, questions have been raised about their efficacy as well as their side effects.[17]

Some of the specific incentives may be counterbalanced by unintended reactions. For example, when foreign joint ventures are allowed to sell their products in China for foreign exchange, they may, perhaps improperly, be asked to pay foreign exchange for inputs supplied domestically. The inducement of low labor costs may be nullified when foreign enterprises are asked to pay artificially high wages.

The Principle of Mutual Benefit

Symptomatic of change in the Chinese attitude toward transnationals is the acceptance of the principle of mutual benefit. The implication is that transnationals should legitimately make a profit even though the Chinese objective may be different. The difference between the objectives of socialist China and those of profit-seeking transnationals should therefore not be an obstacle to business relations.

There remains the question of how much profit is regarded as appropriate. Since the Chinese still do not have much experience with opportunity cost, the profit rate sought by transnationals is often regarded as outrageously high. This is affected by the early Chinese practice of zero-interest investment funds as well as low depreciation charges. The raising of capital charges in line with systemic reforms is gradually changing the Chinese perception of profit.

A related issue is lack of the concept of business risk under the traditional system of central allocation in China. *Ex ante* is not clearly distinguished from *ex post* profit. Thus, when *ex post* profit is high, the Chinese often suspect that they have agreed to the wrong terms. In some cases, they have sought renegotiation in order to reduce the profit. Conversely, in an effort to show transnationals that they are truly welcome, a certain *ex post* profit rate has sometimes been guaranteed. Such treatment ignores the fundamental function of the entrepreneur, who must be prepared to take the risk and thus to suffer any loss due to unforeseen circumstances or internal mismanagement as well as to reap the fruits of greater than expected profits. The inefficiency and waste built into the cost-plus type of government contract in the developed countries should serve as a pertinent lesson.

The Concerted Approach

Under the traditional system, business dealings with transnationals were centralized. A core of experienced personnel had gradually been built up. Knowledgeable transnationals knew whom they should deal with and what to expect from them. However, as long as decisionmaking was shared by many entities, the centralized system did not ensure that the parties with the appropriate functional titles had the real deciding power, nor were the precise roles of the Chinese negotiators or partners made known to the transnationals. Indeed, in negotiating positions, the Chinese routinely claimed that the approval of higher authorities was needed.

The simplification of the decision tree and the decentralization of authority in dealing with foreign enterprises to provincial and municipal entities have facilitated the identification of the appropriate parties. At the same time, during this transitional period, a whole new generation of cadres has entered the picture. In many localities, their expertise and experience cannot compare with those at the center. In other words, they are in the early stages of the learning curve. Their feeling of inadequacy reinforces the usual reluctance of bureaucracies to make decisions, in obedience to the rule "to do nothing is to do no wrong." This reluctance is aggravated by conspicuous errors committed by overzealous or careless bureaucrats. From the point of view of the nation as a whole, especially, instances of cross-hauling, cut-throat competition among Chinese suppliers have become standard jokes. For example, a Chinese product is exported and reimported at an inflated price. Commodities of dubious quality are dumped on the international market at cut rates to obtain scarce foreign exchange through the retention system.

Efforts to restore order and form a united front in relation to transnationals have been made. These include the establishment of one-stop windows by local authorities, where all the relevant decisionmakers are congregated in a single office, and the introduction of central licencing control of selected items for import and export. The nagging question remaining is whether an appropriate balance is being struck so that concerted action does not lead to a return to centralization with all its attendant problems of rigidity and lack of competitive vigor.

International Practice

Concomitant with the gradual establishment of a favorable environment for transnationals has been the increasing Chinese acceptance of international practice. As late as 1978, for example, transnationals were greatly surprised when the Chinese offered to pay cash for the huge initial purchase of the Baoshan steel mill project; today, the Chinese will consider various kinds of credit proposals, including official and mixed credit, variable rates, denomination in different currencies, and leasing. In early contract negotiations, standard concepts and terms, such as *force majeure* and *discounted cash flow*, were unfamiliar to the Chinese and thus required tortuous explanation and negotiation; today, most of them are readily accepted by the Chinese. As a result, the negotiating process has been greatly facilitated.[18]

Even some of the more sophisticated new instruments have been quickly learned. For example, the Chinese have participated in international syndication and issued bonds on the international capital markets. They have earned interest on their gold stored in London by loans to investment banks repayable in gold, taking advantage of the spread between the spot and futures prices. They have also made arrangements for operating on the London metal exchange. However, despite their importance as major producers and traders of a number of primary commodities (including grains, fibers, oil, and metals), the direct use of the futures markets has probably been inhibited by bureaucratic aversion to "speculation." The Chinese have yet to learn the use of such markets in order to minimize risk and, thus, avoid speculation. For instance, if large purchases of grains are envisaged, quiet purchases in the futures market may have a less stimulating effect on the market than official announcements of buying missions. Producers of primary commodities (such as farmers in the United States) can hedge against the risk of a decline in prices by sales in the futures market, while at the same time forgoing the speculative gains of a possible price rise.

The Calculus

The adoption of the principle of mutual benefit discussed earlier implies the calculation of costs and benefits. Certainly, this is an improvement over blind business dealings. At the same time, experience points to great difficulties in this calculus. Four of these difficulties apply particularly to the Chinese.

First, the information needed for serious assessment is usually lacking. On the Chinese side, such simple data as enterprise balance sheets and unit costs are seldom available. Even if these data exist, they are frequently unavailable to the user because of the absence of communication between various units.[19] This illustrates that mere acceptance of broad principles, such as international practice, is not enough. As far as information on transnationals is concerned, even the most elementary aspects are often not possessed by the Chinese. This is reflected in the enormous appetite of the Chinese for gathering information directly from the transnationals, through technical seminars and incessant questioning.

Second, the notion of cost and benefit is often oversimplified. For example, while the Chinese are interested in obtaining the best price from competing sources, they have discovered that a low price may in the end be more expensive. Quality differences may not be easily perceptible, as in the case of more or less durable packaging materials. Some suppliers may be eager to win a foothold in the Chinese market but unable to meet the prescribed delivery requirements. Other low bidders may recoup initial losses by overcharging for spare parts, repair services, and so on.

Third, the cost-benefit calculation often neglects the indirect effects. Prolonged contract negotiations are, for example, a cost to the transnationals that ultimately must be borne by the Chinese. Estimates of impacts in such areas as employment or balance of payments are usually limited to the direct effects. A further problem is the neglect of such issues as environmental and social dislocation.

Fourth, while it is relatively easy to grasp the usefulness of information and of a more comprehensive and sophisticated evaluation, it is far more difficult to put it into practice. The new requirement of feasibility studies raises the question of objectivity and thoroughness. Some executing units have vested interests in certain projects. It is very difficult to obtain an independent assessment of such studies because the validity of data is hard to check and the underlying assumptions are not usually explicitly stated. The top-level decisionmakers in particular rarely have the ability or the time to look critically at these studies. They rarely go beyond the executive summaries and tend to be intimidated by a mass of technical or psuedoscientific arguments. In the final analysis, the outcome of cost–benefit calculus is still greatly influenced by value judgments.

The Bargaining Process

The importance and lengthy process of bargaining reflects inexperience on both sides, as well as the Chinese belief that both general environment and specific incentives are too blunt to be applicable to numerous specific circumstances. It also reflects lack of coordination among the decisionmakers, deviations from international practice, and uncertainty about the possibility or viability of the projects in question. Improvements in all the areas just enumerated have thus tended to economize on bargaining and shortening the period.

It is sometimes argued that, as the Chinese progress along the learning curve, their bargaining position will be strengthened to the detriment of the transnationals. This zero-sum game scenario is not necessarily true because both sides can gain when the Chinese improve. Much of the reluctance on the part of the Chinese to conclude arrangements with the transnationals arises from concern that they may give away too much. There have been numerous reports of bargaining sessions aborted because the Chinese asked exorbitant prices for "antique" plants and equipment, land, labor, and so on. If the Chinese become more confident about a fair division of benefits, many potential opportunities can be realized.

The Diffusion of Knowledge

As in many developing countries, the possible benefits to be derived from relations with transnationals depend on the capacity for diffusion. The impact of transnationals may be severely limited if it is mainly confined to the enclaves in which they operate. This argument has been used, for example, to criticize the usefulness of the Special Economic Zones as well as the Open Cities. It was also invoked in order to object to the introduction of a patent law in China on the ground that technology from the transnationals should be widely diffused in order to achieve maximum effect. After considerable debate, the Chinese have reaffirmed the strategy of differentiated degrees of openness for various localities in accordance with their preparedness. They have also discontinued the practice of copying patented foreign technologies without paying royalties, thereby allaying transnational fears that once a Chinese entity obtains foreign proprietary technology, it will clandestinely pass it on to other entities and thus dissipate it. The Chinese have also learned that the capacity for diffusion does not depend primarily on where transnational activities are actually located, but on internal channels for diffusion. Nor need such channels be contrary to international practice. Reverse engineering, in fact, is unlikely to be practical in many cases. It usually takes a very long time and rarely works from the economic point of view because some essential ingredient is missing. Even if a copy can be made, duplication in quantity is another story. Perhaps more important is the Chinese realization that what is to be learned from transnationals is not largely proprietary in nature. Much of the know-how, such as good management or marketing techniques, is not patented and can be fully diffused. The main concern is how thoroughly the Chinese have learned and how broadly they have managed to diffuse such know-how.

In this connection, the Chinese bias in favor of the hard sciences remains to be overcome.[20] This bias is in itself a reaction against the long historic bias in favor of letters in the examination system and by the literati. It also reflects aversion to risk after decades of political movement. Evidently, questions relating to matters such as engineering are less controversial than those matters affecting people, such as management. A major obstacle to diffusion continues to be limited communication between various vertical units and even within units, as well as lack of movement of personnel. Technical assistance from enterprises in the coastal areas to those in the interior, informal exchanges through professional organizations, and reforms in the personnel system to promote mobility are gradually being introduced in order to overcome these obstacles.

The Adaptation

The Chinese have long emphasized the need for adaptation in learning from the West. The concept of "Chinese learning for fundamental principles and Western learning for application to mundane affairs" is still powerful, at least in intellectual circles today. The main advantage of this attitude is the self-respect it induces. On the other hand, it can also be an excuse for superficiality and for skirting the more fundamental issues.

There are, of course, many cases of incongruity where transnational corporations' methods have been directly transplanted without appropriate adaptation. A conspicuous example is computerization of productive operations without adjustments in the software to permit the use of the Chinese language. A more serious difficulty lies in resistance to change on the ground that foreign ways are inappropriate. Thus, a Chinese chief engineer fired for incompetence by a foreign manager may blame the latter for ignorance of Chinese practices. The real question is which Chinese practices must be discarded. The process of finding an appropriate blend of something old and something new remains unfinished.

Innovation

Whether in the adaptation of methods learned from the transnationals on the factory floor or in the formulation of a modernized Chinese management system, much innovation is needed. Curiously enough, innovation has so far been very little discussed in China. To the extent that it has been, there is fascination with the Schumpeterian variety that determines the Kondratiefs or the megatrends and neglects the thousands of little things that require improvement, be they O-rings in a spacecraft or leaky toilets in hotels.

There is, of course, controversy as to whether innovation can be taught or learned, A more fruitful question is whether conditions are conducive to innovation, for there is no lack of potential innovators in China.

The Chinese have learned that transnationals operating in China must be given a degree of autonomy. While the hands of the transnationals are less tied than those of their Chinese counterparts, their operations are affected by the total Chinese environment, as discussed at the beginning of this chapter. The activities of many transnationals continue to be severely limited. The scope and degree of flexibility is severely prescribed. For example, transnational commercial banks are generally not allowed to accept deposits or make domestic loans; foreign law firms are not permitted to argue for their clients in Chinese courts; foreign accounting firms are also restricted in their professional practices. More important even than explicit proscriptions is the scope for change, for expansion or for the introduction of new methods and products. Without the ability to change, there can be no innovation. Even where specific change is permitted, there are unforeseen changes that cannot be provided for in advance. Moreover, it is frequently not deliberate policy but administrative practices (such as detailed tax audits on suspected irregularities or lack of cooperation by suppliers) that discourage innovation. If the demand for favorable conditions for innovation by transnationals is also met for local enterprises, China's learning curve in its relations with transnationals will have incalculable effects on its modernization.

Notes

1. Wang, N. T., *China's Modernization and Transnational Corporations* (Lexington, Mass.: Lexington Books, 1984); "TNCs in China's Modernization," *CTC Reporter* (New York: United Nations Centre on Transnational Corporations, summer 1983). For the purposes of this chapter, the term *transnational corporations* (or *transnationals* for short) is used interchangeably with *multinational corporations* and *multinational enterprises*. These entities extend their operations to other countries, whether in production or services; they may be incorporated or not, publicly or privately owned, large or small in size. For a discussion of the definitional issue, see *Transnational Corporations In World Development: A Re-examination* (New York: United Nations, 1978), pp. 158–70.

2. The vast literature on transnational corporations amply illustrates this point. Certainly, a macro approach is too broad to delve into the intricacies at the enterprise level. International trade theory is ill-suited to explain international production, and international investment theory oversimplifies the multifarious activities packaged by transnationals. See Wang, N. T., *China's Modernization,* op. cit., pp. 63–88; and Dunning's chapter 1 in this book.

3. See, for example, the listing in the World Bank's *World Tables* and *World Development Report,* recent editions.

4. Cited in World Bank, *China: Long-term Development Issues and Options* (Washington, D.C.: World Bank, 1985), p. 110.

5. For numerous illustrations, see Drucker, Peter, *Innovation and Entrepreneurship* (New York: Harper & Row, 1985).

6. For a theory of packaging and repackaging, see Wang, N. T., *China's Modernization*, op. cit., pp. 65–68.

7. See the forthcoming energy case study by Oksenberg, M., and Liebcrthal, K.

8. The opposition of local elites to transnationals in developing countries is greatly influenced by government policies that foster local monopoly. A parallel may be found in developed countries where protected inefficient producers are vehemently opposed to competition from Third World enterprises.

9. The list may be elaborated to include consulting, management contracts, subcontracting, leasing, processing of imported material for export, processing of imported intermediate products for export, export of goods with foreign trademarks or foreign designs, countertrade, franchising, *produit en main*, coproduction, and various combinations of those forms listed.

10. For an assessment of these policies, see Wang, N. T., "Policies and Procedures Relating to Foreign Private Capital," in *Mobilization of Domestic and External Finance for Development* (New York: United Nations, 1987).

11. See Abernathy, William J., and Wayne, Kenneth, "Limits of the Learning Curve," *Harvard Business Review* (September–October 1974): 109–21.

12. See Leibenstein, H., "Allocation Efficiency vs X-efficiency," *American Economic Review*, vol. LVI (1966): 392–415; Stewart, Frances, and James, Jeffrey, *The Economics of New Technology in Developing Countries* (Boulder, Colo.: Westview, 1982), pp. 6–10, 83–103.

13. See Brown, Lawrence A., *Innovation Diffusion* (New York: Methuen, 1981), pp. 197–228.

14. See Wang, N. T., *Chinese Legal Framework for Foreign Investment and Its Implications* (New York: Columbia University, East Asian Institute, 1986), pp. 8–14.

15. One well-learned lesson is that a massive unilateral cancellation or suspension of contracts is not only costly in terms of the total environment, but also from the point of view of direct indemnity payments.

16. To the extent that the Chinese adopt a policy of reciprocity in handling visa applications, certain delays are calculated responses to those that affect visa applications by Chinese nationals on the other side.

17. See Wang, N. T., "Tax Incentives and Foreign Investment: Policy Consideration for China," *The Chinese Intellectual*, vol. 2, no. 12 (Autumn 1985): 8–12 (in Chinese) and in *China Reforms for Excellence* (Wong Pai-Yee, Vynnis, ed.) (Hong Kong: VIP Management Consultants, 1986).

18. For example, the time required for joint venture contract negotiations when the joint venture law was first promulgated frequently extended to three or four years. In the mid-1980s, some negotiations last no more than a few months. It would be useful to have a systematic reporting on the lag between application and approval by sector, size, form, and locale. Such reporting should also serve as a deterrent to administrative irregularity and corruption. When I was asked to administer an import-quota–allocation system when the currency was grossly overvalued, the first

measure I introduced was a daily report on the status of all applications showing the date of the application, where it had travelled to, and how long it had stayed there. An unusually speedy trip for difficult cases might serve as a warning sign of possible special favors, while inordinate delays might be a signal of possible extortion.

19. A striking illustration of the importance of available information is the surprise expressed by the Chinese at the highest levels about the quality of the World Bank reports on China. The question arises why Chinese economists have been unable to produce such documents. The main reason is that the World Bank people had full access to Chinese information while no Chinese, including central government officials, enjoy such a privilege. Indeed, the Chinese readily admit that specialists on their own country must consult materials issued abroad.

20. A similar bias is beginning to emerge in the social sciences. For example, Chinese students abroad majoring in economics are increasingly drawn to econometrics. This is a healthy reaction against the illiteracy in mathematical and quantitative methods of the old generation of economists as well as risk aversion. In part it is a response to the market mechanism as the Chinese students have discovered that they have a comparative advantage in mathematical skills, which are less culturally determined than verbal skills, and they are lured by offers of scholarships and fellowships. From the national point of view, however, the need for skills other than narrow specialization in econometric methods is greater. It is hoped that the new generation of econometricians will also learn well the limitations of their trade, especially in policy applications. For example, few forecasters in the developed countries would rely entirely on their econometric models.

Appendix 17A: The Learning Curve

The learning curve is used in many disciplines. Psychologists attempt to investigate the learning process over time. As an individual learns a new skill, many errors are made at the beginning, but they decrease in number until learning capacity has been reached. The concept is also used by sociologists and in agricultural and market research to show the diffusion of innovations, such as hybrid corn or a new model, over time.[1] The shape of the curve is downward-sloping if the number of errors or cost (on the Y-axis) is plotted against the time or cumulative number of trials or production, as shown in (A) and (B) in figure 17A–1 (on page 268). It is bell-shaped when the number of adoptions of innovation is plotted over time, as shown in (C). It is S-shaped when plotted on a cumulative basis, as shown in (D) in the figure.[2]

Notes

1. See, for example, Rogers, Everett M., *Diffusion of Innovations* (New York: Free Press, 1962).

2. See Midgley, David F., and Dowling, Grahame R., "Innovativeness: The Concept and Its Measurement," *Journal of Consumer Research,* vol. 4 (March 1978): 229–42; and Dolan, Robert J., and Jeuland, Abel P., "Experience Curves and Dynamic Demand Models: Implications for Optimal Pricing Strategies," *Journal of Marketing* (winter 1981): pp. 52–62.

Figure 17A–1. The Learning Curve

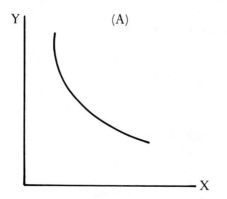

Y: cost per unit or number of errors
X: time or cumulative number of trials

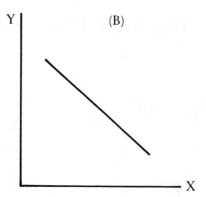

Y: same as (A), log
X: same as (A), log

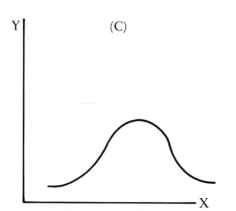

Y: number of people adopting
   new method
X: year

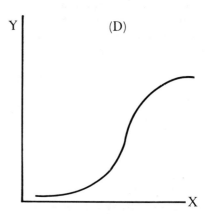

Y: cumulative number of people
   adopting new method
X: year

Subject Index

AEG, 167
Albert, 214
Amax, 65
Aramco, 235
Argentina: foreign investment in, 131; IMF and, 172; investment/trade statistics, 131
Asian Development Bank, 130
Asian Wall Street Journal, 127
Australia: direct investment by, 210; foreign investment in, 4
Austria, foreign investment in, 158

Bahamas, foreign investment in, 100
Bayer, 167
BBC, 166
Bechtel, 66
Beijing Jeep, 234
Bolivia, foreign investment in, 147–148
Bosch, 167
Brazil, 192; direct investment by, 3–4; foreign investment in, 39, 73, 119, 126, 131; IMF and, 172; investment/trade statistics, 131
Britain, 77; direct investment by, 3, 7, 21, 39, 94, 95, 122, 154; direct investment in India, 122; direct investment in Thailand, 154; foreign investment in, 116; investment/trade statistics, 3, 7, 39, 94, 95, 122
Business India, 133

Canada: direct investment by, 112, 212; direct investment in China, 212; foreign investment in, 4, 9, 94, 113, 114, 115, 116, 157–158, 185; U.S. investment in, 9, 113, 114, 115, 116, 185

CEC, 166
Cerro de Pasco, 65
Chevron International Oil, 133
Chile, foreign investment in, 172
China, People's Republic of (PRC), 122; Australian investment in, 210; Bank of, 209, 211, 215, 225; Baoshan steel complex, 203, 210–211, 260; barriers to transnational corporations in, 83, 195–196; Beijing Jeep, 234; Canadian investment in, 212; Central Committee, 183, 199, 206, 218; Chengdu Academic Conference (1985), 208; choosing a foreign strategic model for, 183–190; Economic Commission, 206; Foreign Economic Contracts Law, 223; Foreign Enterprise Income Tax Law, 227; foreign investment in, 8, 21, 25, 59, 116, 118–119, 161–162, 171, 183–190, 191–196, 199–219, 223–232, 233–249, 251–264; French investment in, 214; general economic and social conditions, 200–202; Guang Mei Food Company, 216, 217; Guang Ming Shirt Factory, 211; Guangzhou development zone, 218; Guangzhou First Industrial Corporation, 217; Guangzhou Trust and Investment Corporation, 217; Hong Kong investment in, 195, 210, 221–222; as host country, 191–192; Hainan Dao development mix, 218; Hainan Dao granite factory, 214–215; Hainan Dao nylon zipper factory, 214; Hainan Dao palm oil venture, 215, 216; Hua Nan Computer Company,

Venezuela, foreign investment in, 116
Vietnam, U.S. technology-export ban and, 228
Volkswagen, 217

Wellcome, 167
West Germany, 216; direct investment by, 3, 4, 39, 94, 95, 112, 203, 214; direct investment in China, 203, 214; foreign investment in, 131; investment/trade statistics, 3, 4, 39, 94, 95, 112, 131
World Bank, 86; Hungary and, 166; India and, 130; report on transnational corporations, 39; U.S. and, 110

Xiamen University, 213

Arthur Young International, 233–234
Yugoslavia, foreign investment in, 21, 192

Name Index

About the Contributors

Jack N. Behrman is Luther Hodges Distinguished Professor at the Graduate School of Business Administration, University of North Carolina at Chapel Hill. He was formerly assistant secretary of the U.S. Dept. of Commerce. His recent publications include *Industrial Policies, International Restructuring and Transnationals,* and *The Rise of the Phoenix: The U.S. Role in a Restructured World Economy.*

Murray E. Bovarnick is vice-president of Organization Resources Counselors, a New York–based international consulting firm. He has held adjunct professorships at Tulane University and Pace University. He was principal author of *Multinationals in China: Human Resource Practices and Issues in the PRC.*

Chen Yin-fang is professor of international economics at Nankai University in China. He has taught economic statistics as well as international business and served as deputy chairman of the China International Relations Association. He is coauthor of *Transnational Corporations: An Analytical Study* and has published numerous articles on such corporations.

John Dunning is ICI Research Professor in International Business at the University of Reading, United Kingdom. He was formerly Esmee Fairbairn Professor of International Investment and Business Studies and head of the department of economics at the University of Reading. Professor Dunning has written or edited twenty-one books and reports on international investment and multinational enterprises.

Carsten Thomas Ebenroth is director of the Institute of International Economics at the University of Konstanz in Germany (F.R.). His publications include studies in transfer pricing.

Joachim Karl is research associate at the University of Konstanz in Germany (F.R.).

Anant R. Negandhi is professor of international business in the College of Commerce and Business Administration of the University of Illinois at Urbana-Champaign. He is the author of numerous studies in international business and editor of the series *Research in International Business and International Relations.*

Jun Nishikawa is professor of economics at Waseda University, Japan. He is former president of the Peace Studies Association of Japan. His publications include *North-South Issues* and *ASEAN and the United Nations System.*

S. J. Noumoff is chairman of the executive committee of the Centre for Developing Area Studies at McGill University in Montreal, Canada and was formerly director of its Centre for East Asian Studies. He has authored over one hundred papers on China and other Third World countries and has been the China resource person for the Canadian Federal Government Task Force to review the Canadian International Development Agency.

Suthy Prasartset is a member of the Faculty of Economics at Chulalongkorn University in Thailand. He is the author of many studies on the Thai economy.

Stefan H. Robock is R. D. Calkins Professor Emeritus of International Business at Columbia University. He was formerly director of the International Business Studies at Indiana University and chief economist for the Tennessee Valley Authority. Dr. Robock's recent publications include *International Business and Multinational Enterprises* and *Brazil: A Study in Development Progress.*

Edward Roche is an associate at Booz-Allen and Hamilton in New York. He received his Ph.D. from Columbia University.

Mihály Simai is director of the Institute for World Economy, vice president of the Hungarian Economic Association, and a member of the Development Planning Committee of the United Nations. He was formerly president of the World Federation of U.N. Association. His recent publications include *Power, Technology and Global Cooperation* and *The U.N. Today and Tomorrow.*

Preston M. Torbert is a partner in the international law firm, Baker and McKenzie in Chicago. Dr. Torbert has participated in negotiations and lectured on legal subjects on many occasions in China. His publications include numerous articles on trade and investment with China and a book on *The Ching (Qing) Imperial Household Department.*

Wang Zheng Xian is professor and dean of the School of Management at Zhongshan University in China. His recent papers include "On the Development Strategy of China's Foreign Economic Relations" and "Feudalism and the Chinese Enterprise."

Xian Guoming is lecturer in economics at Nankai University in China. He has published articles on transnational corporations.

Zhang Yangui is lecturer in economics at Nankai University in China. He has published articles on transnational corporations and development economics.

About the Editors

Teng Weizao is advisor, professor of economics, and director of the Research Centre for International Issues of Nankai University in China where he was formerly president and director of its Economic Research Institute. He is expert advisor to the United Nations Commission on Transnational Corporations and has written many books and articles on transnational corporations.

N. T. Wang is the director of the China-International Business Project, senior research scholar of the East Asian Institute, and adjunct professor at the Graduate School of Business of Columbia University in New York. He was formerly a director of the United Nations Centre on Transnational Corporations and has headed a number of United Nations missions to developing countries. Among Dr. Wang's recent publications are _China's Modernization and Transnational Corporations_ and _Economic Development and Transnational Corporations_.